SMALL VICTORIES

Small Victories

Recipes, Advice + Hundreds of Ideas for Home-Cooking Triumphs

JULIA TURSHEN

FOREWORD BY Ina Garten

PHOTOGRAPHS BY Gentl + Hyers

CHRONICLE BOOKS

SAN FRANCISCO

For Grace, who makes *sweet even sweeter*
(thank you, Mary Oliver), and for my Aunt Debby,
who makes the most delicious reservations.

Library of Congress Cataloging-in-Publication Data.
Names: Turshen, Julia, author. | Gentl + Hyers, photographer.
Title: Small victories : recipes, advice + hundreds of ideas for home-cooking triumphs / Julia
   Turshen ; photographs by Gentl + Hyers.
Description: San Francisco : Chronicle Books, [2016] | Includes index.
Identifiers: LCCN 2015039651 | ISBN 9781452143095 (hardcover : alk. paper)
Subjects: LCSH: Cooking. | LCGFT: Cookbooks.
Classification: LCC TX714 .T88 2016 | DDC 641.5--dc23 LC record available at
http://lccn.loc.gov/2015039651

Manufactured in China

MIX
Paper from
responsible sources
FSC™ C008047
www.fsc.org

Designed by Vanessa Dina with contributions from
   Doug Turshen and Rochelle Udell
Prop styling by Andrea Gentl
Food styling by Julia Turshen
Typesetting by Howie Severson
Photograph on page 2 by Alan Richardson.

The photographers wish to thank Meredith Munn,
Monique Baron, Larry Ruhl, and Grace Bonney.

10 9 8 7 6 5 4 3 2 1

Chronicle Books LLC
680 Second Street
San Francisco, California 94107
www.chroniclebooks.com

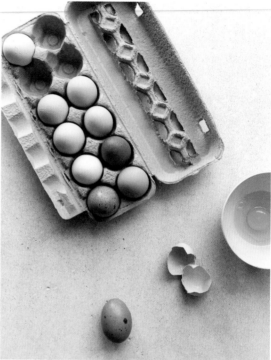

BREAKFAST

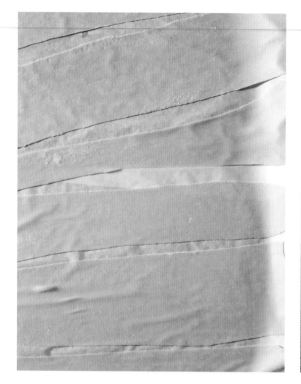

GRAINS, BEANS + PASTA

MEAT + POULTRY

A FEW DRINKS + SOME THINGS
TO KEEP ON HAND

SEVEN LISTS

Foreword

I will always remember the first time I met Julia Turshen. She was catering a party for my dearest friends and when she walked into the room, it simply lit up. I'm not sure if it was her brilliant smile, infectious laugh, or that gorgeous wild hair but the whole picture is truly memorable. She went on to make an amazingly delicious and earthy dinner for all of us, but it was only later when she and I became friends that I came to really understand Julia's special brand of magic.

Julia's love of two things come together in this book—her total delight in great food and she adores cooking for people she loves. She spent a decade as a private chef and coauthoring some of the best cookbooks around. But this book is pure Julia; the recipes she makes for Grace and their friends are ones that we all want to make at home. They're simple to prepare but have great bold flavors.

Julia's book is like her—it's totally accessible. She explains a few unusual ingredients at the beginning, and everything else is available at the grocery store. I adore her notes for recipes like Doug's meat loaf (Doug's her dad) and ways you can "spin-off" each recipe into your own. Julia is a cook who not only trusts her recipes but also her readers. I can't wait to cook my way through this amazing new book, and I'll definitely be starting with those raspberry jam buns!

—Ina Garten

Introduction

It began with celery. As a kid obsessed with everything about cooking, I decided I should be able to chop precisely and sauté effectively. I convinced my parents to buy me endless bunches of celery to practice with. I spent entire weekends perfecting my dice and heating up a little oil in a skillet in which I would attempt to flip the celery without using a utensil, just like I had seen all of my favorite chefs and teachers do on television. My very supportive family ate more sautéed celery than they would probably like to remember. Committing the motions to memory, I eventually grew comfortable with the techniques and continued to build on the celery, turning the sauté into a soup, a stir-fry, and more. Teaching myself to cook wasn't a quick process, but along the way I stopped to celebrate each accomplishment and began to consider them small but very worthwhile victories. The day no celery landed on the floor: Small victory!

Cooking went from being a childhood hobby (I opened my first "restaurant," called Julia's Place, in my parents' apartment when I was about three) to a lifelong passion, really the driving force through my everything. I started my first business, Julia Turshen Catering, complete with business cards, at the age of thirteen, right after I started cooking Thanksgiving dinners for my entire family without any assistance. During college, I interned at a food magazine and assisted a cookbook author and a food television producer. At school, I wrote just about every essay I was assigned on the food in whatever book we were reading. Soon after college, I started working with other people on their cookbooks and, in between writing gigs, I worked as a private chef. Both jobs allowed me to travel frequently, but a couple of years ago I traded other folks' kitchens for my own, where I happily spend every day testing and developing recipes. If I am not cooking, I am thinking about what I'd like to cook, and if you can't find me at the stove, chances are I'm out getting groceries. Even when I'm eating, I am planning my next meal. Cooking has been the most positive influence on my life. It has made me healthier, happier, more connected to my family and friends, and more aware of and kinder to the environment. It's transported me around the world, sometimes literally and often just through trying out a new spice or recipe. As you can imagine, I highly recommend it.

Celebrating small victories is not only how I've marked my life (both in and out of the kitchen), but it's also a sure way of becoming a comfortable and intuitive, even inventive, cook. Which brings us to this very personal collection of recipes and advice, the goal of which is to demonstrate that cooking doesn't have to be complicated to be satisfying, or over-the-top to be impressive. Each recipe in the pages that follow introduces a small victory (often more than one). They range from not always obvious but very useful tips (e.g., how to get the seeds out of a pomegranate without making a mess) to broader ideas about cooking (e.g., the only thing that stands between you and a tender pork shoulder is time, and patience itself is an important ingredient). Every recipe is also accompanied by a number of spin-offs, which are thoughts on how to turn that small victory into many other things besides the main recipe. In other words, if you cook this thing, you can also cook all of these things.

The idea for this book came from a conversation I seemed to be having repeatedly with a lot of people. It went something like this:

I (would) love to cook, but I only know how to make, like, two things.

Well, what are they?

Oh, I don't know . . . (insert two random recipes here).

Well, you actually know how to make 200 things.

The only way to become a cook is to cook, and the road to becoming a good cook is paved not only with repetition but also with the intuition you gain along the way. That intuition will allow you to realize that if you can make spaghetti, you can also make rice, quinoa, or soba noodles. Truly, if you can boil water, you can make just about anything. In fact, you don't even always need the water. If you know how to grill a hamburger, you know how to grill anything. If you know how to roast a tray of sweet potatoes, you can roast just about any vegetable or combination of vegetables. If you can whisk together oil and vinegar, you can dress not only a salad but also that grilled something or roasted whatever.

Cooking is simply a huge and often very fun puzzle of piecing together techniques with different ingredients. Once you know the basics, the world is your oyster (or your clam, chicken thigh, block of tofu—whatever makes you happy). Think of small victories as the corners of the puzzle, the pieces that help us become inspired, relaxed cooks who know how to fill in the rest.

Shall we get started?

Some Things to Keep in Mind

A kitchen requires only **three knives**: A chef's knife with a blade that you keep sharp, a serrated bread knife, and a small paring knife that feels comfortable in your hand. The rest of the options might look nice, but I find they rarely get used. Like clothes you never wear, an excess of inessential knives (all tools, for that matter) usually just end up occupying valuble space and cause you to be unnecessarily indecisive.

The three tools you can never have too many of are **cotton kitchen towels**, **wooden spoons**, and **paper towels**.

A **Microplane grater**, which originated as a woodworking tool, is invaluable. It makes zesting citrus a breeze, turns Parmesan and other hard cheeses into the finest flakes, works as a nutmeg grater, and is excellent for creating flecks of chocolate. A sturdy pair of **stainless-steel tongs** is also invaluable. I like to think of them as an extension of my hand. Once you start using them, you'll wonder how you ever lived without them.

If you really get into baking, a **kitchen scale** is useful. It will make your measurements totally accurate, since there's no room for error (1 cup of flour can vary by a number of grams, depending on how you pack it and how humid the room is, but 120 grams of flour will always be 120 grams of flour). Using a digital scale also means you have less to clean up, because you can simply add all the ingredients to the bowl, bringing the scale back to zero between additions. Note

that while I am pro-scale, if you're not, that's okay. I've provided standard cup measurements throughout the book.

If you're measuring flour without a scale, let's take a second to talk about the good old **spoon-and-sweep**. This method will keep your flour measurement as accurate as possible. First, stir your flour with a large spoon (whether it's in its bag or another container) and then spoon the flour into your measuring cup. This aerates the flour and eliminates any big clumps. Sweep the top of the measuring cup with something flat, like the back edge of a dinner knife, and that's that. Don't tap the cup on the counter—that will just pack the flour down, so you'll end up adding more than you need and your cake or cookies or whatever you're making will be dry, which is a bummer.

Maldon salt is worth splurging on for sprinkling on finished dishes just before you serve them, like a final hurrah. It's got an amazing crunchy texture and a clean flavor that is unrivaled, and I love it. But all you really need for general cooking, and what I call for throughout the book, is regular old **kosher salt** (my preference is Diamond Crystal because it's the least salty of the salts, giving you more control since salt is much easier to add than it is to take away). Because kosher salt is coarser than table salt, it is easier to get an accurate measurement with it since it doesn't clump the way table salt can (moisture in table salt can really skew your measurement). Kosher salt also has a really

clean flavor—there's no iodine-y, metallic thing going on—plus, it's very affordable. I buy it in big boxes and decant it into a little bowl that is near me in the kitchen at all times. Also, while I've given measurements and guidelines throughout the recipes, what tastes properly seasoned to me might not be true for you and, as you're the one doing the cooking in your home, I say salt until something tastes right to you. As I once heard Mark Bittman, the prolific writer and cookbook author, say, knowing how much salt to add to a dish is like knowing how much to turn the steering wheel when you're driving. You just know.

Throughout the recipes, **garlic**, **onions**, **shallots**, **ginger**, and **carrots** should be peeled unless noted otherwise. I always throw the peels and skins into my stockpot for added flavor and color, so go ahead and do that if you'd like. When I'm being especially mindful, I keep a sealed plastic bag full of scraps in the freezer and when it's brimming, I take out the stockpot. Also remember that not all garlic cloves are the same—some are super-strong, others might not be. Use your discretion—add more if needed or use half a clove.

All **eggs** are large, all **milk** is whole, and all **butter** is unsalted. But if you just have medium eggs, 2 percent milk, or salted butter, don't turn the page. Everything is adjustable—add a splash of cream to thinner milk, or a spoonful of yogurt, or just leave it as is. Hold back on the salt if you have salted butter and then adjust accordingly. **Stress makes food taste bad**, so try not to worry much. My dear friend Amelia, who works in the art world, keeps a sticker above her desk that says, "There's no such thing as an art emergency." The same sentiment applies to making dinner.

A thought on **olive oil**, which I pretty much go through by the bucket. While I appreciate a strong-flavored, expensive oil, I don't think you need to spend a fortune on olive oil. If I am lucky enough to have been given a bottle of really nice olive oil, I usually keep it for things where I will really taste it, like drizzling it over an avocado I've smashed on toast or stirring it into spaghetti that will also get some grated cheese and cracked black pepper and nothing else. For general, all-purpose cooking, salad dressing making, etc., I actually love Trader Joe's olive oil, and I have used other store brands with equal success (such as Whole Foods' 365 brand; and if you're in the New York area, Fairway's olive oil is awesome). Wherever you purchase your olive oil, get anything that encourages you to have a generous pour (meaning it needn't break the bank). On a similar note, always buy the bigger bottle. You can never have too much.

Keep your **tomatoes** at room temperature and, for extended periods of time, your **lemons** and **limes** in the fridge. Tomatoes get mealy and lose a lot of flavor when they're refrigerated. And lemons and limes look beautiful set out in a bowl on your counter, but they always get moldy when I leave them out, and who wants that?

It's best to **start cooking meat and poultry when they're at room temperature** rather than right out of the refrigerator so that they cook evenly. In general, you want to shock things as little as possible in the kitchen (imagine how it feels to jump into a freezing swimming pool versus a lukewarm one). A **instant-read thermometer** is a good tool to rely on to test meat and poultry for doneness. Like a scale for measuring flour, a thermometer takes a lot of guesswork out of cooking and can be helpful not just for the sake of precision but for peace of mind (I've offered temperatures throughout and other cues if you don't have a thermometer). On a similar temperature note, don't be afraid to **serve things at room temperature**. The hardest part of making a meal isn't making the individual elements, but timing them so that they're ready at the same time. Lots of things taste just as good at room temperature as they do warm, and some are even better. And remember, **people are coming to your home, not to a restaurant**. That's a wonderful thing and a good reason to embrace a casual, comfortable vibe.

Just because your oven dial says a certain number, that doesn't guarantee that the interior will actually be at that temperature. An **oven thermometer** (available at most grocery and hardware stores) is not expensive, and it is very useful when baking since all ovens, in my experience, are always a little off. That said, my childhood babysitter, Jennie, who is an amazing baker, makes bread and cakes all the time, but her dial broke years ago—she just puts her hand in the oven to see if she thinks it's hot enough—and all of her stuff turns out perfectly. While I don't really advocate this technique, my point in mentioning it is that there's no need to stress too much about a few degrees. People have been baking and roasting since long before everything in our lives became digital and easy to calculate.

In general, anytime you put something in the oven to bake or roast, **keep an eye on it**, just like you would if it were in a pan on your stove top or on the grates of your grill. Look out for how fast (or slow) things are browning, and adjust the temperature if/as necessary. **Also trust your nose**. You can tell when many baked goods are ready when the smell becomes intoxicating. And don't be afraid to **touch your food**. A meat loaf will

be nice and firm to the touch, a cake, too, but it's a different kind of firm, one you'll be able to identify after you make a few (or really just one—trust your instincts, you most likely have more than you know). A pie should bubble with fruit juice and a biscuit should get tall and brown and irresistible. Don't be afraid to **get to know your food** and learn about all the cues it will offer.

On the topic of ovens, note that I never mention using the **convection setting** in your oven for the very simple reason that I don't have a fancy oven and that is not an option for me. I wouldn't feel comfortable suggesting a setting that I haven't used for a recipe, but if you're into convection, go for it.

A drawer away from your stove is the best place to store **spices** since it is cool and dark and also allows you to look at your whole collection instead of just the first row inside of a cabinet. I can't tell you the amount of times I've gone out and purchased something I already own simply because I couldn't find it when I first looked! If your container doesn't already have a label on top, just write it down with a permanent marker (or if the lid is too dark, write the spice name on a piece of masking tape or on a little piece of paper that you attach with clear tape).

When someone invites you over for dinner and tells you that he or she doesn't need anything, **bring something anyway**. Might I suggest breakfast for the next morning, like homemade granola or muffins or something nice from a neighborhood bakery. Or maybe a bag of great coffee beans and a bottle of freshly squeezed orange or grapefruit juice. I've also never seen anyone disappointed to receive a batch of homemade cookie dough . . . just saying.

Unusual Ingredients

I've made a point to only use ingredients that are readily available, and in any instance where I have not (for example, in the Zucchini + Nigella Fritters on page 107), I have explained why I have included something obscure and have also suggested substitutions. The following not-totally-obscure, but also not-totally-obvious ingredients pop up in more than one place throughout the book. While I use them frequently, I understand that they might not be as regularly featured in your kitchen. Here are some thoughts on them.

Buttermilk, readily available in the dairy aisle, is the liquid that's leftover after cream has been churned into butter. It's thick and tangy and remarkably good for you (it's much lower in fat than it appears) and is also wonderful for baking and marinating since its acidity adds flavor and tenderizes everything from cakes to fried chicken. If buying a carton for just a small amount seems off-putting, check out the index to see all the recipes that use it, use extra to marinate a chicken before roasting, or simply substitute an equal amount of whole milk with a little fresh lemon juice or white vinegar stirred into it and let the milk mixture sit for about 10 minutes before using. Buttermilk has the added advantage of keeping, refrigerated, for up to 3 weeks.

Crème fraîche, often found either in the dairy aisle near the sour cream or in the cheese department, is essentially French sour cream. It's not quite as sour as American sour cream and it's got a higher fat content, which makes it wonderfully decadent. I use it in so many things because it's good cold (try a dollop on a slice of cake, such as the Afternoon Cake on page 229) and also works really well in cooked applications, such as a substitution for béchamel in both lasagana (see page 145) and chicken pot pie (see page 184). If you can't find it, simply subsitutute an equal amount of regular sour cream. Feel free to whisk in a little heavy cream or plain cream cheese to up the fat content.

Fish sauce, which I like to think of as Southeast Asian equivalent of Worcestershire sauce (whose main ingredient is, believe it or not, anchovies), is a dark brown liquid made from fermented anchovies. I know that sounds so terrible, but it's truly one of the world's most incredible condiments, totally full of funk and a deep, salty flavor. I use it in many recipes and find it to be so valuable. It's readily available in most supermarkets these days, almost always next to the soy sauce. It's also available in Asian grocery stores and online from redboatfishsauce.com. Nothing really mimics its flavor, but you can substitute half rice vinegar and half soy sauce.

Gochugaru (Korean red chile flakes) and **Aleppo pepper** (Middle Eastern red chile flakes) are two of the dried chiles I adore and use frequently. You can substitute regular red pepper flakes for either (like the ones that are on the counter at pizza joints), but use a bit less as both gochugaru and Aleppo pepper are not quite as spicy as standard red pepper flakes. Both are increasingly available in speciality food stores and are also readily available online through kalustyans.com.

Gochujang, a Korean hot-pepper paste made primarily out of gochugaru (Korean red chile flakes), is one of my all-time favorite condiments. You can use an equal amount of any chile paste in its place, such as Sriracha. To find gochujang, check out your local Asian market or go online to hmart.com.

Kimchi, basically Korean sauerkraut, is an umbrella term that refers to any fermented vegetable, but the most common type, and the one I refer to any time I call for kimchi, is napa cabbage kimchi with plenty of Korean red chile pepper. These days, kimchi is easier than ever to find and you can often locate it in the refrigerated section of the produce department in plenty of grocery stores (near the refrigerated salad dressings) and also near the refrigerated pickles. It is also sometimes, sort of oddly, in the dairy section. Anywhere there's a space in the refrigerator, I guess? Anyway, you can also find kimchi in most Asian grocery stores and also online at hmart.com, milkimchi .com, and Mama O's (kimchirules.com). I am particularly partial to Mama O's Super Spicy variety. They also carry a great vegan version (most kimchi has shrimp, anchovy, and/or other seafood in it). The liquid that the kimchi comes packed in is just as valuable as the kimchi itself, so be sure not to pour it down the drain. See the recipe on page 26 and the Spin-Off on page 27 for more about ways to use the juice.

Pimentón, Spanish smoked paprika, is the most crucial spice in Spanish cooking. It basically tastes like the most amazing peppery, smoky, slightly sweet barbeque sauce in powdered form. It's available in both hot and sweet forms, and my preference is for hot since I like food on the spicy side—but feel free to use whichever you prefer (or have on hand). Pimentón has become so popular in the past decade or so that it's now much easier to find than it used to be. Check the spice aisle in your local grocery store. If you can't find it there, go online to kalustyans .com or latienda.com. You can also substitute regular paprika in its place.

Preserved lemons are whole lemons that have been preserved in salt. Very popular in North African cooking, preserved lemons are packed in jars and look almost like candied fruit floating in brine. They taste like a lemon that bumped into a pickle that then collided with something deeper and richer—maybe an intense olive or something. You can use the whole fruit, skin and pith and everything (such as in the chermoula on page 211), as well as the brine they're packed in (like in the dressing for the zucchini salad on page 91). You can sometimes find them in the ethnic aisle of your grocery store, in most speciality and cheese stores (I think cheese people like the way they look on their shelves?), and also online. You can use a fresh lemon (or lemon juice) in its place and add a little extra bit of salt to compensate, too.

Tahini, a thick paste made from ground sesame seeds, is a great way to get a nutty depth of flavor in dressings (such as the one for the carrot salad on page 84) and in dips (like the eggplant one on page 122). It's widely available in grocery stores, often near the peanut butter (which it's not that dissimilar to) and also online. If you can't find it or don't feel like buying it, feel free to use an equal amount of toasted sesame seeds in its place (you can even bash them using a mortar and pestle) or a bit of toasted sesame oil. Neither of these will give you the same texture, but you will get the right flavor.

BREAKFAST

Avocado + Kimchi Toast

SERVES 4

I know avocado toast is basically an overplayed song, but you need this one! I swear. It uses not just kimchi but also the liquid that kimchi comes packed in to make a ridiculously good dressing (which is, in and of itself, a **small victory**), and the whole thing is so quick and easy and, may I add, especially good with a fried egg on top. A wonderful breakfast for a crowd is a big platter of these toasts and another platter of halved hard-boiled eggs (see page 33) with extra kimchi dressing drizzled on top of them. This toast also gives me a chance to talk about a **small victory** I learned the hard way: How to pit an avocado without cutting yourself. Too often I see people (i.e., me) hold half an avocado in the palm of one hand and whack a large knife into the pit to remove it. This method means the likelihood of that knife slipping just a bit this way or that could too easily result in a serious yet preventable injury. To *safely* pit an avocado, slice it in half all the way around and then put the half holding the pit on your cutting board, pit-side up. With your non-knife-hand securely out of the way, assertively swing your big knife down from a small distance so that the thicker part of the blade lands directly in the pit. Twist the knife to loosen the pit and then pinch two fingers over the top of the knife on either side of the pit to loosen it from the blade's grip—it will fall off like magic, and no extremity will have ever been in contact with the sharp edge of the blade. Phew!

2 Tbsp juice from the kimchi jar, plus 1 cup [200 g] drained cabbage kimchi, roughly chopped

2 Tbsp mayonnaise

Kosher salt

1 ripe avocado, halved, pitted, peeled, and sliced

4 large slices country bread, toasted

1 tsp toasted sesame seeds

A small handful of roughly chopped fresh cilantro

In a small bowl, whisk together the kimchi juice and mayonnaise. Season to taste with salt.

Place one-fourth of the avocado slices on top of each slice of toast and mash the avocado into the toasts with a fork. Sprinkle each one with a generous pinch of salt.

Divide the chopped kimchi evenly among the toasts and drizzle each with one-fourth of the mayonnaise mixture. Sprinkle the sesame seeds and cilantro evenly over the toasts, and slice each one in half. Serve immediately.

SPIN-OFFS

FOR A REFRESHING SALAD, combine cubes of ripe avocado with a diced cucumber (I especially like the slim Israeli ones that aren't too bitter for this, but use whatever you've got) and drizzle with the kimchi juice–mayonnaise dressing. Sprinkle with a few sesame seeds.

FOR A FANCY SALAD, substitute jumbo lump crabmeat for the cucumber and serve with ice-cold glasses of champagne.

THE KIMCHI JUICE–MAYONNAISE DRESSING Is so simple and so useful. Serve drizzled on grilled chicken or skirt steak (see page 159) or on roasted or grilled vegetables (whole scallions, cubed sweet potatoes, asparagus, and broccoli florets all come to mind). Or drizzle over tacos, especially breakfast tacos with scrambled eggs and/or bacon and/or cheddar cheese. Or use it as a dip for chicken nuggets, raw vegetables, even potato chips.

Gravlax with Caper Cream Cheese

SERVES 6

My grandfather wasn't an indulgent man, but there were a handful of things he absolutely loved to eat. The list isn't very long: fresh scallops, pesto, ripe blueberries, and pumpernickel bread. Even though he's been gone for quite a few years, I'm still always in search of a good loaf of pumpernickel and I think of him so fondly when I find one (Russ & Daughters on Manhattan's Lower East Side for the win). My favorite way to enjoy pumpernickel is toasted and spread with a thick schmear of cream cheese and shingled with salty salmon. The **small victory** here has less to do with the nostalgia of pumpernickel and everything to do with homemade gravlax. Once you realize that a simple combination of sugar, salt, and time can effectively cure fish, not only does serving gravlax become infinitely more affordable but you also gain complete control of the quality of the fish you're using and the flavors you infuse it with. It's good to be the one behind the wheel in the kitchen.

GRAVLAX

Packed ¼ cup [50 g] dark brown sugar

½ cup [70 g] kosher salt

½ tsp freshly ground black pepper

1 tsp fennel seeds (optional)

A handful of fresh sprigs of dill, roughly chopped (optional)

One 1-lb [455-g] salmon fillet, skin and any pin bones removed

CREAM CHEESE

8 oz [230 g] cream cheese, at room temperature

Grated zest and juice of 1 lemon

2 Tbsp capers, roughly chopped

2 Tbsp finely chopped fresh chives

½ tsp kosher salt

½ tsp freshly ground black pepper

12 slices pumpernickel bread, toasted, or 6 pumpernickel bagels, split and toasted

A few thinly sliced radishes and/or a sliced cucumber for serving

TO MAKE THE GRAVLAX: In a small bowl, stir together the brown sugar, salt, pepper, fennel seeds (if using), and dill (if using). Use your hands to do this so that you break up any clumps in the sugar.

Put a large piece of plastic wrap on your work surface and put half of the salt mixture on the plastic, spreading it to an even thickness that measures slightly bigger than your piece of salmon. Put the salmon on top of the mixture and cover it with the remaining half of the salt

mixture. Use your hands to pack the mixture on and around the fish. Wrap the salmon tightly in the plastic wrap, using an extra piece if needed, but leave the ends open so some air can circulate and the liquid from the fish can drain easily. Put the wrapped salmon on a wire rack set on a small rimmed baking sheet and put another baking sheet on top of the fish. Put something heavy, like a cast-iron pan or a couple of cans of tomatoes, on top of the baking sheet to weigh the whole thing down. (You could use just about anything in place of the baking sheets, such as two large plates, if you don't have space in your refrigerator for the baking sheets—just be sure whatever is on the bottom has a rim to catch the liquid that escapes from the fish.)

Put the whole shebang in the refrigerator and let the salmon cure for at least 2 days, for a light cure (the salmon will still be moist), or up to 3 days, for a more intense cure (the salmon will lose quite a bit of moisture). Flip the salmon once a day and drain off whatever liquid accumulates on the baking sheet.

TO MAKE THE CREAM CHEESE: Put the cream cheese, lemon zest, lemon juice, capers, chives, salt, and pepper in a food processor and pulse to combine (alternatively, mix everything in a large bowl using a potato masher or a fork). Keep this mixture at room temperature if you're serving it immediately. Otherwise, wrap it tightly and refrigerate for up to 1 week; bring the cream cheese back to room temperature before serving so it's easy to spread.

When the salmon is cured, unwrap it, thoroughly rinse off the salt mixture, and pat dry with paper towels. Thinly slice the salmon on the diagonal. Spread the cream cheese mixture liberally on the toast and top with the gravlax. Serve topped with thin slices of radish and/or cucumber.

SPIN-OFFS

FOR CARAWAY GRAVLAX, substitute 1 tsp caraway seeds for the fennel seeds. Leave the dill in or take it out—up to you.

FOR PASTRAMI GRAVLAX, up the black pepper to a full 1 Tbsp and add 1 tsp each coriander seeds and black mustard seeds. Leave out the fennel seeds and dill.

FOR KOREAN-STYLE GRAVLAX, add 1 Tbsp gochugaru (Korean red pepper flakes) and 1 tsp toasted sesame seeds. Leave out the black pepper and fennel seeds. Substitute two thinly sliced scallions for the dill.

Skip the fish and make **DRY-BRINED PICKLES**. For carrot-and-dill pickles, thinly slice a whole heap of carrots; toss with salt, sugar, and chopped dill; and refrigerate them, loosely covered with plastic wrap, for a few days. Stir them every so often. Actually, make these at the same time as the gravlax and serve them with the gravlax—yum!

Olive Oil–Fried Eggs with Yogurt + Lemon

SERVES 1; EASILY MULTIPLIED

My dad jokes that my way of turning anything into a meal is to put a fried egg on top of it. He even had what he thought was the *best idea in the world!*—for me to figure out a way to remix "Single Ladies (Put a Ring on It)," Beyoncé's seminal song, to "Put an Egg on It" (I'll add that laughing at your own jokes runs in my family). Needless to say, he is right—I do think just about everything is improved with a fried egg on top, and adding one to anything at all, even a bowl of leftover spaghetti, makes for a complete meal. The **small victory** here is adding a few drops of water to the pan to create steam and then immediately covering the pan to trap that steam. This makes perfectly cooked eggs with runny yolks but fully set whites (nothing to me is more off-putting than an uncooked egg white).

¼ cup [60 ml] plain yogurt	Freshly ground black pepper	1 Tbsp roughly chopped leafy fresh herbs, such as basil, dill, chervil, chives, and/or parsley
½ lemon	2 Tbsp extra-virgin olive oil	
Kosher salt	2 eggs	

In a small bowl, combine the yogurt and most of the juice from the lemon half (don't discard the lemon half) and whisk together. Season to taste with salt and pepper. Transfer the mixture to a plate and use a spoon to spread it so that it covers most of the plate.

In a nonstick skillet over medium-high heat, warm the olive oil. Crack the eggs into the pan and sprinkle each egg with a bit of salt and a few grinds of black pepper. Sprinkle a few drops of water (less than 1 tsp) into the skillet, being sure to let the water hit the bottom of the pan and not the eggs, and immediately cover the skillet with a lid.

Let the eggs cook until the whites are cooked through but the yolks are still a bit wobbly, just a minute or two. Transfer the eggs to the prepared plate, setting them on top of the yogurt. Squeeze whatever juice remains in the lemon half over the eggs and scatter over the herbs. Serve immediately.

(Continued)

SPIN-OFFS

FOR EGG-IN-A-HOLE, start by using a juice glass or a cookie cutter to cut a circle out of a piece of bread. Use butter instead of olive oil for cooking, put the slice of bread in the hot buttered skillet, and crack an egg right into the hole that you stamped out. I like to toast the little circle of bread right alongside the egg-in-a-hole (I think of this as like getting a donut hole along with your donut). Sprinkle the egg with salt and pepper, add a couple drops of water to the pan, cover the pan, and cook until the egg is just about set on the bottom (a minute or two), then flip it over to "seal" the other side of the egg and to toast the second side of the bread. Serve immediately, with the circle of bread acting as a little hat.

FOR SHAKSHUKA, a Middle Eastern dish of eggs cooked in an aromatic, often spicy, tomato sauce, sauté a sliced onion in a generous amount of olive oil with plenty of minced garlic, a finely chopped fresh chile pepper (I generally like a jalapeño, mainly because it's readily available), and a few shakes of ground cumin. Once the onion and garlic are soft, add a 28-oz [794-g] can of tomatoes, crush with a potato masher, and simmer the whole mix until it's thick and saucy, about 20 minutes. Season with salt, then crack a few eggs into the pan, right onto the sauce, cover with a lid, and cook until the eggs are just cooked through, about 5 minutes (the sauce creates the steam that cooks the eggs beautifully). Serve sprinkled with chopped herbs (parsley and/or dill is nice) and some crumbled feta. And warm pita bread. Yum.

Green Eggs With (or Without) Ham

SERVES 4

The funny thing about hard-boiled eggs is that the best ones, the ones without that dark line bordering a chalky egg yolk, aren't boiled at all—the eggs start in cold water which is simply brought to a boil and then the pot gets covered and the eggs just sit in that warm, cozy hot tub. This gentle cooking, a true **small victory**, is something I learned from watching Julia Child, my beloved hero, on television (you should know that when I was growing up and had elected to spend all of my time in the kitchen, I was affectionately called "Julia-the-Child"). While I advise using the freshest ingredients as a baseline rule, the second **small victory** here is that older eggs (by which I mean at least a week or two after you bought them) not only work well, they work *better* and are much easier to peel than fresh eggs. Served with an easy, punchy parsley sauce and a little bit of salty country ham (which you can absolutely skip but I couldn't resist the recipe name), these savory eggs are one of my favorite breakfast items.

Packed ½ cup [20 g] fresh Italian parsley leaves, finely chopped

1 small garlic clove, minced

1 tsp red or white wine vinegar, plus more as needed

¼ cup [60 ml] olive oil

Kosher salt

8 old eggs (*at least* a week old)

4 oz [115 g] sliced country ham for serving (optional)

In a small bowl, combine the parsley, garlic, vinegar, olive oil, and a pinch of salt and stir everything together. Taste for seasoning, adding a bit more salt and/or vinegar if you'd like. Let the sauce sit at room temperature while you prepare the eggs (this rest will allow the ingredients to really get to know each other, a good thing).

Put the eggs in a saucepan that's taller than it is wide and cover them with 1 in [2.5 cm] cold water. Set the pan over high heat and bring to a boil. The moment it comes to a full boil, turn off the heat, cover the pan, and let it sit for exactly 10 minutes. Meanwhile, fill a large bowl with half water and half ice and set it aside.

Using a strainer or a slotted spoon, transfer the eggs to the ice-water bath and let them chill until they're cool enough to handle. Then, working with one egg at a time, crack the egg on your work surface and peel it (I like to rinse the peeled eggs under running water to make sure there's no lingering shell).

Cut the eggs in half or into quarters, whatever you prefer, and transfer them to a serving platter. Spoon the parsley sauce over the eggs and pile the ham alongside, if desired. Serve immediately.

(Continued)

SPIN-OFFS

FOR DEVILED EGGS, halve the hard-boiled eggs and put all the yolks in a medium bowl. Mash them together with mayonnaise (use plenty), a little mustard, and a few drops of hot sauce and then whisk it all together until it's really smooth. Season the mixture with salt. Transfer to a plastic bag, snip off a bottom corner, and pipe the mixture into the hollowed-out egg whites. Top with snipped chives or parsley and/or a shake of paprika.

FOR DEVILED-ISH EGGS without much work, halve the hard-boiled eggs, spread the surface of each one with a generous amount of mayonnaise, douse them with hot sauce, and call it a day!

Instead of the parsley sauce, **SPRINKLE WITH DUKKAH**, a mixture of ground nuts and spices popular throughout the Middle East. I like to do one part each pistachios and sesame seeds pulsed in the food processor with a bit of ground coriander, fennel seeds, cumin seeds, and lots of freshly ground black pepper and kosher salt. This mixture is also really good on avocado toast or sprinkled over a bowl of any cooked grain. Keep any leftover dukkah in a jar and leave it out where you can see it so you don't forget about it. You'll be pleasantly surprised by how good it makes just about anything.

TURN THE EGGS INTO SAUCE GRIBICHE, a classic French sauce that's great with steamed asparagus, poached fish, or chicken. I also really like it on ham sandwiches. It's also very good simply served on toast (preferably a slice that's been rubbed with a raw garlic clove), which makes an excellent snack and an unexpected bite to have with cocktails. Simply chop a few hard-boiled eggs and mix them together with chopped capers, chopped parsley, mustard, a splash of vinegar, and plenty of olive oil. Mix and match these ingredients as you like, and feel free to try other herbs like tarragon, chives, and/or chervil.

Chilaquiles with Roasted Tomato Salsa

SERVES 4

Chilaquiles are crispy corn tortillas that are softened and flavored with salsa and served warm, often for breakfast with fried eggs on top. A great example of transforming something that has seemingly gone bad (stale tortilla chips) into something totally memorable, the **small victory** here is all about figuring out the best way to turn something old into something entirely new. If you don't want or have time to fry your own chips, simply substitute six large handfuls of store-bought tortilla chips. Note that the roasted tomato salsa is also a **small victory** unto itself. It's my go-to salsa that I use for everything from a dip for chips to a taco topping.

1 lb [455 g] tomatoes, cored and roughly chopped

1 jalapeño chile, stemmed, roughly chopped (seeds and all—or seed it, or use less than a whole chile if you're not into super-spicy food, or leave it out if you don't like spice at all)

1 small yellow onion, thinly sliced

Canola oil for drizzling and frying

Kosher salt

Packed ¼ cup [10 g] fresh cilantro leaves, plus more for serving

5 Tbsp fresh lime juice

3 Tbsp sour cream

12 corn tortillas, cut into thick strips or wedges

¼ cup [50 g] drained Pickled Red Onions (page 267)

¼ cup [80 g] finely crumbled Cotija cheese (or crumbled feta cheese)

4 fried eggs (see page 31; optional)

Preheat your oven to 425°F [220°C]. Line a baking sheet with parchment paper.

Place the tomatoes, jalapeño, and onion on the prepared baking sheet. Drizzle the vegetables with 1 Tbsp canola oil and sprinkle with ½ tsp salt. Roast, stirring now and then, until the vegetables are softened and browned in spots, about 20 minutes.

Transfer the roasted vegetables to a blender or a food processor and add the cilantro and 3 Tbsp of the lime juice. Puree until smooth. Season the salsa to taste with salt and set aside.

In a small bowl, whisk together the sour cream and the remaining 2 Tbsp lime juice. Season to taste with salt. Set aside.

In a large heavy pot over medium-high heat, warm ½ in [12 mm] canola oil. Once the oil is nice and hot (it should bubble vigorously if you dip the edge of a tortilla into it), add a large handful of tortilla strips, just enough to form a single layer, and cook, turning each one once, until crispy and golden brown, about 1 minute per side. Use tongs or a slotted spoon to transfer the chips to a paper towel–lined baking sheet and continue cooking the remaining tortilla

(Continued)

chips, adding more oil to the pot as necessary. Season to taste with salt. The chips will crisp as they cool.

Once you've crisped all of your tortillas, pour off and discard whatever oil remains in the pot (for easy and safe disposal, pour it into a bowl, let it cool, and then pour it into a bottle or jar, seal, and throw it away). Add the reserved salsa to the pot and bring it to a boil. Lower the heat to a simmer, add the tortilla chips, and cook, stirring now and then, until the chips have softened and absorbed some of the salsa,

about 5 minutes. At first it will look like a lot of chips and not much salsa, but the tortillas will quickly absorb the sauce and become almost a bit wilted. You want the final chilaquiles to be soft but not soggy.

Divide the chilaquiles evenly among four plates and drizzle each portion with one-fourth of the sour cream mixture. Scatter the pickled onions, Cotija, and cilantro over the chilaquiles and top each portion with a fried egg, if desired. For vegan friends, simply omit the sour cream and Cotija (and the eggs). Serve immediately.

SPIN-OFFS

To make **CHILAQUILES WITH SALSA VERDE**, substitute toma-tillos (papery layers removed, cored, washed, and roughly chopped) for the tomatoes and proceed as directed, roasting the tomatillos with the onion and garlic.

USE THE ROASTED TOMATO MIXTURE AS A JUMPING OFF POINT for dinner. When you take it out of the oven, put thin fish fillets (such as flounder), peeled shrimp, or chicken tenders on top of the mixture and drizzle with olive oil and sprinkle with salt. Continue to roast until the fish (or shrimp or chicken) is cooked through, about 10 minutes. Serve with cooked rice and lime wedges for squeezing over.

The only thing that rivals chila-quiles in terms of a way to use leftover tortilla chips is **DOUG'S FAMOUS TEX-MEX MEAT LOAF** (Doug is my father). To make it, combine 1 lb [455 g] ground beef or ground turkey with 1½ cups [125 g] crushed tortilla chips (crush them in a food processor or in a plastic bag with the help of a rolling pin), 2 beaten eggs, ½ cup [120 ml] store-bought salsa, and ½ cup [50 g] grated cheddar cheese. Season with salt and pepper. Shape into a loaf on a parchment paper–lined rimmed baking sheet,

Bake in a 375°F [190°C] oven until the meat loaf is firm to the touch, about 45 minutes, depending on its dimensions. If you'd like, you can put some extra grated cheese or even a thin layer of ketchup on top of the meat loaf halfway through baking for extra umph. By the way, the only thing that's better than a slice of this meat loaf is a sandwich made the day after with melted cheddar cheese on a toasted English muffin.

Bread, Sausage + Apple Hash

SERVES 4

I adore simplicity and I think restraint, especially when it comes to cooking, is one of the most elegant things to practice. I haven't always been this way. True story: I am a recovered snob. When I first started cooking Thanksgiving dinner for my entire family and our extended tables of friends, which was when I was in middle school, I insisted that everyone try my *warm panzanella with sausage and autumnal vegetables*. I threw a fit when my brother insisted it was just stuffing . . . which, in fact, it was. As I've gotten older, I've toned down the pretension and embraced the comfort of familiarity. I have also continued to tweak my stuffing recipe, as it's my favorite item on the Thanksgiving menu, especially when the leftovers are crisped in a frying pan the next morning and topped with a runny fried egg. **Small victory**: Special holiday foods can be made any day of the year. This is something I make often, especially for friends when they visit for a weekend. It's at once comforting and surprising. Another **small victory**: Leftover bread, an often-neglected ingredient, is the springboard to so many incredibly satisfying and flavorful dishes. I've included more stale-bread ideas in the Spin-Offs.

4 thick slices relatively plain day-old bread, such as sourdough or a sesame loaf, torn into bite-size pieces

2 Tbsp extra-virgin olive oil

8 oz [230 g] sweet Italian sausage, casings removed

2 Tbsp unsalted butter

1 small green apple, halved, cored, and cut into ½-in [12-mm] dice

½ small yellow onion, finely diced

Kosher salt

Freshly ground black pepper

6 fresh sage leaves, finely chopped

1 garlic clove, minced

¾ cup [180 ml] chicken or vegetable stock

A small handful of finely chopped fresh Italian parsley

4 fried eggs (see page 31)

Preheat your oven to 400°F [200°C].

Put the bread on a baking sheet and toast, stirring now and then, until it is browned and crisp, about 10 minutes. Set aside.

Meanwhile, in a large skillet over medium-high heat, warm the olive oil. Once it's good and hot, crumble the sausage into the pan and cook, stirring, until the meat is browned and its fat is rendered, about 10 minutes. Use a slotted spoon to transfer the sausage to a plate, leaving the fat in the pan.

Turn the heat to medium-low; add the butter, apple, and onion to the pan; and season with a generous pinch of salt and a few grinds of pepper. Cook, stirring now and then, until the vegetables begin to soften, about 10 minutes. Add the sage and garlic and cook, stirring, until the garlic has lost its raw edge and smells fragrant, about 1 minute.

(Continued)

Add the chicken stock to the pan and bring to a boil. Use a wooden spoon to scrape the bottom of the pan, picking up any browned bits. Add the toasted bread and sausage, along with any liquid that accumulated on the sausage plate, and cook, stirring now and then, just until the bread is slightly softened, all of the liquid has evaporated, and it smells like Thanksgiving, 5 minutes or so. Stir in the parsley and season to taste with more salt and pepper. Serve immediately, topped with the fried eggs.

SPIN-OFFS

To turn leftover bread into **CROUTONS**, simply tear up your loaf (any kind you have) into shaggy bite-size pieces, toss with olive oil, and season with kosher salt. Feel free to add fresh herbs (such as thyme, oregano, or rosemary), minced garlic, and/or grated Parmesan cheese. Bake in a 400°F [200°C] oven, stirring now and then, until browned and crisp.

To turn leftover bread into **ROMESCO SAUCE**, make croutons as instructed above and blend them in a food processor or a blender with roasted red peppers (see page 61 or use store-bought), toasted almonds or hazelnuts, a little minced garlic, olive oil, a splash of sherry vinegar, salt, and pepper. You want everything to be well-combined and nearly smooth, but not super smooth—a little texture is nice. Serve with roasted onions or leeks or grilled fish or chicken. For about 1 cup [240 ml] sauce, I'd recommend 1 cup [30 g] croutons, a single roasted pepper, a small handful of nuts, a small garlic clove, a healthy drizzle of oil, and about 1 tsp vinegar. But this is a relaxed thing—mix and match and taste and see what you like.

To turn leftover bread into **THE EASIEST, "I-JUST-THREW-IT-TOGETHER! BREAD PUDDING,"** start with dried-out slices of bread, preferably something soft and rich like challah or brioche or croissants. Tear into large pieces until you have enough to fill whatever size baking dish you want to use. Make a custard with equal amounts of eggs and dairy (preferably half-and-half, but whole milk is just fine, as is coconut milk or sour cream thinned with milk) and sweeten with whatever you like—brown sugar, granulated sugar, maple syrup. I usually do ½ cup [100 g] sugar, more or less, for every 3 eggs. Add a pinch of salt and whatever other flavorings you'd like (vanilla, cinnamon, and bourbon come to mind) and soak everything in the dish while your oven heats to 350°F [180°C]. Feel free to add chopped nuts, raisins, chocolate chips, fresh berries, and/or sliced bananas. Bake the bread pudding until browned and puffy, about 45 minutes, depending on the amount of pudding and the size of the baking dish.

Sour Cream Pancakes with Roasted Blueberries

SERVES 2 TO 4, DEPENDING ON HOW HUNGRY YOU ARE
(I.E., 4 IS THE RECOMMEND SERVING SIZE, 2 IS THE REALISTIC ONE)

I have always been a savory-breakfast person (leftover soup, sure! spicy sausage with salted yogurt and herbs, yes!), but my wife, Grace, has made me a total pancake convert. She not only loves them, she also makes the most incredible ones, often studded with so many banana slices and chunks of dark chocolate that you're already halfway into your nap before you finish your plate. One weekend morning, Grace slept in late (very unusual for her) and I got to make them for us. I was almost finished with the batter when I went to reach for milk and realized we had none. There was, however, a container of sour cream. Then I went to get the baking powder and realized we were out of that too. I added the sour cream and a shake of baking soda and made a wish. The pancakes didn't just work out, we loved them.

I did a bit of research to understand exactly why they worked and once I'd demystified leavening, the whole world of raised pancakes and baked goods became a lot more comprehensible—a **small victory** of the nerdiest kind. Baking powder and baking soda are both leavening agents that, when combined with liquid, form carbon dioxide, the gas that helps baked goods rise. Baking soda needs something acidic (sour cream, buttermilk, lemon juice, or yogurt, for example) to kick it into gear, but once it is in effect it works really well and doesn't leave an off-taste the way baking powder sometimes can. It expires quickly, though, so it's important to make sure it's within its sell-by date (or test it by making sure it fizzes when a small amount is mixed with a little vinegar). Baking powder is essentially baking soda with an acid mixed into it, so it's guaranteed to work, but using too much can leave a bit of a metallic taste. That's why, in my opinion, for flatter things like pancakes, you should use just a little baking soda and an acidic ingredient; for anything where you desire more height, such as biscuits, use a bit of both soda and powder—a double hit of leavening to guarantee a good rise.

1¼ cups [160 g] blueberries, rinsed and drained

Packed 3 Tbsp dark brown sugar

¾ cup [90 g] all-purpose flour

1 tsp baking soda

½ tsp kosher salt

2 eggs

1 cup [240 ml] sour cream

Unsalted butter for cooking and serving

(Continued)

Preheat your oven to 400°F [200°C].

In a baking dish, combine the blueberries with 2 Tbsp of the brown sugar and stir to mix. Roast, pulling the baking dish out of the oven a few times to stir the berries, until their skins burst and they have released lots of juice, about 20 minutes. Using a fork or a potato masher, crush the berries a bit so that they become jammy. Set aside.

Meanwhile, in a large bowl, combine the flour, baking soda, and salt and whisk to combine. Crack the eggs into a medium bowl, add the sour cream and remaining 1 Tbsp brown sugar, and whisk until the mixture is uniform. Pour the sour cream mixture into the flour mixture and use a wooden spoon to mix everything together. It's okay if the batter isn't perfectly smooth—it's better to undermix than overmix.

Set a large cast-iron skillet, a griddle, or your largest nonstick pan over medium heat and add 1 Tbsp butter. Once the butter melts, swirl the pan or brush the griddle to evenly coat the surface. Pour the batter into the pan in ¼-cup [60-ml] increments to form pancakes that are roughly 4 in [10 cm] in diameter; cook only as many pancakes at a time as can fit comfortably in your pan. The minute that pancakes become too precise is the minute they become no fun, so don't stress over this—it's okay if they're not all the same size. Cook the pancakes until small bubbles appear on the surface and the undersides are nicely browned, 1 to 2 minutes. Flip the pancakes over and cook until the second sides are nicely browned, another minute or so. Transfer the pancakes to warm plates and continue making pancakes, adding more butter as you go, until you've used up all the batter.

Serve the pancakes immediately, with more butter on top and the warm roasted blueberries.

SPIN-OFFS

FOR BUTTERMILK, YOGURT, OR CRÈME FRAÎCHE PANCAKES, substitute 1 cup [230 g] of one of these for the sour cream.

SHAKE UP THE TOPPING ROUTINE by roasting just about any fruit in place of the blueberries, or use a mix of berries (berries will be the most jammy, but all fruit benefits from the concentrated caramelization that happens in the oven). Roasted blackberries, sliced bananas, sliced peaches, and thinly sliced apples or pears are all really delicious. Or rhubarb! Just keep an eye on the fruit while it's roasting, as some types (e.g., apples) take a little longer than others and some (e.g., sliced bananas) take not much time at all.

THE ROASTED FRUIT TOPPING IS VERY VERSATILE; serve it over ice cream for dessert, on toast spread with ricotta for breakfast, or on waffles for any time. Stir it into yogurt. Or serve alongside a roasted or grilled rich meat like pork shoulder or pork chops. Or lamb! Lamb loves fruit.

Apple + Toasted Oat Muffins

MAKES 12 MUFFINS

I've gathered everything I know about muffins into this single recipe, which offers not just one, but three **small victories**. *First*, scooping the muffin batter into the tin using an ice-cream scoop (the kind with a lever) means evenly sized muffins and no extra batter flinging itself onto the spaces between the muffin cups (you know, the bits that always burn and are a nag to get off). *Second*, tossing add-ins such as chopped apples with flour before stirring them into the batter keeps them from sinking to the bottom—think of the flour coating as a little raincoat (this goes for nuts and chocolate chips and other things like that, not only in muffins but also in cakes and loaves). *Third*, toasting oats before cooking them, even if just for oatmeal, adds an extra layer of nutty flavor—an ingenious tip that comes straight from my dear friend chef Jody Williams (of Buvette fame).

½ cup [50 g] rolled oats

1½ cups [180 g] all-purpose flour, plus 2 Tbsp

1 tsp baking powder

1 tsp baking soda

1 tsp ground cinnamon

1 tsp ground ginger

1 tsp kosher salt

A pinch of ground cloves

¾ cup [150 g] sugar

½ cup [110 g] unsalted butter, melted and cooled

½ cup [120 ml] milk

1 egg, beaten

1 tsp vanilla extract

1 large apple (use whatever type you like for apple pie; I like Granny Smith, Fuji, or Gala apples best here), peeled, cored, and cut into small dice or coarsely grated

½ cup [70 g] golden or regular raisins

Preheat your oven to 350°F [180°C]. Line a standard 12-well muffin tin with paper liners and set it aside.

Put the oats on a baking sheet and bake them, stirring them now and then, until they smell toasty and are golden brown, 5 to 8 minutes.

In a large bowl, combine the oats with the 1½ cups [180 g] flour and whisk in the baking powder, baking soda, cinnamon, ginger, salt, and cloves. Add the sugar, butter, milk, egg, and vanilla and stir to combine.

Toss the diced apple with the raisins and remaining 2 Tbsp flour so that each piece is coated, then gently stir into the batter.

Use an ice-cream scoop to distribute the batter evenly among the prepared muffin wells.

Bake the muffins until they're nicely browned and a toothpick inserted in the center of a muffin comes out clean, 25 to 30 minutes. Let the muffins cool before eating.

Leftovers can be stored in an airtight container at room temperature for up to 4 days. Split and toast under the broiler or in a toaster oven to refresh.

SPIN-OFFS

FOR BANANA AND WALNUT (AND CHOCOLATE) MUFFINS, mash two very ripe (i.e., covered with dark freckles) peeled bananas with a fork or a potato masher so that they're basically a puree and substitute that for the chopped apples and raisins. Add the mashed bananas with the milk. After mixing the batter, fold in a handful of roughly chopped walnuts (and chocolate chips), tossed with 2 Tbsp flour.

FOR ZUCCHINI AND PECAN MUFFINS, coarsely grate a large zucchini and wrap it in a clean dishcloth. Twist the dishcloth to squeeze out excess liquid and then fold the zucchini into the batter. Leave out the chopped apples and raisins. After mixing the batter, fold in a handful of roughly chopped pecans, tossed with 2 Tbsp flour.

FOR GLUTEN-FREE MUFFINS, use gluten-free oats and flour (plus 1 tsp xanthan gum if the flour doesn't already have it).

FOR DAIRY-FREE MUFFINS, use almond or rice milk instead of cow's milk and olive oil instead of butter.

Raspberry Jam Buns with Crème Fraîche Frosting

MAKES 12 BUNS

When I was in high school, I took a weeklong bread baking intensive at the French Culinary Institute (now called the International Culinary Center). Not only did I feel like I had a better and closer understanding of my maternal grandparents, who ran a bread bakery in Brooklyn long before I was ever even a thought, I also learned so much about the chemistry behind baking, which helped me to overcome my fear of yeast. Prior to the course, anytime I saw yeast as an ingredient in a recipe, I turned the page. Yeast? It seemed over my head and too easy to mess up. What I can offer you in a condensed space is this: Don't be afraid. It's a tool, just like any other leavening ingredient (like baking powder). The other thing I learned, a true **small victory**, is that once you stop being afraid of yeast, mastering a basic yeasted dough, like the one I've included here, means that everything from cinnamon buns to dinner rolls is within your reach. This rendition employs raspberry jam, which is spread on top of the rolled-out dough so that when you roll it up and slice it, the jam is spiraled throughout the individual buns. Served with a generous amount of sweetened crème fraîche drizzled on top, this version is my personal favorite, but, as you'll see in the Spin-Offs, the possibilities are limitless.

¾ cup [180 ml] whole milk	2 Tbsp granulated sugar	¼ cup [30 g] powdered sugar
2¼ tsp active dry yeast	1 tsp kosher salt	½ cup [115 g] crème fraîche
2 eggs	4 Tbsp [55 g] unsalted butter, at room temperature	½ tsp vanilla extract
3¼ cups [390 g] all-purpose flour	⅔ cup [200 g] raspberry jam	

In a small saucepan over medium heat, warm the milk until it is body temperature (you can also use the microwave for this). Transfer the warm milk to a large bowl and stir in the yeast. Let the mixture sit until the yeast is dissolved and looks cloudy (almost like miso soup), about 5 minutes. A few bubbles on the surface is also a good sign that your yeast is ready.

Crack one of the eggs into a small bowl and beat with a fork. Add the beaten egg to the milk-yeast mixture, along with the flour, granulated sugar, salt, and butter. Use a wooden spoon to mix everything together until the dough starts to pull away from the sides of the bowl. (If after a minute or two of mixing it doesn't pull away from the bowl, add a little

(Continued)

more flour, 1 Tbsp at a time, until it does. On the other hand, if the dough seems far too dry and impossible to mix, add a little more milk, 1 Tbsp at a time, until it becomes a little more forgiving. This is the nuanced part of baking where all the tiny variables—how humid the air is, how you measured your flour, etc.—all come into play. Don't worry too much and trust your instincts.)

Transfer the dough to a lightly floured work surface. Shape the dough into a large ball and knead it by pressing it with the heel of your hand and pushing it away from you, then immediately pulling it back, folding the top of the dough back on itself. Kneading is all about this push-and-pull. Turn the dough clockwise a little bit each time you push and pull it so that it gets evenly worked, and knead it until its surface is completely smooth and the whole thing feels both solid and soft at the same time, not unlike a baby's bottom (probably my favorite line in this book). It will take a solid 5 minutes of kneading.

Put the dough back in the large bowl and cover the bowl with plastic wrap. Let the dough sit in the warmest spot in your kitchen until it's soft and puffy and just about doubled in volume, about 1 hour.

Return the dough to the lightly floured work surface and use a floured rolling pin to roll it into a large ovalish rectangle measuring roughly 18 in [46 cm] long and 12 in [30.5 cm] wide. If the dough resists while you are rolling it, simply let it rest until it yields to the rolling pin; dough responds well to patience. Spread the surface of the dough evenly with the raspberry jam,

leaving a ½-in [12-mm] border. Starting from a long side, roll the dough up tightly so you end up with an 18-in [46-cm] rope. Cut the rope into a dozen even slices (I like to cut it in half and then cut each half in half, and so forth, so that it's easy to get even pieces). The ends might not have much jam—you can still add them to the bunch to make a baker's dozen.

Line a baking sheet with parchment paper. Arrange the buns, spiraled-jam-side up, on the prepared baking sheet in relatively even rows. The buns should be touching each other but not shoving each other and the seams on the rolls should be facing inward in the "huddle" so that they don't unravel in the oven. Cover the buns loosely with plastic wrap and let rise at room temperature until they've risen a bit and are soft and puffy, about 1 hour. Or, so you can prepare them the night ahead, let them rise at room temperature for just 30 minutes, cover in plastic wrap, and refrigerate overnight. The next morning, pull them out and let return to room temperature, about 1 hour, before proceeding.

Meanwhile, preheat your oven to 350°F [180°C].

Crack the remaining egg into a small bowl and whisk it with 1 Tbsp water. Uncover the buns and brush them with the egg mixture (I use my hands for this so I get to be very gentle, achieve even coverage, and don't have to wash a brush afterward). Discard whatever egg mixture is left over (or save for another use such as a tiny omelet).

(Continued)

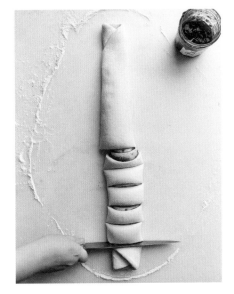

Bake the buns until they're beautifully browned and the exposed jam is caramelized, 25 to 30 minutes.

While the buns are in the oven (ha!), in a small bowl, whisk together the powdered sugar, crème fraîche, and vanilla.

Drizzle the hot buns (yeow!) with the crème fraîche mixture—this should be a wonderfully messy moment. Serve immediately (an even more wonderfully messy moment). These buns are best served warm out of the oven rather than at room temperature.

If you know you will have extra buns, don't top them with the crème fraîche. Store in an airtight container at room temperature for a couple of days or wrap tightly in plastic and freeze for up to 1 month (thaw at room temperature). Warm in a 350°F [180°C] oven for 10 minutes. Top the warmed buns with the crème fraîche mixture and serve.

SPIN-OFFS

FOR CINNAMON ROLLS, instead of spreading the dough with raspberry jam, sprinkle the surface evenly with a thin layer of brown sugar and shake over a very thin dusting of cinnamon, then roll it up and proceed as instructed. Substitute cream cheese for the crème fraîche in the frosting mixture.

FOR TERRIFIC GARLIC BUNS, instead of spreading the dough with raspberry jam, brush it with ½ cup [110 g] melted butter and then sprinkle over six minced garlic cloves, a generous sprinkle of salt, and a handful of finely chopped parsley. Roll up the dough and proceed as instructed. Skip the frosting!

FOR HERB–GOAT CHEESE BUNS, instead of spreading the dough with raspberry jam, dot it with 8 oz [230 g] plain goat cheese and sprinkle over a small handful of finely chopped thyme, rosemary, and/or sage. Roll up the dough and proceed as instructed. Skip the frosting!

FOR MONKEY BREAD, divide the dough into a dozen even pieces and roll each piece in melted butter and then in cinnamon-sugar (this will be a messy job, very well suited for children). Pack the pieces into a loaf pan, cover with plastic wrap, and let rest and rise for 1 hour. Uncover it, brush with beaten egg, and bake in a 350°F [180°C] oven until golden brown, about 20 minutes.

FOR SALAMI OR PROSCIUTTO BREAD, instead of spreading the dough with raspberry jam, shingle 4 oz [115 g] thinly sliced salami or prosciutto over it. Roll up the dough, *don't slice it*, and let it rest and rise for 1 hour, then brush the loaf with the egg and bake it. Thinly slice it while it's warm. So good!

FOR BUTTERY DINNER ROLLS, divide the dough into a dozen evenly sized pieces and form each into a little ball by rolling it between your hands. Transfer the balls to a parchment paper–lined baking sheet, arranging them so that they're touching each other. Cover with plastic and let them rest and rise for 1 hour. Uncover, brush with egg, and bake in a 350°F [180°C] oven until golden brown, about 20 minutes. Brush with melted butter instead of frosting.

Everything Biscuits

MAKES 12 BISCUITS

Reading the late, great Edna Lewis's seminal book *The Taste of Country Cooking* so many years ago helped me, a young New York Jew whose entire family lives in the TriState area, begin to understand the nuances, depth, and incredible appeal of Southern cooking traditions and techniques. One of the stories about Edna that I love the most is when tasked with making a huge amount of biscuits for an event, she did so one batch at a time. She said it was only way she would do it, because she did it by feel. If she scaled up the recipe, the biscuits just wouldn't be the same. She worked with a true understanding of the physicality of baking—the intuition that comes when you let your hands tell you when the dough is right.

Biscuits are a great introduction to the wonderful **small victory** of making dough without any tools except your own two hands and learning "the feel." By using your fingers to work the butter into the flour, you can create little pockets of fat that, in turn, create steam when the biscuits are in the oven, which result in the flakiest baked goods (this skill also translates to making pie dough and scones). Here, I cover the biscuits with all the toppings you would typically find on top of an everything bagel (and put some inside the dough, too). A mash-up of my two favorite carbohydrates, this is my New York nod to a Southern gem.

2 tsp poppy seeds

2 tsp sesame seeds

2 tsp onion flakes

4 cups [480 g] all-purpose flour

1 Tbsp baking powder

1 tsp baking soda

2 tsp kosher salt

8 Tbsp [110 g] unsalted butter, cut into ½-in [12-mm] cubes and chilled

1½ cups [360 ml] buttermilk, plus more for brushing

Line a baking sheet with parchment paper and set aside. (You can skip this if you'd like, since all of the butter in the dough will keep the biscuits from sticking, but I love anything that makes cleaning up easier).

In a small bowl, stir together the poppy seeds, sesame seeds, and onion flakes. Set aside.

In a large bowl, whisk together the flour, baking powder, baking soda, and salt. Whisk more than you think you should—this isn't just to combine the ingredients but also to aerate them. Plus, how much easier is it to clean a whisk than a sifter, *amiright??* Using your hands, work the butter into the flour mixture, rubbing it between your fingers until the mixture turns into coarse crumbs. Using a wooden spoon, gently stir in the buttermilk until the mixture becomes a shaggy dough—no need to overmix here. Stir in half of the poppy seed mixture.

Turn the dough out onto a lightly floured work surface and pat it out so that it's about 1 in [2.5 cm] thick. Using a 2½-in [6-cm] round

(Continued)

cutter (or a juice glass), stamp out biscuits as close together as possible. Transfer the biscuits to the prepared baking sheet, spacing them evenly. Pat the dough scraps together (do not overwork the dough), reroll, and cut out more biscuits. You should end up with a dozen biscuits.

Place the baking sheet in the refrigerator and chill the biscuits for about 1 hour. Baking them from cold will yield flakier biscuits (the butter will be slower to melt and will create more distinct layers); but if you don't have time, don't worry—the biscuits will still be very good.

Meanwhile, preheat your oven to 450°F [230°C].

Right before baking, brush each biscuit lightly with buttermilk and then sprinkle evenly with the remaining poppy seed mixture.

Bake the biscuits until they're risen and golden, 15 to 20 minutes, turning the baking sheet halfway through baking. Serve warm!

SPIN-OFFS

Skip the seeds inside and on top of the biscuits and try all sorts of **DIFFERENT TOPPINGS** (or just brush with buttermilk and leave them plain). Before baking, brush the biscuits with maple syrup and sprinkle with cinnamon and sugar. Or go sweet-and-savory with a brush of maple syrup and a sprinkle of coarsely ground black pepper. Or spread with mustard and top with a bit of grated cheese.

FOR CHEDDAR AND SCALLION BISCUITS, add a handful each of thinly sliced scallions and coarsely grated cheddar cheese to the dough (leave out the poppy seed mixture).

FOR JALAPEÑO POPPER BISCUITS, leave out the poppy seed mixture and substitute ½ cup [120 g] cream cheese for ½ cup [120 ml] of the buttermilk and add a small handful each of chopped pickled jalapeños and coarsely grated cheddar cheese to the dough.

FOR CROQUE MONSIEUR BISCUITS, add a handful each of diced ham and coarsely grated Gruyère cheese to the dough. Don't add the poppy seed mixture to the dough.

FOR CHICKEN AND BISCUITS, add an extra ¼ cup [60 ml] buttermilk to the dough (leave out the poppy seed mixture) and drop it by large spoonfuls on top of a pot of simmering chicken soup (filled with shredded meat and vegetables), cover the pot, and cook over low heat until the topping is cooked through, 10 to 15 minutes. Or cut out biscuits, put them on top of a baking dish filled with pot-pie filling (such as the one on page 184), and bake at 400°F [200°C] until the filling is bubbling and the biscuits are gorgeously browned, about 25 minutes.

SOUPS + SALADS

A Bowl of Anything Soup, Anytime

SERVES 2; EASILY MULTIPLIED

When I was in college, my favorite form of procrastination was to make a big pot of soup (true story). I got into the habit of enjoying a single bowl and then portioning the rest of the pot in airtight plastic bags that I would line up in my freezer as if it were a little filing cabinet. I would take out a bag whenever I wanted a warm meal. Nowadays I do the same thing but, instead of freezing soup, I freeze homemade stock that I can turn into any kind of soup my leftovers dictate. To make stock, simply gather the bits and pieces you've got around (e.g., the bones left from a roasted chicken and/or a few dried mushrooms, the ends from carrots and celery, a whole onion [peel and all], parsley stems) in a pot, cover with cold water, and add a bit of salt. Simmer for at least half an hour, or up to a couple of hours, then strain the stock, let it cool, decant into plastic bags, and freeze. Your future self will thank you. A well-stocked freezer (pun absolutely intended) is a **small victory**. This recipe is really more of a frame of mind—feel free to be creative.

2 Tbsp extra-virgin olive oil

A handful of finely chopped onion (any color), shallots, or leek

1 garlic clove, minced

Kosher salt

Freshly ground black pepper

4 cups [960 ml] chicken or vegetable stock, preferably homemade (see headnote)

2 large handfuls roughly chopped raw or cooked vegetables

A large handful of leftover cooked protein, such as shredded roast chicken, thinly sliced grilled pork, or steamed shrimp (optional)

A large handful of cooked starch, such as rice, quinoa, or small pasta

A handful of roughly chopped fresh herbs for serving

In a large pot over medium heat, warm the olive oil. Add the onion and garlic and sprinkle with a pinch of salt and a few grinds of pepper. Cook, stirring now and then, until the onion is soft and translucent, about 10 minutes.

Add the chicken stock and bring to a boil, then lower the heat to a simmer and add the vegetables. If the vegetables are raw, cook until they're tender, then add the protein (if using) and the starch and cook until heated through. If the vegetables are cooked, add with the protein and starch and cook just until everything is heated through. Season to taste with salt. Serve hot, sprinkling each bowl with some herbs.

(Continued)

SPIN-OFFS *(WELL, IN THIS CASE, JUST SOME FAVORITE COMBINATIONS)*

FOR A HEARTY VEGETABLE AND RICE SOUP, start with leeks and garlic, then add chicken stock with sweet potatoes and kale, shredded chicken, and wild rice. Garnish with thinly sliced scallions and chopped parsley.

FOR THE BEST MUSHROOM AND BARLEY SOUP, start with shallots and garlic, then add vegetable stock made with dried mushrooms, along with roasted mushrooms (see page 116) and cooked barley. Garnish with lots of chopped fresh dill.

FOR A BROTHY ASIAN SOUP WITH VEGETABLES AND SHRIMP, start with onions and garlic and add some ginger, then add vegetable stock, snap peas and frozen peas, and shrimp. Serve over rice and top with chopped fresh cilantro.

FOR A STICK-TO-YOUR-RIBS PORK AND CABBAGE SOUP, start with onions and garlic, then add chicken stock, shredded red cabbage, and sliced leftover cooked pork. Serve over cooked noodles and top with chopped parsley.

Roasted Red Pepper + Pear Soup

SERVES 6 TO 8

My mother made this soup many years ago for Thanksgiving, and it's become the custom in my family to start the holiday meal with it. My brother is so tied to this soup that, try as I might to shake it up, I've now accepted the roasted pepper soup as required. Traditions are simply repetitions, no? The **small victories** here, beyond making my big brother very happy, are twofold: *First*, a way to prepare roasted peppers without standing over the stove and taking up all of your burners (hello, broiler!). *Second*, how to puree hot soup without Jackson Pollock-ing your kitchen or injuring yourself. Both techniques, outlined in the recipe, will give you a tremendous leg up in the world of vegetable and soup cookery. This soup tastes even better the day after you make it. Simply cool it down, refrigerate it, and then gently reheat it before serving.

4 red bell peppers, halved, cored, seeded, and deribbed

3 Tbsp unsalted butter

1 yellow onion, finely diced

3 garlic cloves, minced

2 carrots, finely diced

3 fresh thyme sprigs

Kosher salt

Freshly ground black pepper

1 russet potato, peeled and roughly diced

2 semifirm pears, peeled, cored, and roughly diced

6 cups [1.4 L] chicken or vegetable stock, preferably home-made (see headnote, page 58)

Sour cream and finely chopped fresh Italian parsley for serving

Set your oven rack so it's 6 in [15 cm] from the broiler and preheat your broiler to high. Line a baking sheet with aluminum foil.

Put the bell pepper halves skin-side up on the prepared baking sheet and broil, turning the baking sheet so they broil evenly, until the skins are completely blackened, 10 to 15 minutes depending on the strength of your broiler. Immediately transfer the pepper halves to a large bowl and cover tightly with plastic wrap to trap all the steam (the steam will help loosen the skins). Let the peppers sit until they're cool enough to handle. Rub off and discard the charred skins under running water. Roughly chop the roasted, peeled peppers and set them aside.

Meanwhile, in a large pot over medium heat, melt the butter. Add the onion, garlic, carrots, and thyme and sprinkle with a generous pinch of salt and a few grinds of black pepper. Cook, stirring now and then, until the vegetables are softened but haven't taken on any color, about 15 minutes.

Add the roasted peppers, along with the diced potato and pears, to the pot. Give everything another sprinkle of salt and pepper and then add the chicken stock. Turn the heat to high and bring the mixture to a boil. Then turn the heat to low and let the soup simmer until the potatoes can be easily pierced with the tip of a paring knife, 15 to 20 minutes.

(Continued)

Fish out and discard the thyme stems (most of the thyme leaves will have fallen off into the soup, which is A-OK!). Puree the soup with an immersion blender (be sure to keep it submerged so hot soup doesn't splash around) or with a regular blender. If using the latter, transfer only enough soup at a time to the blender to fill the container no more than one-third full, place the lid on the blender, and put a kitchen towel on top of the blender in the event any hot liquid or steam wants to escape.

Start on low speed and slowly work your way up to high to completely puree the soup. Transfer the blended soup to a clean pot and reheat. (Or, if you don't have another large pot, transfer it to a bowl or pitcher and then, once all the soup is pureed, rinse the original pot and return the pureed soup to it). Season to taste with more salt and/or pepper.

Serve the soup hot, topping each portion with a generous spoonful of sour cream and a sprinkle of chopped parsley.

SPIN-OFFS

One of my other favorite uses for roasted red peppers is to puree them with chickpeas and yogurt for a **HUMMUS-ESQUE DIP**; season with salt, Aleppo pepper (or any chile pepper), and fresh lemon juice. Or puree them with mayonnaise or cream cheese for **A GREAT SANDWICH SPREAD**.

Roasted peppers can also be pureed with canned tomatoes for a **SOUP OR SAUCE**.

Or don't puree them! **SERVE THEM ON THEIR OWN**, adorned with feta cheese and slices of crisp cucumber and dressed with olive oil, red wine vinegar, and fresh oregano. Or dress with olive oil, balsamic vinegar, and torn fresh basil leaves, get some good mozzarella and a loaf of bread, and call it a day!

Use the same onion, garlic, carrot, bay, thyme, and stock base for a pureed **SQUASH SOUP**, substituting roasted squash for the peppers, potatoes, and pears. A few minced fresh sage leaves go really nicely with butternut squash, and spicy harissa is a great complement to kabocha squash.

Or try **ROASTED LEEKS AND CAULIFLOWER** in place of the peppers, potatoes, and pears. Or **ROASTED CARROTS WITH SOME CURRY POWDER**—substitute 1 cup [240 ml] full-fat coconut milk for the same amount of stock. The possibilities are quite limitless.

Parmesan Soup with Tiny Pasta + Peas

SERVES 4

This soup is a love letter to the "Garbage" chapter in Gabrielle Hamilton's cookbook *Prune* with recipes from her restaurant of the same name, which I think is pretty much one of the best restaurant cookbooks out there. Using your Parmesan rinds is a **small victory** that celebrates the flavor that lurks everywhere in our ingredients, even in the bits that normally find themselves in the trash bin. Likewise, leaving the peel on the onion adds not only more flavor here, but also a deep golden color. Cooking the pasta in the soup at the last minute thickens it slightly with starch, a good thing.

The cheese rinds have a tendency to leave their mark on the bottom of the pot. To eliminate the residue after cooking, add 1 cup [240 ml] each of water and white vinegar to the pot and bring to a boil. Turn off the heat and let the pot sit for 10 minutes before pouring the mixture out and washing the pot. The stuck-on cheese will come off really easily . . . another **small victory**.

6 cups [1.4 L] water or very light, not-too-salty chicken stock

1 large yellow onion, unpeeled, roughly chopped

4 large garlic cloves, unpeeled, crushed

1 cup [110 g] 1-in [2.5-cm] pieces Parmesan cheese rinds, plus grated Parmesan for serving

Kosher salt

1 cup [160 g] small pasta, such as ditalini or orzo

1 cup [130 g] frozen peas

Freshly ground black pepper

In a medium pot over high heat, combine the water, onion, garlic, and Parmesan rinds. Bring to a boil, then lower the heat and simmer until the liquid is really fragrant and heady and your whole kitchen smells like melted cheese (you're welcome), about 45 minutes.

Strain the soup into a clean pot (or, if you don't have another medium pot, strain into a bowl and then return it to your pot) and press down on the contents of the strainer to get every last bit of broth out. Discard the contents of the strainer (everything in it will have given all it can offer). Season the soup to taste with salt. (At this point, you can let the soup cool to room temperature and refrigerate it for up to 1 week or freeze it for up to 1 month before proceeding.)

When you're ready to eat, bring the soup to a boil and add the pasta. Cook for 2 minutes less than the pasta package says to, then add the peas and cook until they're bright green and cooked through, 2 minutes.

Divide the soup among four bowls. Sprinkle each bowl with some grated Parmesan and a few coarse grinds of pepper. Serve immediately.

(Continued)

SPIN-OFFS

FOR A BEANS AND GREENS SOUP, add a can of rinsed and drained white beans to the soup and a bunch of roughly chopped kale or Swiss chard, and you'll have yourself a meal.

FOR AN OUT-OF-THIS-WORLD ONION SOUP, add a few caramelized onions (see page 112) to the soup base and omit the pasta and peas. Top each bowl of soup with a piece of toast you've rubbed with a garlic clove and drizzled with olive oil—and, if you'd like to go all the way, broiled with some grated Parmesan cheese on top.

USE PARMESAN RINDS when you're cooking beans from scratch, or chicken soup, or any braised dish, even beef stew. The rinds will impart great flavor wherever they go.

Spring Pea, Leek + Herb Soup

SERVES 4 TO 6

The **small victory** here is learning to embrace water as an ingredient. When you use it as your cooking medium, the flavors of whatever you're cooking in it come through in a way that's so totally honest and straightforward. There's no hiding behind chicken stock. In this soup, the stems from the herbs and the tops and tails of the vegetables flavor the water, which becomes the base of the soup, harnessing all of the possible flavor of each ingredient. If you can get fresh peas, feel free to substitute those for the frozen peas. You will need about 1 lb [455 g] of peas in their shells. Go ahead and throw the shells into the water too to get whatever flavor they can offer to the soup. For a vegan soup, substitute olive oil for the butter and skip the crème fraîche when serving (an extra drizzle of olive oil is nice in that case). Serve this ice-cold if it's hot out or warm if there's a chill in the air.

2 large leeks, split in half lengthwise and washed

A handful of fresh Italian parsley sprigs, stems and leaves separated

A handful of fresh mint sprigs, stems and leaves separated

A handful of fresh basil sprigs, stems and leaves separated

6 cups [1.4 L] cold water

Kosher salt

3 Tbsp unsalted butter

1½ cups [180 g] frozen peas

Crème fraîche and finely chopped fresh chives for serving

Roughly chop the dark green tops, root ends, and tough outer layers of the leeks (all of the parts you would normally throw out) and put them in a large pot. Roughly chop the remaining leeks (the parts you would typically use!), wash them (see page 172), and set aside. Add the stems from the parsley, mint, and basil to the pot along with the water and 1½ tsp salt and bring to a boil. Lower the heat to a simmer and let the stock cook quietly for 30 minutes. Strain the stock through a fine-mesh strainer into a large bowl and set aside. Discard the contents of the strainer.

Wipe the pot dry and put it over medium heat. Add the butter, the reserved chopped and washed leeks, and a large pinch of salt and cook, stirring, until the leeks are softened and translucent, about 10 minutes. If they begin to brown, simply turn down the heat—you want them soft and tender without any color on them. Add the peas. Slowly pour in the warm stock, being mindful to leave any grit at the bottom of the bowl (the leek tops tend to hold on to dirt). Turn off the heat and let the soup cool to room temperature (the residual heat will cook the peas).

(Continued)

Once the soup has cooled, add the leaves from the parsley, mint, and basil to the pot. Puree the soup with an immersion blender, or with a regular blender. If using the latter, transfer only enough soup at a time to the blender to fill the container no more than one-third full, place the lid on the blender, and put a kitchen towel on top of the blender in the event any hot liquid or steam wants to escape. Start on low speed and slowly work your way up to high to completely puree the soup. Either way, season to taste with salt.

Reheat the soup and serve warm, or chill it thoroughly, at least 3 hours or up to overnight (season again before serving as cold temperatures tend to mute flavors). Whether you are serving the soup warm or cold, top each bowl with a spoonful of crème fraîche and a sprinkle of chopped chives.

SPIN-OFFS

FOR TOMATO, BASIL, AND GARLIC SOUP, simmer the skins and seeds of 2 lb [900 g] fresh tomatoes and the stems from a large handful of basil sprigs in 4 cups [960 ml] water. Then strain the stock and puree it with the chopped tomato flesh, the basil leaves, and a clove or two of minced garlic. Puree and finish with a little heavy cream. Serve hot or cold.

FOR A LIGHT WINTER SOUP, make a stock with the peelings and ends of carrots and parsnips and some thyme stems and then cook the chopped carrots and parsnips in that stock, with the thyme leaves. Puree and serve each bowl topped with a swirl of browned butter (see page 109).

FOR A SUPERB ONION SOUP, simmer the peels of onions and garlic in water. Meanwhile, slice the onions and garlic, and caramelize slowly in plenty of olive oil. Add the onion peel stock to the onions and stir well. Serve topped with grated Parmesan and/or Gruyère cheese.

Snow-Day Udon Soup

One extremely cold winter day, I was desperate for something hot and comforting and noodle-y, but when I opened the fridge to see what I could finagle, I realized it contained barely anything except for a few lonely scallions and half a block of tofu. With some help from the pantry and very little effort, I had this nourishing soup made from seemingly nothing. The **small victory** here is about keeping dried mushrooms and dried kombu (a type of seaweed widely available in Asian grocery stores) on hand. They require zero work—just add hot water—and add incredible depth of flavor wherever they go. Think of them like bouillon cubes without that long list of ingredients that defy pronunciation. If you can't find them, just substitute a strong chicken or vegetable stock for the water and feel free to whisk in a spoonful of miso paste, too. For the noodles, I particularly love frozen, precooked udon noodles, which are wonderfully thick and chewy (dried udon are perfectly acceptable, though). You can find the frozen ones in most Asian grocery stores. Feel free to substitute soba, rice noodles, even spaghetti.

6 cups [1.4 L] water

4 dried shiitake mushrooms, rinsed

Two 3-by-6-in [7.5-by-15-cm] sheets dried kombu, rinsed

One 3-in [7.5-cm] piece peeled fresh ginger, roughly chopped

2 garlic cloves, crushed

3 Tbsp soy sauce

2 Tbsp mirin or 1 Tbsp sugar

1 tsp toasted sesame oil

8 oz [230 g] firm tofu, cut into ½-in [12-mm] dice

1 large head bok choy, roughly chopped

1 cup [120 g] frozen peas

Kosher salt

4 servings frozen, fresh, or dried udon noodles, boiled, rinsed, and drained

2 scallions, roots and dark green tops trimmed off, white and light green parts thinly sliced

1 Tbsp toasted white or black sesame seeds

In a large pot over high heat, bring the water to a boil. Lower the heat to a simmer; add the shiitakes, kombu, ginger, and garlic; and cook until the mushrooms are softened and the broth smells very aromatic, about 15 minutes.

Use a slotted spoon or a strainer to remove all the solids from the broth; discard everything but the mushrooms and keep the broth at a simmer. Let the mushrooms cool, then trim off and discard their stems. Thinly slice the caps.

Return the sliced caps to the broth. Stir in the soy sauce, mirin, sesame oil, tofu, bok choy, and peas and cook until the vegetables are tender and bright green, about 2 minutes. Season to taste with salt.

Meanwhile, divide the udon noodles evenly among four soup bowls. Ladle the hot broth over the noodles, being sure to get vegetables in each bowl, and sprinkle with the scallions and sesame seeds. Serve immediately.

SPIN-OFFS

BULK UP THE SOUP—poach 1 lb [455 g] of fish (salmon, halibut, whatever) in the broth and substitute it for the tofu. Or add shrimp, frozen dumplings, and/or cubes of cooked kabocha squash or sweet potatoes.

DRIED MUSHROOMS ADD GREAT FLAVOR TO MUSHROOM SOUP—to make my favorite version, put the roasted mushrooms from page 116 into a pot and add hot chicken or vegetable stock, or even water, to cover, then add a few dried mushrooms and simmer until the dried mushrooms are tender. Remove and discard the stems of the mushrooms, slice the caps, and return them to the pot. Finish the soup with a little splash of heavy cream. Serve as is, puree half for some body, or puree the whole thing for a super-smooth soup.

Clam, Sweet Potato + Miso Soup

SERVES 4

Like so many of my favorite cookbooks, Nancy Singleton Hachisu's *Japanese Farm Food* is full of a lifetime of recipes and stories. Her clam and miso soup was one of the first recipes in the book that struck me for both its simplicity and its distinctiveness. She simply steams clams with sake and adds hot water and miso paste, and that's that—the result is remarkably good. The following is my I-can't-help-but-add-sweet-potatoes-to-everything version, really a subtle nod to the tradition of combining potatoes and shellfish for chowder. The **small victory** here is all about embracing the idea of "pot liquor"—the Southern term for the broth that collects at the bottom of a pot of cooked greens. In this soup, the liquid that the clams release is just as valuable as the clams themselves. Sometimes ingredients are actually twofold, and it's up to us cooks to harness everything they have to offer.

1 lb [455 g] small clams, such as littlenecks or Manila clams, scrubbed

½ cup [120 ml] white wine

4 cups [960 ml] water

3 Tbsp white miso paste

1 large sweet potato, peeled and cut into ½-in [12-mm] dice

Kosher salt

A small handful of minced fresh chives

In a large saucepan over high heat, combine the clams, white wine, and water. Cover the saucepan, bring the contents to a boil (listen closely, you'll hear it happen, and steam will also escape from under the lid), and cook until the clams open, 5 to 10 minutes from start to finish. Uncover the pot and use tongs or a slotted spoon to transfer the clams to a bowl (discard any clams that didn't open—there are invariably a few, so don't sweat it). Cover the clams to keep them warm and set aside.

Whisk the miso paste into the hot broth, then add the sweet potato, turn the heat to low, and simmer until the potato is tender, about 15 minutes. Season to taste with salt (you might not need any, depending on how salty your clams and miso are).

Distribute the clams among four soup bowls and ladle the hot broth and sweet potato over them. Depending on how well the clams were washed, there might be some grit at the bottom of your pot—be sure to leave it there. Sprinkle each bowl with some of the chives. Serve immediately.

SPIN-OFFS

FOR MUSSEL CHOWDER, substitute mussels for the clams and use regular potatoes instead of sweet potatoes.

FOR SHRIMP AND BACON CHOWDER, peel 1 lb [455 g] shrimp. Put the shells (and heads, if you've got them), ½ cup [120 ml] white wine, and 4 cups [960 ml] water in a pot and boil for 15 minutes. Strain the stock into a bowl (discard the solids). Add 4 oz [115 g] chopped bacon to the empty pot and cook until the fat is rendered and the bacon is crispy, about 5 minutes. Use a slotted spoon to remove the bacon and set aside. Add a diced onion and a diced potato to the bacon fat remaining in the pot and cook until the onion is soft, 10 minutes. Add the shrimp broth and simmer until the potatoes are soft, 15 minutes. Add the peeled shrimp and cook just until they're firm, 2 to 3 minutes. Add a splash of heavy cream, if you'd like. Serve the soup topped with the cooked bacon and snipped chives.

Aunt Renee's Chicken Soup

SERVES 6

My dearly departed Aunt Renee, who was quite a character, was famous for many things (from her fake Louis Vuitton bags to her stories about working in the hair salon in the basement of her Brooklyn apartment building), but her chicken soup looms large. When she left us, I put an obituary in the *New York Times* that read simply, "I will take care of the soup." Here it is. It is unequivocally my favorite food in the world. The **small victory** here is not just carrying on traditions, but also learning how to make a good chicken soup; because in doing so, you learn to make chicken stock—the backbone (no pun intended) for so many things in the kitchen. You can put a whole chicken directly in the pot, but I like to separate it so that the white meat is easy to retrieve early on and, also, the whole pot is easier to stir during cooking.

One 4-lb [1.8-kg] chicken, cut into 8 pieces (2 breasts, 2 wings, 2 thighs, and 2 legs), backbone reserved

1 lb [455 g] chicken wings

2 large yellow onions, unpeeled, roughly chopped

4 celery stalks, roughly chopped

1 head garlic, halved horizontally so that the cloves are exposed

A handful of fresh Italian parsley sprigs, stems reserved and leaves finely chopped

1 Tbsp black peppercorns

Kosher salt

8 carrots, peeled and cut into 2-in [5-cm] pieces

3 qt [2.8 L] water

2 parsnips, peeled and cut into 2-in [5-cm] pieces

A handful of roughly chopped fresh dill

In the largest pot you have, combine the chicken pieces, chicken wings, onions, celery, garlic, parsley stems, peppercorns, and 1 Tbsp salt. Add half of the carrots to the pot and cover with the water. Bring to a boil, then lower the heat to a simmer and cook, skimming off and discarding any foam that rises to the top, until the chicken breasts are firm to the touch, about 25 minutes.

Use tongs to remove the chicken breasts from the pot and set them aside in a bowl. Continue simmering the stock, stirring it every so often and skimming any foam that rises to the top, until everything in the pot has given up all of its structural integrity (the vegetables should be totally soft and the chicken should look well past

its prime—this is all great, it means these things have given all of their flavor to the water) and the stock is a rich golden color, about 3 hours.

While the stock is simmering, let the chicken breasts cool to room temperature, and then discard the skin, remove the meat from the bones (discard the bones), and shred the meat. Set the meat aside.

Ladle the stock through a fine-mesh sieve into a clean pot (or, if you don't have another large pot, ladle it into a bowl, clean the pot you started with, and return the stock to the pot). Discard the contents of the sieve (everything in it will have given all it can by this point).

(Continued)

Bring the stock back to a boil and season to taste with salt (be bold, it will need quite a bit!). Add the remaining carrots and the parsnips, lower the heat, and simmer until the vegetables are tender, about 10 minutes.

Add the reserved chicken breast meat to the soup and let it warm up for a minute or two. Ladle the soup into bowls, and top each with some of the chopped parsley and dill. Serve immediately.

NOTE: This soup is even better the next day. Do not discard the hardened fat that will have formed on top after the soup has been refrigerated. The rich pools of chicken fat on top of your soup are essential (at least in my book, but no hard feelings if you would rather discard the fat).

SPIN-OFFS

FOR ITALIAN WEDDING SOUP, leave out the parsnips and extra carrots and save the cooked chicken breasts for something else. Poach little meatballs (try the ones on page 168) in the soup and wilt in some chopped escarole right before serving. Each bowl should get lots of grated Parmesan cheese.

FOR THAI CHICKEN SOUP, add a crushed large piece of fresh ginger, a bunch of scallions, some cilantro stems, and a chopped chile to the broth. Adjust the water to 10 cups [2.4 L] and add a 13½-oz [398-ml] can of full-fat coconut milk. Leave out the parsnips and extra carrots and simply serve the broth with the shredded chicken. Top with sliced scallions and cilantro leaves.

My Colombian friend Luz Gerstein serves a grand meal of chicken soup known as **AJIACO** with assorted toppings. To serve your own, set your table with bowls of shredded chicken from the broth, fried onions, rounds of cooked corn on the cob, cubed boiled potatoes (regular and/or sweet potatoes), diced avocadoes, cilantro leaves, and lime wedges and then give every guest a large bowl of the hot chicken broth. Everyone can adorn their soup to their liking. Also put a small pitcher of cream on the table for anyone who wants to swirl a bit into their soup. This is a really fun meal, and everything can be done ahead of time.

FOR CHICKEN AND VEGETABLE SOUP, simply add whatever kinds of vegetables you like to the strained broth (with or without the parsnips and extra carrots). Add the shredded white meat or save it for something else, like chicken salad sandwiches. Some of my favorite combinations include diced beets and shredded red cabbage (stunning!), finely diced leeks and roughly chopped potatoes, and shredded Savoy cabbage with chopped tomatoes (serve with grated Parmesan).

Corn + Potato Chowder

SERVES 6

There's more to an ear of corn than just the kernels. In this chowder, which is basically an ode to sweet summertime, I walk you through two **small victories**. The *first* is how to easily and efficiently cut kernels from the cobs without them flying all over your kitchen. The *second* one is how to infuse the soup with tons of flavor from the corncobs. As shown throughout all of the soup recipes in this chapter, I'm a big believer in extracting all of the potential bits and pieces of flavor from any ingredient, wherever they may be hiding. If you'd like the chowder to be a bit thicker, you can puree up to half of the soup in a blender or use an immersion blender to puree some, but not all, of the soup. The sage mixture that gets drizzled on top complements the corn really well, but feel free to skip it if you prefer things a bit simpler.

1 small garlic clove, minced

12 large fresh sage leaves, minced

¼ cup [60 ml] extra-virgin olive oil

Kosher salt

6 ears corn, shucked

3 cups [720 ml] whole milk

3 cups [720 ml] water

6 fresh thyme sprigs

3 Tbsp unsalted butter

1 large yellow onion, finely diced

2 russet potatoes, peeled and cut into ½-in [12-mm] dice

In a small bowl, combine the garlic, sage, and olive oil and stir. Season to taste with salt. Set aside.

Break each ear of corn in half (this should make you feel like you are *the strongest person alive!* By breaking the ears in half, you shorten the distance from the top of the ears and thereby minimize how many kernels can potentially fly out all over your cutting board.) Working with one piece of corn at a time, stand the half ears up on your cutting board (put the broken, flat side on the board) and carefully cut off the kernels. Transfer the kernels to a medium bowl and set aside. Scrape the cobs with the blunt edge of your knife to get all the milky bits. Put the corn milk into the bowl with the kernels.

Put the spent corncobs in a large pot, along with 1 Tbsp salt, the milk, water, and thyme. Set the pot over high heat and bring to a boil. Turn the heat to low and simmer until the mixture is very fragrant, about 20 minutes.

Meanwhile, in a separate pot, melt the butter over medium heat. Add the onion and a generous pinch of salt and cook, stirring, until the onion is soft, about 10 minutes. Add the potatoes and pour the milk mixture through a sieve into the pot, discarding the cobs and thyme. Bring to a boil, then lower the heat and simmer until the potatoes are tender, about 15 minutes. Add the reserved corn kernels and cook just until they're tender, 2 to 5 minutes, depending on how fresh they are.

Season the soup to taste with salt, ladle into bowls, and top each portion with a swirl of the sage mixture. Serve immediately.

SPIN-OFFS

FOR A VERY CHIC COLD CORN SOUP, cool the soup and puree it in a blender (or with an immersion blender) until completely smooth. To achieve the texture of cashmere, pass the soup through a fine-mesh sieve. Season one final time before serving, as cold temperatures tend to mute flavors. Very nice on a hot day.

FOR ANOTHER VEGETABLE SOUP that is the essence of the vegetable it features, sauté a diced onion, two minced garlic cloves, and 2 Tbsp minced fresh ginger in olive oil and then add 1 lb [455 g] carrots that you've roasted until soft and caramelized along with 4 cups [960 ml] carrot juice. Puree, season with salt, and serve hot or cold. I like a swirl of browned butter on top of this if I'm eating it hot, or a spoonful of crème fraîche if it's cold (or hot . . . really, I like crème fraîche on anything).

Bibb Lettuce with Garlic Dressing

SERVES 4

A few years ago, I spent a weekend in Portland, Oregon, with my best friend, Cleo, and we ate as much in two days as most people do in about a week. Our final meal was at the venerable restaurant Le Pigeon and the dish that has stuck with me to this day was a very simple salad slicked with a pickled garlic dressing. I started making this version and it is probably the salad I make most often, since it comes together quickly and goes perfectly with just about everything. The **small victory** here lies in the mashed garlic that requires no extra gadgets. Simply put a peeled garlic clove on your cutting board, turn your chef's knife so that the flat side of the blade hovers over the clove, and give the side of the blade a whack to crush the garlic. Sprinkle the crushed clove with a generous pinch of kosher salt (which acts as an abrasive) and then use the flat side of the knife to press and smear the garlic into a puree. I do this just about each time I use garlic in anything. Which is often.

2 garlic cloves, mashed to a paste with a bit of kosher salt (see headnote)

1 Tbsp white wine vinegar (or red wine or sherry vinegar, whatever's open)

¼ tsp kosher salt

Freshly ground black pepper

3 Tbsp extra-virgin olive oil

1 Tbsp mayonnaise (or plain yogurt or crème fraîche—again, whatever's open)

1 large head Bibb lettuce, roughly torn, washed, and dried (note that Bibb lettuce also goes by the names butter or Boston— "a rose is a rose is a rose")

2 radishes, cut into wedges or thinly sliced

In a small mixing bowl, whisk together the garlic, vinegar, salt, and a few grinds of pepper. Let sit for 5 minutes to allow the garlic to bloom and flavor the vinegar, which in turn will slightly mellow the garlic. (This is a good moment to wash and dry your lettuce if you haven't already done that.)

Whisk the olive oil and mayonnaise into the garlic-vinegar mixture.

Put the lettuce in a large bowl and pour nearly all of the dressing over it. Coat the greens with the dressing (there's no better tool for this than your hands—get in there). Transfer the greens to a serving platter or to individual salad plates. Distribute the radishes evenly over the greens and drizzle over the remaining dressing. Serve immediately.

SPIN-OFFS

FOR SPAGHETTI AGLIO E OLIO, warm ½ cup [120 ml] extra-virgin olive oil in a small skillet set over low heat with eight garlic cloves that you've mashed to a paste, and then toss with 1 lb [455 g] cooked spaghetti. Add some chopped parsley, if you'd like, and mix in plenty of freshly ground black pepper and finely grated Parmesan. Thin with some reserved pasta cooking water as necessary so that the spaghetti is coated nicely. Serve with extra cheese on top.

FOR SHRIMP SCAMPI, warm ½ cup [120 ml] extra-virgin olive oil in a large skillet set over medium-high heat with four garlic cloves that you've mashed to a paste. Add 1 lb [455 g] peeled and deveined shrimp and cook, stirring, until the shrimp are pink and firm to the touch. Squeeze over the juice of a lemon, add a handful of chopped parsley, and season with lots of salt and pepper. This is great over pasta or served with crusty bread.

FOR GARLIC YOGURT, mix two garlic cloves that you've mashed to a paste with 1 cup [240 ml] plain yogurt and the juice of half a lemon. Season with salt and pepper. Serve this alongside grilled meats (especially lamb) or fish, cooked rice, and/or store-bought stuffed grape leaves.

Julia's Caesar

SERVES 4

When I used to work regularly as a private chef, the most requested item I prepared for lots of different families was Caesar salad dressing. I was often asked to leave containers in refrigerators all over New York City! My master plan is to one day put it in a bottle (my mother is convinced that it will sell well and then my whole family can live in the "house that Julia's Caesar built"). But, in the meantime, here's the most direct way to get it from my kitchen to yours. The **small victory** here is abandoning convention and swapping a spoonful of mayonnaise for the customary raw egg to make a creamy, thick, luscious dressing without any worry about salmonella or anything like that. Plus, what isn't improved by a spoonful of mayonnaise?

1 small garlic clove, minced

4 olive oil–packed anchovy fillets, drained

1 Tbsp fresh lemon juice

1 Tbsp red wine vinegar

¼ cup [60 ml] extra-virgin olive oil

2 Tbsp mayonnaise

¼ cup [25 g] finely grated Parmesan cheese

Kosher salt

Freshly ground black pepper

3 hearts of romaine lettuce, trimmed, washed, dried, and cut into bite-size pieces

A handful of cherry tomatoes, halved

In a blender or food processor, puree the garlic, anchovies, lemon juice, vinegar, olive oil, and mayonnaise until smooth. Add the Parmesan and give the dressing a few pulses just to incorporate the cheese. Season to taste with salt and pepper. (Alternatively, finely chop the anchovies, put them in a bowl with the rest of the ingredients, and whisk everything together.)

Put the lettuce in a large bowl and drizzle nearly all of the dressing over it. Use your hands to mix everything together, making sure each and every piece of lettuce is coated with dressing.

Divide the dressed lettuce among four plates. Divide the tomatoes evenly among the salads and drizzle the last bit of dressing over the salads. Serve immediately.

SPIN-OFFS

FOR A VEGETARIAN VERSION, use 1 Tbsp drained capers in place of the anchovies.

FOR A VEGAN VERSION, use 1 Tbsp drained capers in place of the anchovies and Vegenaise instead of regular mayonnaise, and leave out the Parmesan.

FOR THE EASIEST CREAMY MUSTARD DRESSING, whisk together 1 Tbsp mayonnaise, 1 Tbsp Dijon mustard, 1 Tbsp seeded mustard, 3 Tbsp red wine vinegar, and ¼ cup [60 ml] extra-virgin olive oil. Season with salt and pepper.

Shaved Carrot + Avocado Salad with Tahini

SERVES 4

Sometimes the best thing to do with a vegetable is to thinly slice it and dress it smartly. To achieve thin slices without losing a finger, the **small victory** here is to first cut a slice off your vegetable so it can lie flat and securely on your cutting board and you don't risk having it roll around under your knife. Also, **small victory of all small victories**, put a damp paper towel under your cutting board to hold it in place. Do this every single time you use your cutting board. It's like glue. Back to slicing. . . . You can also use a mandoline. I honestly don't think any home cook needs a mandoline, but if you want one, use it safely. As with most things in the kitchen, I'm not that into bells and whistles and highly recommend a simple plastic Japanese mandoline with a single secure blade instead of the fancier (and more expensive) French ones that have a variety of parts and blades. Pay close attention while you're slicing, use the root ends of vegetables to hold on to them, and don't be a hero—it's better to leave a bit of vegetable at the end than get dangerously close to your fingers. Between the rich tahini and the creamy avocado, this salad is very substantial and, I should note, totally vegan.

1 Tbsp tahini, stirred

2 Tbsp boiling water

2 Tbsp extra-virgin olive oil

2 Tbsp fresh lemon juice

Kosher salt

¾ lb [340 g] carrots, thinly sliced on the diagonal into coins

1 ripe avocado, halved and pitted (see headnote, page 26)

2 tsp toasted sesame seeds (see Note)

2 scallions, roots and dark green tops trimmed off, white and light green parts thinly sliced

2 Tbsp roughly chopped fresh cilantro (optional)

In a medium bowl, whisk together the tahini, boiling water, olive oil, and lemon juice. Season to taste with salt. Put the carrots in a large bowl, add half of the dressing, and toss to combine.

Transfer the dressed carrots to a serving platter. Use a spoon to artfully scoop the avocado from its shell into pieces and place them over the carrots. Season the avocado pieces to taste with

salt and then drizzle the salad with the remaining dressing. Scatter the salad with the sesame seeds, scallions, and cilantro (if using). Serve immediately.

NOTE: If your sesame seeds aren't already toasted, put them in a dry skillet over medium heat and cook, stirring, until they're golden brown, about 4 minutes.

(Continued)

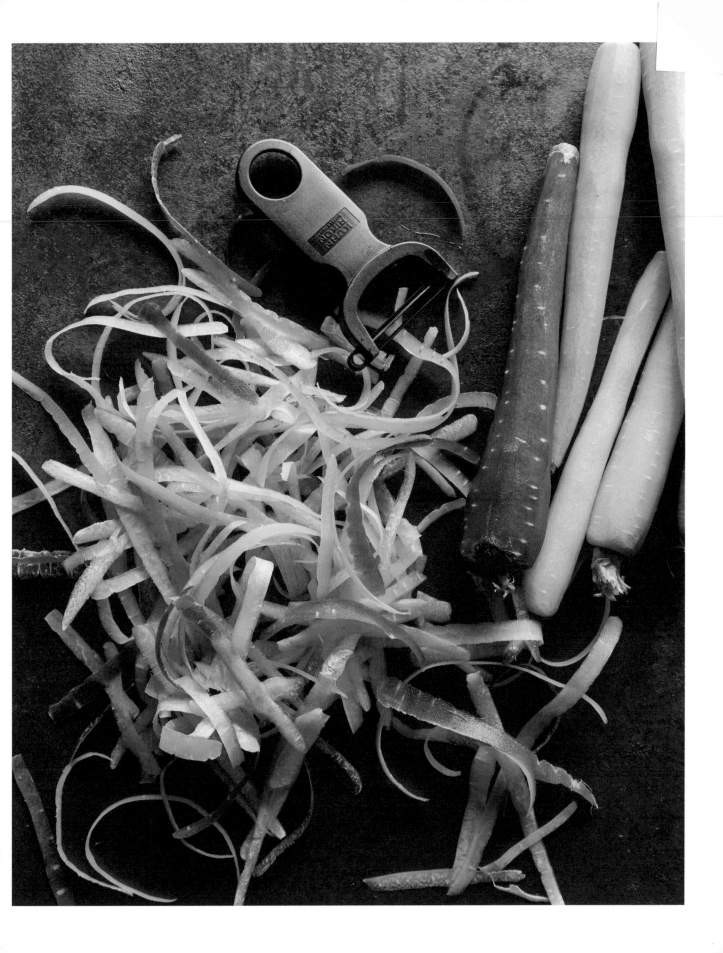

SPIN-OFFS

TOSS SHAVED FENNEL, thinly sliced kumquats, and sliced scallions with kumquat and/or lemon juice and olive oil. Garnish with fennel fronds, toasted Marcona almonds, and lots of shaved Parmesan.

DRESS SHAVED CELERY, toasted walnuts, and chopped Italian parsley with lemon juice and olive oil.

DRESS SHAVED CABBAGE with sesame seeds, rice wine vinegar, and sesame oil.

DRESS SHAVED GREEN APPLES with fish sauce, lime juice, and brown sugar. Stir in salty peanuts and thinly sliced fresh red chile.

Gus's House Salad

One of my favorite restaurants in the world is Gus's (officially called Gus's Franklin Park Restaurant, but I have never heard anyone use its whole name) in Harrison, New York, the town I grew up in after my parents traded the city for the suburbs. Just about everyone who goes there orders the house salad, a mix of crispy iceberg lettuce, sharp onions, sweet tomatoes, and plenty of assertive blue cheese, all dressed with oil and vinegar, heavy on the vinegar. The salad, not to mention the restaurant itself, hasn't changed in decades, and I love that. The **small victory** with this salad is learning how to dress a salad without making a dressing. Just like making biscuits (see page 53), dressing a salad "freestyle" means using your hands and knowing the feel of when something is right. It also means tasting as you go, an essential practice for anyone who steps foot in the kitchen.

1 head iceberg lettuce, outer leaves discarded, cut into 1-in [2.5-cm] pieces

¼ cup plus 2 Tbsp [90 ml] olive oil, plus more as needed (no need to use anything fancy here)

¼ cup [60 ml] red wine vinegar, plus more as needed

Kosher salt

Freshly ground black pepper

1 large ripe tomato, roughly chopped

½ small red onion, very thinly sliced

1 cup [100 g] crumbled dry blue cheese

Put the lettuce in a large bowl and drizzle with the olive oil and vinegar. Sprinkle with ½ tsp salt and a few grinds of pepper. Using your hands (just go for it), mix everything together. The lettuce should be very well dressed (taste for seasoning and add more olive oil, vinegar, salt, and/or pepper as needed). Add the tomato, onion, and blue cheese and gently toss everything together (you can use salad spoons or tongs now if you don't want your hands to smell like blue cheese). Serve immediately.

SPIN-OFFS

TOSS PEPPERY ARUGULA with olive oil and fresh lemon juice and top with large, thin shards of Parmesan.

DRESS THINLY SLICED RAW MUSHROOMS with olive oil and fresh lemon juice and top with chopped hazelnuts and grated pecorino cheese.

DRESS SLICED PEELED ORANGES, torn black olives, and thinly sliced red onions with olive oil and red wine vinegar.

Beet + Just-Barely-Pickled Cucumber Salad

SERVES 6

This salad is my rendition of my grandmother's wonderful cucumber salad, which I will forever associate with my cousin Jenette, as it was one of the only things she ate without question when we were kids. Sometimes my grandmother would run the tines of a fork down the outside of the cucumber so that when she sliced it, the rounds would come out with perforated edges, a bit of flair that I remember thinking was the *most sophisticated thing I had ever seen in my life!* Anyway, enough about cucumbers. The **small victory** here has nothing to do with them and everything to do with the beets that go along with them. Peel cooked beets using paper towels to make the slightly clumsy task way less clumsy (paper towels = grip) and way less messy (no stained hands!).

1 English cucumber, ends trimmed, thinly sliced

Kosher salt

1 tsp sugar

2 Tbsp sherry vinegar

1 lb [455 g] red beets, scrubbed

2 Tbsp extra-virgin olive oil

2 Tbsp finely chopped fresh dill, plus more for sprinkling

3 Tbsp crème fraîche, sour cream, or plain yogurt

In a large bowl, combine the cucumbers with 1 tsp salt and the sugar. Drizzle the vinegar over the cucumbers and use your hands to combine everything. Set aside to lightly pickle.

Meanwhile, bring a large saucepan of water to a boil and add the beets (the water should cover the beets—if it doesn't, add more). Cook the beets, turning them every so often, until they're tender (test with a paring knife), about 45 minutes (it may be a bit less or a bit longer depending on the size and age of the beets, so start testing at 30 minutes).

Drain the beets, transfer to a paper towel–lined cutting board, and use the paper towels to rub the skins off the beets. Trim off and discard the root ends of the beets.

Slice the warm beets into thin rounds and transfer them to a large serving bowl or platter. Drizzle with the olive oil and sprinkle with a generous pinch of salt. Use your hands or a slotted spoon to transfer the cucumbers to the beets and gently combine.

Put the dill and crème fraîche in the bowl that the cucumbers were in and whisk together with the juice from the cucumbers. Pour the mixture over the salad and sprinkle with additional dill. Serve immediately.

(Continued)

SPIN-OFFS

MAKE A QUICK DRESSING OF EQUAL PARTS SOY SAUCE, toasted sesame oil, and rice vinegar and dress the sliced beets and cucumbers with it. Sprinkle with toasted sesame seeds and a few sliced scallions.

Beet and goat cheese salads are a bit cliché these days, but I love clichés! I find that they often became clichés for a good reason—in this case, beets and goat cheese taste great together. To put a little spin on the cliché, make a **GOAT CHEESE DRESSING** by whisking together room-temperature goat cheese with sherry vinegar and olive oil until smooth; season with salt and pepper. Dress sliced beets with it and adorn with a few chopped toasted nuts or poppy seeds and/or chopped dill or parsley.

Zucchini, Red Onion + Pistachio Salad

SERVES 4

Once upon a time, I bought my first-ever jar of preserved lemons and was instantly hooked. I started stuffing them into roasted chickens, tucking slices into a whole fish for roasting, and watching whole preserved lemons totally collapse into braised lamb. The only thing I didn't love was the huge amount of liquid left in the jar after I used up the lemons. It seemed every recipe I ever encountered gave instructions for how to use only the lemons and not all of the fragrant liquid that comes with them. Reluctant to pour it down the drain and move on to the next jar, I started coming up with ways to use the juice and found that it could stand on its own as an ingredient. Whisked together with olive oil, it's now one of my favorite dressings, especially for raw zucchini. This discovery helped me realize that all preserved products (e.g., anchovies, capers, and pickles) lend tremendous flavor to whatever they're packed in, usually olive oil or brine. I get very happy whenever you can get two ingredients for the price of one (ahem, **small victory**). Needless to say, you don't need to buy a whole jar of preserved lemons just to get a little juice for this recipe. Feel free to substitute fresh lemon juice in its place.

2 Tbsp extra-virgin olive oil, plus ¼ cup [60 ml]

¼ cup [40 g] shelled pistachios

Kosher salt

¼ small red onion, thinly sliced

A pinch of sugar or 1 tsp honey

3 Tbsp juice from a jar of preserved lemons, plus more as needed

2 zucchini, ends trimmed and sliced as thinly as possible

A small handful of fresh soft herb sprigs (a mixture of dill, cilantro, and mint is really nice, but use whatever you've got), chopped

In a medium skillet over medium-high heat, warm the 2 Tbsp olive oil. Add the pistachios, give them a good sprinkle of salt, and cook, stirring now and then, until lightly browned and fragrant, about 3 minutes. Transfer the pistachios to a plate and set aside.

Meanwhile, in a small bowl, stir together the onion with the sugar, a pinch of salt, and 1 Tbsp of the preserved lemon juice. Set aside.

In a large bowl, whisk together the remaining 2 Tbsp preserved lemon juice, a pinch of salt, and the ¼ cup [60 ml] olive oil. Add the zucchini and stir gently to combine. Taste the zucchini for seasoning and add more salt and/or preserved lemon juice if you think it needs it.

Transfer the zucchini to a platter. Scatter the onion with its liquid, the pistachios, and herbs over the zucchini. Serve immediately.

(Continued)

SPIN-OFFS

Use pickle, caper, or preserved lemon brine to **PICKLE OTHER THINGS**, such as cucumber slices, whole string beans, sliced carrots, and/or peeled pearl onions. Pour the brine over the vegetables, cover, and refrigerate for at least 24 hours or up to 2 weeks. They will get more intense as the days go by.

FOR A GREAT POTATO SALAD, boil potatoes in a mixture of three parts water and one part pickle or cornichon brine; drain. Meanwhile, whisk together some more of the brine with some mayonnaise. Mix the cooked potatoes with the dressing and chopped celery, minced parsley and/or minced dill, and a few diced pickles or cornichons.

Use the brine from a jar of pickled onions or jalapeños to make **A GIMLET OR A MARTINI**. Pickle brine is also delicious in **BLOODY MARYS**. As is the juice from a jar of kimchi.

Make a **GRAB-AND-GO SALAD DRESSING** by pouring an equal amount of olive oil into a jar of leftover brine. Keep in the fridge for up to 2 weeks. Just shake it and pour anytime you need to dress something. I learned this from my friends Sarah and Sheila who run Gordy's Pickle Jar, a wonderful pickle company.

USE LEFTOVER PICKLE BRINE to brine a chicken or turkey for roasting. You need a lot of brine for this, so feel free to cut it with some water (up to half the amount you need) and/or put the bird or pieces of poultry in a resealable bag so you don't need as much liquid to cover.

Radicchio Slaw with Warm Bacon Dressing

SERVES 4

My adoration for coleslaw means you can find me making it, and variations of it, regularly. This version, with bitter radicchio and a warm bacon dressing, is particulary satisfying. It works not only as a side dish but could also get a fried egg or two to be a complete meal. The **small victory** here is all about massaging radicchio (and other similar vegetables like shredded kale, cabbage, Brussels sprouts, and even dandelion greens) with salt and olive oil before dressing them. It really helps to soften the seemingly tough vegetables. Don't be afraid to really scrunch them.

2 heads radicchio (each about 6 oz [70 g]), unattractive outer leaves and cores discarded, finely shredded

4 Tbsp [60 ml] extra-virgin olive oil

Kosher salt

4 oz [115 g] bacon, finely diced

3 Tbsp sherry vinegar or apple cider vinegar

2 Tbsp crème fraîche or heavy cream

1 Tbsp Dijon mustard

Freshly ground black pepper

Put the radicchio in a large serving bowl, drizzle with 2 Tbsp of the olive oil, and sprinkle with ¼ tsp salt. Use your hands to massage the oil and salt into the radicchio, softening it a bit. Set aside.

In a large skillet over medium-high heat, warm the remaining 2 Tbsp oil. Add the bacon and cook, stirring, until the fat is rendered and the bacon is crisp, 5 to 10 minutes. Turn off the heat and stir in the vinegar, crème fraîche, and mustard. Be mindful that the vinegar might be very pungent when it hits the hot pan.

Pour the bacon dressing over the radicchio and stir to combine. Season to taste with plenty of salt and pepper. Serve immediately.

SPIN-OFFS

FOR AN ITALIAN VERSION OF THIS SALAD, substitute pancetta for the bacon, and use red wine vinegar. Use a vegetable peeler to cut long, thin slices from a wedge of Parmesan cheese, and scatter them over the salad.

FOR THE BEST KALE CAESAR, massage chopped kale with the oil and salt, dress it with Julia's Caesar dressing (see page 83), and top with anchovy bread crumbs (see page 118).

VEGETABLES

Tin-Foil Kale + Cherry Tomatoes

SERVES 6

Once, during a summer vacation in a small rental house with no air-conditioning, I became determined to cook using only the outdoor charcoal grill so as not to heat up the house and to avoid washing too many pots and pans. That's when I discovered a wonderful **small victory**: Wrapping kale, cherry tomatoes, olive oil, and garlic in a huge piece of tin foil and grilling it gives you the effect of sautéed greens without having to wilt the kale in batches in a pan. Plus, there is no pan to wash. You also get great smoky flavor from the grill (though you could also park the packet in a 425°F [220°C] oven for about 15 minutes). If you're at all concerned about cooking in foil, simply line the foil with a piece of parchment paper before adding the kale.

1 lb [455 g] curly kale, stems trimmed off, roughly chopped or torn, washed, and still damp

2 Tbsp extra-virgin olive oil

Kosher salt

2 garlic cloves, thinly sliced

1 pt [325 g] cherry tomatoes, halved

1 lemon, halved

Prepare your grill for medium-high heat (or heat a large grill pan set over a couple of burners) and make sure your grates are super-clean.

Meanwhile, tear off two 24-in [60-cm] pieces of aluminum foil from a standard roll. Turn these two pieces into one supersize piece of foil by overlapping their long edges ever so slightly and folding the overlap over a couple of times to make a secure seam. Put the kale in the center of the foil. Any water clinging to the kale from washing it is a good thing, as it'll create some steam; if your kale seems dry, sprinkle it with 2 Tbsp water. Drizzle the kale with the olive oil, sprinkle with ½ tsp salt, and scatter the sliced garlic over it. Use your hands to combine everything, almost as if you were dressing salad. Top the kale with the cherry tomatoes.

Wrap the kale and cherry tomatoes in the foil, keeping the vegetables in a relatively thin layer so that they cook evenly; wrap the entire bundle in another large piece or two of foil if necessary to make a neat, totally enclosed package. The final package should measure about 9 by 15 in [23 by 38 cm].

Put the foil package on the grill and cook, turning it now and then, until the smell of garlic wafts through the air and the kale is tender and bright green (check by carefully opening the foil with the help of your tongs), 10 to 15 minutes.

Unwrap the package and transfer the contents to a serving bowl or platter. Squeeze the juice from the lemon halves over the kale and tomatoes and season to taste with salt. Serve immediately.

SPIN-OFFS

FOR AN ASIAN BENT, add 1 Tbsp minced peeled ginger along with the garlic, and drizzle the cooked kale and tomatoes with soy sauce and a little toasted sesame oil right before serving. A few toasted sesame seeds and/or sliced scallions sprinkled on top would be nice, too.

SUBSTITUTE ANY STURDY GREEN FOR THE KALE, including, but not limited to, the greens from beets or turnips, Swiss chard, and/or dandelion greens.

MANY VEGETABLES CAN BE COOKED THIS WAY, including mushrooms (toss with olive oil, garlic, and thyme) and asparagus (substitute butter for some or all of the olive oil and throw in a handful of black olives).

FOR AN ITALIAN BENT, use broccoli rabe (blanched first to remove some of its bitterness) or its less-bitter cousin, spigariello (if you can find it). Dress with olive oil, salt, and garlic, and add a thinly sliced lemon. Wrap in foil and grill. So, so good and brought to you by Sarah Billingsley, who edited this book!

FOR GRILLED TOMATO SAUCE, simply make a foil package of cherry tomatoes dressed with oil, salt, and garlic. They will release a lot of delicious juice. Open the package carefully! Use on pasta.

Swiss Chard with Ginger + Coconut

SERVES 4

The **small victory** here is making greens easy to cook at any instant by cleaning them ahead and storing them wrapped in paper towels in a plastic bag in the refrigerator, where they'll stay fresh for about a week. Then they're ready to be cooked at a moment's notice. By switching up the type of green and the flavorings (check out the Spin-Offs), you can have a healthful side dish that suits just about any meal, even a frozen pizza. This chard goes especially well with rice and a diced avocado or grilled fish.

2 Tbsp neutral oil, such as canola, grapeseed, or safflower

One 2-in [5-cm] piece fresh ginger, peeled and minced

1 lb [455 g] Swiss chard, stems and leaves, separated and thinly sliced

Kosher salt

¼ cup [60 ml] full-fat coconut milk, shaken

1 Tbsp fish sauce

A small handful of toasted, shredded unsweetened coconut for serving (optional)

In a large pot over high heat, warm the oil. Add the ginger and cook, tilting the pot so that the ginger really fries in the oil, until golden brown and crisp, 1 to 2 minutes.

Immediately add the chard stems to the hot, gingery oil and sprinkle with a generous pinch of salt. Cook, stirring, until the stems just begin to wilt, about 1 minute. Add the leaves and cook, stirring, until they begin to wilt, about 1 minute. Drizzle the coconut milk and fish sauce over the chard and cook, stirring, until it's totally tender and still retains some vivid color, 2 minutes more.

Season the chard to taste with salt. Transfer to a serving platter and sprinkle with the toasted coconut. Serve immediately.

SPIN-OFFS

If you substitute olive oil for the neutral oil, garlic for the ginger, and kale for the chard (and leave out the coconut milk and fish sauce), you'll have **GARLICKY KALE** that goes perfectly with just about everything.

SUBSTITUTE SPINACH OR SHREDDED GREEN CABBAGE for the chard, or any other dark leafy green for that matter. And feel free to **VARY THE TOPPINGS**. Chopped salted peanuts or cashews and/or chopped cilantro all complement the flavors really nicely. You can also **TOAST SPICES** like cumin and coriander in the oil along with the ginger for added flavor. Lastly, feel free to **MIX UP THE LIQUID**. You can use chicken or vegetable stock, plain yogurt, or crème fraîche instead of the coconut milk (or just a splash of water).

String Beans with Pork, Ginger + Red Chile

SERVES 4 AS A SIDE DISH, 2 AS A MAIN COURSE

I used to travel for work frequently and I got into a real routine of ordering Chinese takeout when I was almost back to my apartment, timing the call so the food would arrive soon after I did. After cooking on the road for long stretches of time, it was so nice to do absolutely nothing! My regular go-to order was dry-sautéed string beans with brown rice on the side and spicy pork-and-ginger dumplings doused in red chile oil. This stir-fry combines all of those flavors and demonstrates the **small victory** of how to properly stir-fry, which is to say: Don't crowd your pan and don't be afraid of high heat.

¼ cup [60 ml] neutral oil, such as canola, grapeseed, or safflower

1 lb [455 g] string beans, tipped, tailed, and halved

4 oz [115 g] ground pork

2 Tbsp minced peeled fresh ginger

1 fresh red or green chile (such as a jalapeño or a serrano), stemmed, seeded, and minced, or ½ tsp red pepper flakes

2 tsp soy sauce

2 Tbsp chicken stock, white wine, or water

Kosher salt

Freshly ground black pepper

Cooked brown or white rice for serving

In the largest skillet you have (at least 12 in [30 cm] in diameter) over high heat, warm 2 Tbsp of the oil. Let it get nice and hot (it will *smile*). Add the string beans and cook, stirring, until they're charred in spots and just tender, about 5 minutes. Transfer the beans to a bowl and set aside.

Add the remaining 2 Tbsp oil to the pan, along with the pork, and cook, stirring occasionally, until the pork loses its rawness and is on its way to being browned, 2 to 3 minutes. Add the ginger and chile and cook, stirring, until the pork is browned and a little bit crisp, about 5 minutes.

Return the string beans to the skillet and drizzle over the soy sauce and chicken stock. Cook, stirring, just until everything is nicely combined and the liquid is mostly evaporated, a couple of minutes. Season the beans to taste with salt and pepper. Serve immediately, next to or on top of rice.

SPIN-OFFS

Stir-fry **ASPARAGUS WITH GINGER AND RED CHILE** and finish the dish with a handful each of torn basil leaves (preferably Thai basil) and roughly chopped salted peanuts. Also try stir-frying **SNOW PEAS, SNAP PEAS, AND ENGLISH PEAS** together with some minced shallots or green garlic—all so green!

Stir-fry **SHREDDED BRUSSELS SPROUTS** with lots of garlic and finish with a splash of fish sauce and a spoonful of minced pickled chile peppers.

Stir-fry fresh **CORN KERNELS** with ginger and finish with chopped fresh cilantro.

Creamed Corn

SERVES 4

This tastes like corn with the volume turned all the way up. It is great as a side dish or as a bed for seared scallops or roasted fish or barbecued chicken (coincidentally, all of my favorite things to eat during the summer). The **small victory** here is that by pureeing half of a vegetable dish, you get tremendous body and richness without having to make a roux or adding tons of cream, half-and-half, or butter (but I do call for some, because . . . come on!). A little basil, sage, thyme, or cilantro wouldn't be unwelcome here, but I really love the simplicity of just corn, dairy, and salt.

6 ears corn, shucked

3 Tbsp unsalted butter

Kosher salt

¼ cup [60 ml] half-and-half or 2 Tbsp each heavy cream and whole milk

Break each ear of corn in half. Working with one piece of corn at a time, stand the half ears up on your cutting board (put the broken, flat side on the board) and carefully cut off the kernels. Transfer the kernels to a large bowl. Scrape the cobs with the blunt edge of your knife to get all the milky bits. Put the corn milk into the bowl with the kernels. Discard the scraped cobs or use them to make corn stock (see page 78).

In a large saucepan over medium-high heat, melt the butter. Add the corn kernels and a generous pinch of salt. Cook, stirring, until the corn is tender and bright yellow, about 5 minutes depending on the age of the corn.

Transfer half of the corn mixture to a blender, add the half-and-half, and puree until smooth. (Alternatively, use an immersion blender to blend some, but not all, of the corn.) Transfer the pureed corn to the saucepan, turn the heat to medium, and let everything get nice and hot, about 2 minutes. Season to taste with salt. Serve immediately.

SPIN-OFFS

FOR CREAMED CORN CONGEE, cook rice (white or brown) with twice as much water as you normally would and let it cook well past your typical stopping point, so that it's very soft. Fold in the creamed corn and serve topped with sliced scallions and a splash of soy sauce.

FOR CREAMED LEEKS AND/OR ONIONS, finely chop them and sauté them in butter, just like the corn. Puree half the mixture in a blender with a splash of heavy cream or half-and-half, and stir it back into the rest of the vegetables (or use an immersion blender to puree some, but not all, of the vegetables). This makes a delicious bed for roast chicken, grilled steak, or pork chops.

FOR CREAMED SPINACH, sauté a finely chopped onion in butter and then add lots and lots of spinach (it wilts like you wouldn't believe, so use quite a bit more than you think you should) and cook it until the liquid it releases evaporates. Add a splash of heavy cream or half-and-half. Puree half of the mixture in a blender and stir it back into the rest of the spinach (or use an immersion blender to puree some, but not all, of the spinach). Season with salt, pepper, and ground nutmeg.

Zucchini + Nigella Fritters

SERVES 4

The **small victory** here is nailing a basic fritter batter, which means you can start any meal off on a memorable note. Plus, fritters are the greatest vehicle for little bits of things lurking in the fridge—chopped kimchi, leftover roast pork, grilled corn cut from the cob, grated cheese—anything can be a fritter! I've included nigella seeds here because I love them, they're onion-y and striking looking (they resemble black sesame seeds and are sometimes labeled "black caraway seeds," "onion seeds," or "kalonji"), and they remind me of the way Syrian string cheese tastes, something my mother adores. I am fully aware that they are hard to track down, and I don't expect you to lose your mind looking for them, but if you see them, try them! They're also great on hummus, eggplant dip (see page 122), or sprinkled on a simple tomato and onion salad. You can also leave them out of the fritters. Or add two thinly sliced scallions or a minced shallot to the batter (either will add the pleasant onion-flavor vibe). Another **small victory** is to be sure to keep the fritters little and thin so that by the time they get crisp on the outside, they are fully cooked inside. Note that you can make these ahead and warm and re-crisp them on a baking sheet in a 400°F [200°C] oven for about 10 minutes.

GARLIC SAUCE

½ cup [120 ml] sour cream

1 small garlic clove, minced

2 Tbsp minced fresh mint or dill, or a combination

1 Tbsp fresh lemon juice

½ tsp kosher salt

FRITTERS

Kosher salt

1 Tbsp nigella seeds (see headnote)

½ cup [60 g] all-purpose flour

½ tsp baking powder

1 lb [455 g] zucchini, ends trimmed, coarsely grated

1 egg, beaten

Neutral oil, such as canola, grapeseed, or safflower, for frying

Lemon wedges for serving

TO MAKE THE SAUCE: In a small bowl, whisk together the sour cream, garlic, mint, lemon juice, and salt. Set aside.

TO MAKE THE FRITTERS: In a large bowl, combine 1 tsp salt, the nigella seeds, flour, and baking powder and whisk together. Wrap the zucchini in a clean kitchen towel and wring out all the liquid over the sink. Transfer the zucchini to the bowl with the nigella seed mixture, add the egg, and stir until everything is well combined.

Line a plate with paper towels and set aside.

In a large heavy skillet, preferably old and well-seasoned cast-iron or heavy nonstick, set over medium-high heat, warm enough oil to completely cover the surface, but it shouldn't be more than ¼ in [6 mm] deep. Once the oil is hot (a little bit of the fritter mixture will sizzle upon contact), drop tablespoonfuls of the batter into the skillet, without crowding them, and use the back of the spoon to press each mound into a flat pancake. Cook the fritters until the

(Continued)

undersides are browned, about 3 minutes, then carefully turn them and cook until the second sides are nicely browned, about 2 minutes. A thin, flexible spatula, such as a fish spatula, or two forks are the best tools for this. Transfer the fritters to the prepared plate and fry the remaining batter in batches, adding more oil to the pan as necessary.

Sprinkle the warm fritters with a little salt. Serve immediately, with the sauce for dipping and the lemon wedges for squeezing over.

SPIN-OFFS

Substitute a peeled and coarsely grated **SWEET POTATO** for the zucchini (leave out the nigella seeds). Fry and top with applesauce!

Substitute 8 oz [230 g] **JUMBO LUMP CRABMEAT AND A HAND-FUL OF CORN KERNELS** for the zucchini (leave out the nigella seeds). Serve topped with sour cream mixed with lime juice, hot sauce, and chopped cilantro.

Substitute 1 cup [150 g] **FINELY CHOPPED CABBAGE KIMCHI AND FOUR THINLY SLICED SCALLIONS** for the zucchini (leave out the nigella seeds). Serve with a dipping sauce made of equal parts soy sauce and rice wine vinegar with a little toasted sesame oil.

Asparagus with Browned Butter + Hazelnuts

SERVES 4

This recipe, where the asparagus is doused in browned butter with crunchy hazelnuts (which taste like browned butter) is an ode to the moment the asparagus arrives in the spring and the promise of the warmer weather that will soon follow. The **small victory** in this recipe is learning how to brown butter, taking its flavor from clean and pure to somewhere deeper and nuttier—not unlike toasting nuts before eating them. Topped with fried or poached eggs (or served alongside scrambled eggs), this makes an excellent breakfast or light lunch.

1 lb [455 g] asparagus, tough ends snapped off and discarded

3 Tbsp unsalted butter

¼ cup [30 g] crushed hazelnuts (a rolling pin makes quick work of this)

Kosher salt

1 Tbsp fresh lemon juice

Fill a large skillet halfway with generously salted water (it should taste like seawater) and bring it to a boil. Add the asparagus and cook until the stalks are bright green and just tender, 2 to 3 minutes. Drain the asparagus in a colander and set aside.

Wipe off any remaining water in the skillet, put it over medium-high heat, and add the butter. Once the butter melts, add the hazelnuts and cook, stirring, until both the hazelnuts and the butter brown, about 4 minutes. Add the asparagus to the pan and stir to coat the spears with the butter.

Transfer the asparagus to a serving platter and scrape all of the butter and hazelnuts over it. Sprinkle with a generous pinch of salt and drizzle with the lemon juice. Serve immediately.

SPIN-OFFS

DRIZZLE PIECES OF ROASTED CARROTS OR SQUASH with browned butter, squeeze over some fresh lemon or even orange juice, and sprinkle with flaky sea salt. You can also crisp up a few leaves of chopped sage in the butter and add those, too.

TOP SAUTÉED OR ROASTED FLOUNDER (or another flatfish) with browned butter, capers, and lemon juice. Classic and delicious!

Kinda, Sorta Patatas Bravas

SERVES 4

This dish includes all the best parts of *patatas bravas*, the crispy potatoes you get in Spain with garlicky aioli and spicy tomato sauce. It combines the flavors of the two sauces into a single easy one and trades the fryer for the oven. The **small victory** here is the magical effect of boiling the potatoes before roasting them in a preheated cast-iron skillet (or you could use a baking sheet), which gives you potatoes that are simultaneously crunchy on the outside and soft on the inside without the hassle of frying them.

¼ cup [60 ml] mayonnaise

1 Tbsp tomato paste or ketchup

2 tsp red wine vinegar

1 small garlic clove, minced

¼ tsp cayenne pepper or a few dashes Tabasco sauce

1 tsp hot pimentón (Spanish smoked paprika)

Kosher salt

1½ lb [680 g] fingerling or small creamer potatoes, halved if larger than bite-size

2 Tbsp extra-virgin olive oil

2 Tbsp finely chopped fresh Italian parsley

In a small bowl, whisk together the mayonnaise, tomato paste, vinegar, garlic, cayenne, and ½ tsp of the pimentón. Season the sauce to taste with salt and set aside.

Place a large cast-iron skillet in the over and preheat to 425°F [220°C].

Put the potatoes in a large pot of salted water, bring to a boil, and cook until they're barely tender, about 10 minutes (start counting once the water comes to a boil); the potatoes should still have a little resistance when you test one with a paring knife. Drain the potatoes in a colander, turn them out onto a dish towel, and pat them dry.

Transfer the well-dried potatoes to a large bowl. Drizzle with the olive oil, sprinkle with a generous pinch of salt and the remaining ½ tsp pimentón, and toss everything together. Carefully remove the hot skillet from the oven and add the potatoes. Return to the oven and roast the potatoes, stirring occasionally, until they are super-browned and crispy, about 40 minutes.

Transfer the potatoes to a serving platter, drizzle with the reserved sauce, and sprinkle with the parsley. Serve immediately.

SPIN-OFFS

FOR SOUR CREAM–CHIVE POTATOES, roast potatoes as directed (but leave out the pimentón) and serve them topped with ½ cup [120 ml] sour cream, a large handful of finely chopped chives, and plenty of salt.

FOR CRISPY, CHEESY POTATOES, roast potatoes as directed (but leave out the pimentón). Once they're nice and crispy, scatter over a large handful of finely grated pecorino, Parmesan, or cheddar cheese (whatever mood you're in!) and return them to the oven for a few minutes, just to melt the cheese.

FOR POTATO SKIN-STYLE POTATOES, melt cheddar cheese over the crispy potatoes and serve dolloped with sour cream and scattered with chopped cooked bacon and thinly sliced scallions.

Grace's Sweet Potatoes

SERVES 4

The **small victory** here is the honest admission about how long it takes to truly caramelize onions. I don't for the life of me understand why in so many cookbooks and television shows we're told it takes just 15, or even 5, minutes. The most important ingredient in caramelized onions is *time*. The sweet reward is a depth of flavor that can't be imitated by a quick sauté or a bit of color achieved with high heat. My wife, Grace, likes to combine the onions with roasted sweet potatoes and crispy pancetta. A favorite side dish, I ask her to make these all the time.

2 lb [900 g] sweet potatoes, unpeeled, scrubbed and cut into ½-in [12-mm] dice

2 Tbsp extra-virgin olive oil

Kosher salt

½ tsp red pepper flakes (optional)

4 oz [115 g] pancetta, finely diced

1 large red onion, thinly sliced

2 Tbsp dark brown sugar, honey, or maple syrup

2 Tbsp red wine vinegar

Preheat your oven to 425°F [220°C]. Line a baking sheet with parchment paper.

Put the sweet potatoes on the prepared baking sheet. Drizzle with the olive oil, sprinkle with ½ tsp salt and the red pepper flakes (if using), and toss everything together. Roast the sweet potatoes, stirring a couple of times, until tender and browned, about 45 minutes. Set aside.

Meanwhile, in a large skillet over medium-high heat, cook the pancetta, stirring, until the fat is rendered and the pancetta is crisp, 5 to 10 minutes. Using a slotted spoon, transfer the pancetta to a bowl and set aside.

Add the sliced onion to the skillet (add a little olive oil if there's not enough fat in the pan—it will depend on how much fat is in the pancetta, so trust your instincts here). Turn the heat to medium-low and cook the onion, stirring now and then, until the onion has collapsed and is very soft and browned in spots, about 45 minutes. Stir in the brown sugar and vinegar and cook until the liquid has evaporated, about 5 minutes. Season to taste with salt.

Add the reserved pancetta and sweet potatoes to the skillet and stir everything together. Serve warm.

SPIN-OFFS

FOR A GREAT BITE TO SERVE WITH DRINKS, slather little pieces of toast with ricotta and top with the onion mixture.

FOR AN EASY CHUTNEY, make the onions as directed, and add a handful of golden raisins, a tiny bit of minced peeled fresh ginger, and a chopped tomato along with the brown sugar and vinegar. Let everything simmer for 10 minutes.

Roasted Radishes with Kalamata Dressing

I once spent a few weeks cooking for a client who was vegan and ate no processed foods whatsoever. I loved the job because within those strict boundaries, I got to focus primarily on vegetables and explore any and every preconceived idea I ever had about cooking them without being distracted by the infinite possibilities of a full pantry. One of the dishes I made for him, that I still continue to make, are these roasted radishes with black olives, which add a depth and richness that you don't often get with vegan cooking. The **small victory** here is all about cooking vegetables that are almost always served raw. Not only will you discover a new angle for something like a radish, you will also add a bit of variety to your regular routine—not to mention guarantee that you will impress your dinner guests. The olive dressing, by the way, is good on many things. Try spooning it on top of goat cheese (serve with toast or crackers), sliced tomatoes, or grilled chicken or fish.

1½ lb [680 g] radishes, split lengthwise (it's okay to leave a little of the stem)

5 Tbsp extra-virgin olive oil

Kosher salt

1 small garlic clove, minced

1 Tbsp sherry vinegar

12 pitted Kalamata olives (or other dark olives), finely chopped

1 Tbsp finely chopped fresh Italian parsley or chives or 1 tsp finely chopped fresh oregano

Preheat your oven to 425°F [220°C]. Line a baking sheet with parchment paper.

Put the radishes on the prepared baking sheet, drizzle with 2 Tbsp of the olive oil, sprinkle with a large pinch of salt, and use your hands to toss everything together. Roast, stirring occasionally, until the radishes are tender and browned, about 45 minutes.

Meanwhile put the garlic, a large pinch of salt, and the vinegar in a small bowl and let them sit and get to know each other for 10 minutes (this quick-pickle moment will tame the bite of the garlic and also infuse the vinegar with the garlic). Slowly whisk in the remaining 3 Tbsp olive oil and then stir in the olives.

Transfer the roasted radishes to a serving platter, spoon over the olive dressing, and scatter over the parsley. Serve immediately.

SPIN-OFFS

TRY STIR-FRYING ICEBERG LETTUCE; it sounds really out there, but it is very good. Get a large skillet nice and hot over high heat and add a slick of oil and some finely chopped peeled ginger, garlic, and fresh red chile. Once those sizzle, add a couple handfuls of chopped iceberg lettuce and cook, stirring a bit. Serve drizzled with soy sauce and fish sauce.

FOR BRAISED CELERY, sauté a sliced onion in olive oil in a large skillet or saucepan. Once it's soft, add a few minced garlic cloves, a couple of anchovies (if you're into them, but okay if not), and a head of celery cut into 2-in [5-cm] pieces. Add enough vegetable or chicken stock to reach halfway up the celery. Cover and simmer until the celery is soft, about 20 minutes. Season with salt and serve drizzled with high-quality olive oil and fresh lemon juice.

ENDIVE OR RADICCHIO cut into wedges and coated with olive oil and salt like a sear on a hot grill for a few minutes on each side until they're nice and charred. Serve with lemon wedges for squeezing over.

Roasted Mushrooms on Toast

I was once invited to a mushroom-themed dinner (I was tasked with dessert and made a chocolate cake in the shape of a mushroom!) cooked by my friend Tamar Adler. For one part of the meal, she served the most beautiful wild mushrooms that she had roasted, and I thought, *well, isn't that smart?* Roasting mushrooms instead of sautéing them gives you all the concentrated flavor of sautéed mushrooms without having to work in tons of batches and without having to use your entire olive oil supply . . . hello, **small victory**. Keep in mind that the mushrooms will shrink a ton in the oven since they're so full of water (not unlike spinach), so don't be alarmed when you see the mountain of them reduced to a flat layer on your sheet pan. I like to serve these on toast that's been rubbed with garlic and slicked with crème fraîche because life is short, and everything should be delicious. These are great to serve with drinks, or as a first course with a little arugula salad next to them, or as a main course topped with fried or poached eggs.

2 lb [900 g] assorted mushrooms, tough stems discarded, torn into bite-size pieces

¼ cup [60 ml] extra-virgin olive oil, plus more for drizzling

Kosher salt

2 tsp minced fresh thyme

Twelve ¼-in- [6-mm-] thick slices baguette or country bread

1 garlic clove

½ cup [115 g] crème fraîche

1 Tbsp finely chopped fresh Italian parsley

Preheat your oven to 425°F [220°C]. Line a baking sheet with parchment paper.

Spread the mushrooms on the prepared baking sheet, drizzle with the olive oil and sprinkle with a large pinch of salt and the thyme. Use your hands to toss everything together. Roast the mushrooms, stirring occasionally, until they are tender and well browned, about 40 minutes.

When you take the mushrooms out of the oven, toast the bread and rub one side of each piece of toast with the garlic clove (the toast will act almost as sandpaper and will catch little bits of the garlic). Spread the garlic-rubbed side of the toasts with the crème fraîche.

Divide the roasted mushrooms among the toasts. Drizzle each toast with a little bit more olive oil and sprinkle each one with a little pinch of salt and some of the parsley. Serve immediately.

SPIN-OFFS

FOR A GREAT VEGETARIAN MEAL, serve the roasted mushrooms on soft polenta and top with a fried or poached egg and some grated Parmesan or pecorino cheese. Some wilted greens and/or roasted tomatoes would be really nice here, too. If you're vegan, leave out the egg and cheese and top with chopped hazelnuts that you've toasted in olive oil.

FOR MUSHROOM SPAGHETTI, toss the roasted mushrooms with 1 lb [455 g] cooked spaghetti, along with 3 Tbsp butter (but feel free to add more . . . neither a strand of spaghetti nor a roasted mushroom can have *too much* butter). Serve topped with lots of grated Parmesan or pecorino cheese and plenty of chopped parsley.

Cauliflower with Anchovy Bread Crumbs

SERVES 4

As much as I love roasted cauliflower, the anchovy bread crumbs (crunchy! salty! umami!) are really the heroes here. I made them for the first time when I was fixing a simple dinner, and a platter of plain roasted cauliflower just seemed to be begging for something special. There was a stale loaf of bread on the counter and a tin of anchovies in the cupboard. Done and done. Learning to repurpose old bread into bread crumbs is a **small victory** that feeds my hate-to-throw-out-useful-things soul. To make them, simply break stale bread into small pieces and pulse them in a food processor until they're as fine or as coarse as you'd like them. Coarse is best for this recipe.

1 head cauliflower, cored and cut into small florets

½ cup [120 ml] extra-virgin olive oil

½ tsp kosher salt

1 garlic clove, minced

4 oil-packed anchovies, drained

1½ cups [210 g] coarse bread crumbs (see headnote)

¼ tsp freshly ground black pepper

2 Tbsp finely chopped fresh Italian parsley

Preheat your oven to 425°F [220°C]. Line a baking sheet with parchment paper.

Put the cauliflower on the prepared baking sheet, drizzle with 3 Tbsp of the olive oil, sprinkle with the salt, and toss everything together. Roast, stirring occasionally, until the cauliflower is tender and well browned, about 40 minutes. Transfer to a serving platter.

Meanwhile, in a large heavy skillet over medium-high heat, warm 3 Tbsp olive oil. Add the garlic and anchovies and cook, stirring, until the

anchovies have completely disintegrated into the oil. Add the bread crumbs and cook, stirring frequently, until they've absorbed all of the oil and are brown and a bit crisp, about 5 minutes. Stir in the pepper and parsley and remove from the heat.

Scatter the bread crumbs evenly over the cauliflower and drizzle everything with the remaining 2 Tbsp olive oil. Serve immediately.

SPIN-OFFS

SERVE THE ANCHOVY BREAD CRUMBS ON TOP OF SPAGHETTI in lieu of or in addition to cheese. It can be plain spaghetti that's simply been tossed with olive oil and garlic, or just with tomato sauce, or even white clam sauce.

TURN THE ROASTED CAULIFLOWER INTO SOUP by pureeing it with 6 cups [1.4 L] chicken stock. Serve each bowl topped with anchovy bread crumbs.

You can make bread crumbs the same way using **DIFFERENT FLAVORINGS**, substituting chopped rosemary for the anchovies, for

example, or substituting fresh oregano for the parsley. For a **VEGAN VERSION**, use capers instead of anchovies. For a **CHEESY VERSION**, you can add some finely grated Parmesan or pecorino at the last minute. These are excellent on top of tomato soup.

Roasted Scallion + Chive Dip

I know I said previously that my favorite food is chicken soup, but I think it might actually be potato chips. And do you know the only thing better than a perfect potato chip? A potato chip with dip. This ultimate oniony dip made with sweet roasted scallions and fresh chives makes any chip moment extra special. There are two **small victories** here. The *first* is that when you have older scallions and herbs that don't have freshness going for them, instead of throwing them out, roast them and/or puree them to create a dip. The *second* is a very small one but a very useful one—when emptying anything out of a food processor bowl, you can keep the blade from dangerously tumbling out by holding it in place from underneath the bowl with one of your fingers. Holding the blade this way will not only keep things safer but it will also guarantee that you won't lose any of whatever you've pureed by lifting out the blade and opening an escape route for the contents of your food processor.

24 scallions, roots and dark green tops trimmed off, white and light green parts roughly chopped

2 Tbsp extra-virgin olive oil

Kosher salt

¼ cup [60 ml] mayonnaise

½ cup [120 ml] sour cream

1 tsp sherry vinegar, plus more as needed

¼ cup [10 g] minced fresh chives, plus more for serving

Freshly ground black pepper

Potato chips for serving, preferably plain or salt and vinegar

Preheat your oven to 425°F [220°C]. Line a baking sheet with parchment paper.

Put the scallions on the prepared baking sheet, drizzle with the olive oil, and sprinkle with 1 tsp salt. Rub everything together so the scallions are coated with olive oil and spread them out so they're in a single, even layer. Roast, stirring once, until they're softened and browned in spots, 15 to 20 minutes. Let cool to room temperature.

Transfer the cooled scallions to the bowl of a food processor. Add the mayonnaise, sour cream, vinegar, chives, and ½ tsp pepper. Pulse to combine. You want the dip to be relatively but not completely smooth; a little texture is welcome. Taste the dip for seasoning, and add more salt, pepper, and/or vinegar as needed.

(Store in an airtight container in the refrigerator for up to 3 days; I actually prefer it cold. If you serve it cold, season again before serving, as cold temperatures tend to mute flavors.)

Transfer the dip to a bowl, top with additional chives, and serve with potato chips.

(Continued)

SPIN-OFFS

FOR BEET AND ALMOND DIP, puree
1 lb [455 g] roughly chopped cooked
beets with 1 cup [140 g] roasted
almonds, the juice of 1 lemon, and
½ cup [120 ml] extra-virgin olive oil.
Season with salt. This is very good with
warm pita bread or seeded crackers.

FOR WHITE BEAN AND PARSLEY DIP,
puree a rinsed and drained can of white
beans with a large handful of chopped
parsley, a minced garlic clove, the juice
of 1 lemon, and ½ cup [120 ml] extra-
virgin olive oil. Season with salt. This is
really good on thick slices of toasted
country bread that have been rubbed
with a garlic clove.

**FOR WHIPPED FETA AND YOGURT
DIP**, put 4 oz [115 g] crumbled feta
cheese in a food processor and puree
until smooth. Add 1 cup [240 ml]
Greek yogurt, the juice of 1 lemon,
and 3 Tbsp extra-virgin olive oil and
let the food processor run until the
mixture is extremely smooth and
slightly aerated, about 2 minutes;
scrape down the sides of the bowl
a few times with a rubber spatula.
Season with salt and pepper. Transfer
to a bowl, drizzle with extra-virgin olive
oil, and sprinkle with dried oregano
or za'atar. Serve with cut-up raw vegetables and/or warm pitas.

FOR EDAMAME DIP, puree a bag of
defrosted edamame (the shelled ones)
in a food processor. Add a scoop of
silken tofu to make it smooth and
creamy and season with miso paste,
grated fresh ginger, and/or soy sauce.
Serve with rice or seaweed crackers
and/or cucumber slices.

Smoky Eggplant Dip with Yogurt + Za'atar

MAKES ABOUT 2 CUPS [480 ML]

The **small victory** here is learning how to go past the point where you think you should stop. It's essential to burn the eggplant on the outside to transform the inside to the totally yielding softness needed for this baba ghanoush–ish dip. Cooking is often not only about learning how to trust your instincts, but also about how to discover new ones. The za'atar, a Middle Eastern spice blend that often has some combination of herbs, spices, and seeds (typically oregano, sumac, sesame seeds), can be swapped out for an equal amount of toasted sesame seeds and/or a pinch of minced, fresh thyme leaves.

1 lb [455 g] eggplant

Kosher salt

1 Tbsp tahini

2 Tbsp fresh lemon juice, plus more as needed

3 Tbsp plain full-fat Greek yogurt

1 Tbsp extra-virgin olive oil

1 Tbsp torn fresh mint

1 tsp za'atar

Warm pita for serving

Prepare your grill for medium-high heat (or heat a large grill pan set over a couple of burners) and make sure your grates are super-clean.

Prick the eggplant in a few spots with a fork and grill it, turning now and then, until the skin is completely blackened and the flesh feels soft when you pierce the eggplant with a paring knife, about 45 minutes. Transfer the eggplant to a plate and let cool to room temperature. (Alternatively, you can roast the eggplant whole in a 425°F [200°C] oven; turn it over halfway through roasting or char over the flames of a gas stove.)

Cut the eggplant in half lengthwise and use a spoon to scoop the soft flesh into the bowl of a food processor. Discard the eggplant skin. Add ½ tsp salt, the tahini, lemon juice, and yogurt to the eggplant and pulse everything a few times just to combine. Do not let the machine run for longer than a couple of seconds at a time—you want the dip to have a bit of texture and not be completely smooth. Taste the dip for seasoning and add more salt and/or lemon juice if needed.

Transfer the dip to a shallow bowl and smooth the surface with the back of a spoon. Drizzle the dip with the olive oil and sprinkle with the mint and za'atar. Serve immediately, with plenty of warm pita for scooping and dipping.

SPIN-OFFS

**FOR A BABA GHANOUSH–
HUMMUS HYBRID**, puree a rinsed
and drained can of chickpeas in
the food processor before adding
the eggplant. Add a bit more
tahini and lemon to taste.

**FOR ROASTED PEPPER AND
EGGPLANT DIP**, puree three
cleaned roasted red peppers (see
page 61, or use store-bought) in
the food processor before adding
the eggplant. Leave out the tahini
and yogurt and substitute red
wine vinegar for the lemon juice.
Serve topped with capers and/or
chopped pitted olives.

**FOR A PSEUDO-INDIAN EGG-
PLANT DIP**, make the dip as
directed, but leave out the tahini.
Heat 3 Tbsp canola or vegetable oil in a small skillet and add
½ tsp each cumin seeds and black
mustard seeds, and toast until
fragrant and the seeds begin to
pop. Pour this mixture over the
eggplant dip.

GRAINS, BEANS + PASTA

Kimchi Fried Rice with Scallion Salad

SERVES 4

There's a theory out there in the ether that even the best cooks struggle with cooking rice (Kim Severson once wrote a great piece about this in the *New York Times*). I'm afraid I've suffered from poor rice cooking for a long time. The fail-proof method (**small victory**) I've grown to love, especially for long-grain rice, with grains that are best when kept separate (as opposed to cozy short-grain rice, where the grains hug their neighbors), is to cook rice just as you would pasta. Bring a large pot of salted water to a boil, add the rice, and boil until the grains are tender (10 to 15 minutes for most types of white rice, 35 to 40 for most types of brown rice). When the rice is done, drain it in a fine-mesh sieve and serve immediately with butter and salt, or let it cool and use it the next day for the one of the best foods in the world: fried rice.

Leftover rice is best for making fried rice because the grains become very dry and then act as sponges for whatever flavors you combine them with (another **small victory**). My favorite is cabbage kimchi, the fermented condiment that's eaten with every meal in Korea. I came to love it when I worked on *Kimchi Chronicles*, the companion cookbook to the PBS program of the same name. Served with a simple scallion salad (a popular accompaniment to Korean barbecue), this is one of my favorite side dishes, and it makes for a wonderful, savory meal on its own if you top it with a fried or poached egg.

SCALLION SALAD

4 scallions, roots and dark green tops trimmed off

1 tsp toasted sesame oil

1 tsp rice wine vinegar

1 tsp toasted sesame seeds

Kosher salt

FRIED RICE

One 16-oz [448-g] jar cabbage kimchi, including juice

3 Tbsp canola or vegetable oil, plus more as needed

1 small yellow onion, finely diced

2 garlic cloves, minced

Kosher salt

4 cups [560 g] day-old cooked brown or white rice

1 Tbsp soy sauce, plus more as needed

TO MAKE THE SCALLION SALAD: Cut the scallions thinly on the diagonal or into small matchsticks. The best way to do this is to cut each scallion into three even pieces and then cut each piece in half lengthwise. Put each piece flat-side down on your cutting board and cut into thin strips. Put the scallions, sesame oil, rice wine vinegar, and sesame seeds in a medium bowl and stir to combine. Season to taste with salt and set aside.

(Continued)

TO MAKE THE FRIED RICE: Put a sieve or colander over a bowl and drain the kimchi. Reserve the juice. Finely chop the kimchi and set it aside.

In a large nonstick skillet over medium-high heat, warm the canola oil. Add the onion and garlic and sprinkle with a large pinch of salt. Cook, stirring now and then, until the onion just begins to turn translucent, about 5 minutes. Turn the heat to high, add the chopped kimchi, and cook, stirring now and then, until the edges of the kimchi become ever so slightly crisp and stick to the pan, about 5 minutes.

Crumble the rice into the skillet and stir thoroughly to combine. Add the reserved kimchi juice and cook, stirring, until the rice is warmed and red through and through from the kimchi juice, about 3 minutes. Turn off the heat, drizzle over the soy sauce, and taste for seasoning, adding a bit more salt and/or soy sauce if needed.

Transfer the fried rice to a serving bowl (or portion straight from the skillet) and top with the scallion salad. Serve immediately.

SPIN-OFFS

ADD BACON! Pork and kimchi are very good friends. Start the dish by cooking 4 oz [115 g] roughly chopped bacon until all of its fat is rendered and the bacon is crisp. Add the onion, garlic, and kimchi and proceed as directed.

FOR ONE OF THE MOST SATISFYING FRIED-RICE VARIATIONS, crisp up some diced bacon in a skillet, then remove it, using a slotted spoon, and set aside. Cook some diced parsnips in the bacon fat until they're browned on the outside and tender when you test them with a paring knife. Add leftover cooked rice to the skillet rice and cook until the rice is saturated with bacon fat and warm. Return the bacon to the mix, stir everything together, and add plenty of chopped parsley or cilantro.

FOR A GREAT SUMMERTIME LUNCH DISH, combine leftover cooked rice with chopped tomatoes, chopped fresh basil, and lots of high-quality canned or jarred tuna (the ones imported from Spain and Italy are especially good). Stir together with a little olive oil and red wine vinegar and serve at room temperature.

Best Rice Pilaf with Roasted Red Cabbage

SERVES 6

The single item of food I requested most often when I was a kid was Rice-A-Roni (boxed rice pilaf). In an effort to create a version that matches its salty, savory flavor without any of the ingredients I don't recognize on the package, I worked on this recipe for a long time to nail a crowd-pleasing result. There are two **small victories** here. The ***first*** is when you break the spaghetti into small pieces, do yourself an enormous favor and put it into a zip-top plastic bag before you break it so that the pasta doesn't fly all over your kitchen (I figured this out the hard way). The ***second*** is roasting shredded cabbage until it almost, but not quite, burns—it makes the cabbage remarkably crunchy and gives the pilaf a pleasing slow-cooked flavor (not to mention beautiful color). This cabbage is so good that I often serve it on its own as a side dish—that is, if it even makes it to a serving bowl, as I have a tendency to eat it straight out of the pan. If you're averse to gluten, you can either leave out the pasta or use gluten-free spaghetti.

4 cups [300 g] finely shredded red cabbage

3 Tbsp extra-virgin olive oil

Kosher salt

2 Tbsp unsalted butter

½ cup [35 g] 1-in [2.5-cm] pieces of spaghetti or angel hair pasta

1 cup [200 g] long-grain white rice

1¾ cups [420 ml] chicken stock or water

Pinch of saffron threads (optional)

Preheat your oven to 425°F [220°C]. Line a baking sheet with parchment paper.

Put the cabbage on the prepared baking sheet, drizzle with 2 Tbsp of the olive oil, sprinkle with ½ tsp salt, and use your hands to toss everything together. Spread the cabbage over the surface of the baking sheet. Roast the cabbage, stirring it every so often, for longer than you think you should, until it's quite shriveled and crispy and on the very thin line between dark red and burnt, about 30 minutes. Set aside.

In a large saucepan over medium-high heat, warm the remaining 1 Tbsp olive oil and the butter. Add the pasta and rice and cook, stirring, until the pasta turns golden brown, the rice turns opaque, and everything smells toasty and vaguely nutty, about 5 minutes. Add 1 tsp salt, the stock, and saffron (if using) and bring the mixture to a boil, then turn the heat to low, cover the pan, and simmer until the rice just loses its starchy bite and the liquid has completely evaporated, 10 to 15 minutes, depending on your brand of rice.

(Continued)

Put a paper towel between the pan and the lid and set aside for 10 minutes to rest. The paper towel will absorb excess liquid from the residual steam and leave you with the fluffiest rice.

Once the pilaf has rested, uncover it and fluff with a fork. If your saucepan is large enough, add the reserved cabbage to the pilaf, stir everything together, and then transfer to a serving bowl. If your pan isn't large enough, simply transfer both the pilaf and the cabbage to a large serving bowl, stir, and season to taste with salt. Serve immediately.

SPIN-OFFS

FOR BROWN RICE PILAF, substitute long-grain brown rice for the white rice and increase the liquid to 2½ cups [600 ml]. Keep everything else the same, or feel free to swap the cabbage for roasted mushrooms (see page 116). The cooking time will be more like 40 minutes.

FOR MUJADARA, the Middle Eastern equivalent of rice and beans, swap the roasted cabbage for caramelized onions (see page 112) and fold in cooked brown or green lentils at the end, too. Serve with garlicky yogurt (see page 81).

FOR TOMATO SOUP RICE, use 1 cup [240 ml] tomato soup and 1 cup [240 ml] water or stock. Serve with grated cheese (cheddar or Parmesan work well) on top.

Potluck Quinoa

SERVES 4

I love grain salads for lunch and I also find them perfect for potlucks and holiday meals, because you can make them ahead (they don't suffer at all if they sit for a while) and they're great at room temperature. It's best to use grains that are fluffy and stay separate when cooked. A **small victory** for guaranteeing this texture is to spread out the hot cooked grains on a baking sheet as soon as possible. This cools them down quickly and lets all the excess steam evaporate. Another **small victory** here is planning ahead. Just as it takes about the same amount of time to roast two chickens as it does to roast one, making extra grains guarantees you're always a step closer to easily preparing something healthful and wholesome at home.

1 cup [180 g] quinoa

Kosher salt

¼ cup [60 ml] extra-virgin olive oil, plus more for drizzling

½ cup [70 g] whole raw hazelnuts, crushed (a rolling pin makes quick work of this)

2 Tbsp fresh lemon juice

2 large handfuls baby arugula and/or soft, leafy herbs (parsley, dill, chives, etc.), roughly chopped

4 oz [115 g] fresh goat cheese, crumbled

Rinse the quinoa thoroughly in a fine-mesh strainer (this may sound like an annoying step, but don't skip it since quinoa's natural coating tastes soapy). Put the rinsed quinoa in a medium saucepan with 1¾ cups [420 ml] water and 1 tsp salt. Bring to a boil, then lower the heat, cover, and simmer until the quinoa has absorbed all of the water, softened, and each grain has "spiraled," about 12 minutes.

Transfer the quinoa to a baking sheet and use a spoon to spread it out. Let cool to room temperature, then transfer to a large bowl and set aside.

Meanwhile, in a skillet over medium-high heat, warm the olive oil. Add the hazelnuts, sprinkle with a large pinch of salt, and cook, stirring frequently, until the nuts are dark brown, about 5 minutes.

Transfer the hazelnuts and all of their fragrant oil to the bowl with the quinoa, along with the lemon juice and arugula. Stir everything together and season to taste with salt. Scatter the goat cheese on top of the quinoa and drizzle the whole thing evenly with a good glug of olive oil. Serve immediately.

SPIN-OFFS

MIX COOKED QUINOA with chopped and roasted zucchini and black sesame seeds and dress with a mixture of equal parts extra-virgin olive oil, soy sauce, and rice wine vinegar.

FOR A SUPER-RETRO COMBINATION, combine cooked quinoa with perfectly diced carrots and frozen peas that you've cooked in salted water. Stir everything together with plenty of butter and serve warm.

FOR A REALLY SATISFYING SIDE DISH, mix cooked quinoa with roasted mushrooms (see page 116) and top with a few Pickled Red Onions (page 267). For a main course, top each serving with a fried or poached egg.

Kasha + Mushrooms with Crispy Salami

SERVES 4

There are some Jewish classics that I grew up with that I adore, mostly things that my family would order at places like the long-gone Rascal House in North Miami Beach, where my great-grandmother (who I was lucky enough to know as a child) lived. Family favorites included mushroom and barley soup, kasha knishes eaten with lots of mustard, and eggs scrambled with bits of crispy kosher salami. This dish, a mash-up of all of those, is almost like Jewish fried rice. It could be served as a side dish or be topped with fried eggs for a complete meal (maybe with a little salad next to it to offset its richness). The **small victory** here is all about the cooking of the kasha—coating it in beaten egg and toasting it before adding liquid is like giving each grain its own little blanket and keeps the kasha from becoming extremely mushy (as it's prone to do).

¼ cup [60 ml] sour cream

1 Tbsp Dijon mustard

2 Tbsp red wine vinegar

2 Tbsp water

A small handful of finely chopped fresh dill

Kosher salt

1 egg

1 cup [180 g] kasha (sometimes labeled buckwheat groats)

4 Tbsp [60 ml] extra-virgin olive oil

1½ cups [360 ml] chicken stock or water

1 tsp caraway seeds

6 oz [170 g] kosher beef salami (preferably Hebrew National), diced

12 oz [340 g] cremini mushrooms, tough stems trimmed off, thinly sliced

In a small bowl, whisk together the sour cream, mustard, vinegar, water, and dill. Season to taste with salt and set aside.

In a small bowl, beat the egg. Add the kasha and stir to combine.

In a large saucepan over medium heat, warm 2 Tbsp of the olive oil. Add the egg-coated kasha and cook, stirring, until the pan is dry and the kasha smells nutty, about 2 minutes. Add the chicken stock, along with a large pinch of salt, and bring to a boil. Then, lower the heat, cover the pan, and simmer the kasha until it's tender, about 10 minutes. Turn off the heat, put a paper towel between the pan and the lid (to absorb the excess steam), and set the kasha aside.

Meanwhile, in a large skillet over medium-high heat, warm the remaining 2 Tbsp olive oil. Add the caraway seeds and salami and cook, stirring, until the caraway seeds smell fragrant and the salami is crisp, about 5 minutes.

Add the mushrooms to the pan and sprinkle with a large pinch of salt. (If your pan isn't big enough to hold them all in a single layer, cook in batches, or you'll end up with steamed mushrooms—which aren't that wonderful.) Cook, stirring now and then, until the mushrooms are softened and a bit browned and any liquid that they released has evaporated, about 10 minutes.

Add the kasha to the mushrooms, stir everything together, and season to taste with salt.

Transfer the kasha to a serving bowl and drizzle the sour cream mixture over it. Serve immediately.

SPIN-OFFS

FOR ANOTHER CLASSIC JEW-ISH COMBINATION, mix together barley and mushrooms. I like to warm leftover cooked barley in butter and add the sautéed mushrooms from this dish or roasted mushrooms (see page 116). A little chopped parsley or dill wouldn't hurt here.

FOR A GREAT FALL DISH, warm cooked kasha in a skillet with olive oil and garlic and add diced roasted root vegetables.

FOR A SORT OF '80S RIFF ON FRIED RICE, warm leftover cooked wild rice in a skillet with butter and add chopped roasted hazelnuts and dried cranberries. Serve dotted with goat cheese.

Curried Red Lentils with Coconut Milk

SERVES 4

When I was in college, I would often end up cooking dinner at friends' apartments using whatever they had on hand, which always seemed to be curry powder, a can of something, and an old onion. Something from nothing, these meals hit the spot in the most nourishing of ways. It felt as though even if we didn't know what we were doing with our lives in the long run, we could have the immediate comfort of something warm and homemade for dinner. This dish, almost like a thick soup or a dal of sorts, is an ode to those nights when my friends and I drank wine from a box and stayed up late watching *Strangers with Candy* on our hand-me-down televisions. Note that this is also completely vegan (just skip the yogurt when you serve the lentils). The **small victory** here is not only making something healthful and easy on the cheap, it's also about the first step of the dish; toasting spices in oil allows them to bloom and make themselves known. I always think of dried spices as sleeping in the cupboard. When they hit hot oil, they wake up. You'll find that almost any dish made with spices is better if you can take a moment to warm and reinvigorate them.

3 Tbsp extra-virgin olive oil

1 Tbsp minced peeled fresh ginger

2 garlic cloves, minced

1 shallot, minced

½ tsp ground coriander

1 tsp cumin seeds or ground cumin

1 tsp ground turmeric

1 cup [180 g] split red lentils

One 13½-oz [398-ml] can full-fat coconut milk, shaken

Kosher salt

Cooked basmati rice, plain yogurt, and chopped fresh cilantro for serving

In a large saucepan over medium heat, warm the olive oil. Add the ginger, garlic, shallot, coriander, cumin, and turmeric and cook, stirring now and then, until the vegetables are softened and the spices are very fragrant, about 10 minutes. Add the lentils, coconut milk, and 2 tsp salt, then fill the empty coconut-milk can with water and add that to the saucepan. It will look like a lot of liquid, but the lentils will absorb it as they cook. Stir everything together, turn the heat to high, and bring the mixture to a boil. Turn the heat to low and let the lentils simmer, stirring now and then, until they're completely soft, about 20 minutes. Season to taste with salt.

Serve the lentils hot over rice. Top each serving with a spoonful of yogurt and a sprinkle of cilantro.

SPIN-OFFS

FOR VEGETABLE AND/OR CHICKEN CURRY, substitute 1 lb [455 g] chopped vegetables (such as cauliflower, carrots, potatoes, peas, or anything, really) and/or cubes of boneless chicken thighs or breasts for the lentils. Feel free to brown the chicken first for added flavor. Everything else stays the same.

FOR AN EASY THAI-STYLE CURRY, keep the lentils or substitute 1 lb [455 g] vegetables, shrimp, chicken, or tofu. Leave out the cumin and add a minced chile pepper along with the garlic and ginger. When you add the coconut milk and water, also add the stems from a handful of fresh cilantro (discard these later), and finish the dish with a splash of fish sauce. Serve with lime wedges, Sriracha, and cilantro leaves.

Chopped Chickpea Salad

SERVES 4

I love canned chickpeas. LOVE. When there's a can of chickpeas in my cupboard, I feel secure—I know that a hearty, satisfying, quick, inexpensive meal of just about any persuasion (they're ubiquitous in Italian, Middle Eastern, and North African cuisines and more) is within reach (check out page 275 for more on this). While I fantasize about being the type of cook who regularly shops at Kalustyan's (the incredible spice and specialty food store in Manhattan) for dried beans, soaks them overnight, and lovingly simmers them on the back burner with onion peels and bay leaves while I do the crossword puzzle and drink milky tea . . . I'm just not. And that's okay—I've got Goya on my side. The **small victory** here is about identifying a worthwhile shortcut and taking advantage of it. Sometimes cooking isn't about doing every step—sometimes it's about knowing where your effort counts and dressing up a shortcut ingredient to make it feel fresh.

1 Tbsp Dijon mustard

2 Tbsp red wine vinegar

Kosher salt

Freshly ground black pepper

¼ cup [60 ml] olive oil

One 15-oz [425-g] can chickpeas, rinsed and drained

8 small or 6 medium radishes, cut into rounds, half-moons, or matchsticks (whatever!)

½ English cucumber, seeded and diced

4 scallions, roots and dark green tops trimmed off, white and light green parts thinly sliced

A large handful of finely chopped arugula

A small handful of finely chopped dill

½ cup [60 g] crumbled feta cheese

In a large bowl, whisk together the mustard, vinegar, a large pinch of salt, and a few grinds of black pepper. While whisking, slowly drizzle in the olive oil to make a thick dressing.

Add the chickpeas, radishes, cucumber, scallions, arugula, and dill to the bowl. Gently stir everything together and season to taste with salt and pepper. Gently stir in the feta. Serve immediately or let the salad sit for up to 3 hours at room temperature or overnight in the refrigerator (bring to room temperature before serving). This is one of those dishes that gets better as it sits.

SPIN-OFFS

MIX WHITE BEANS WITH SHAVED FENNEL, chopped fresh parsley, a little chopped fresh oregano, and shards of Parmesan. Dress with fresh lemon juice and olive oil.

COMBINE BLACK-EYED PEAS and shredded raw collard greens with chopped roasted peanuts and finely diced red onion. Dress with apple cider vinegar and olive oil.

STIR TOGETHER PINTO OR BLACK BEANS with chopped tomatoes, jalapeños, chopped cilantro, and thinly sliced white onion. Dress with olive oil and fresh lime juice.

Crispy Hominy +
Cheddar Fritters

SERVES 4

When I worked on *The Kimchi Chronicles*, the companion cookbook to the PBS show of the same name about Korea and its food, I grew to love *bindatteok*—crunchy, savory fritters made of ground mung beans seasoned with seasame oil and soy sauce, and often punctuated with bits of kimchi and scallions. Inspired by them, I've continued to make fritters with different beans, grains, and legumes. **Small victory**: They all work and they're all delicious. I especially love using canned hominy to get the great flavor of corn—sort of like corn fritters without all the shucking—but feel free to try all sorts of different beans and grains (check out the Spin-Offs for more ideas). By the way, these are a great thing to make for gluten-free friends or family (or for yourself if you're gluten-averse).

One 15-oz [425-g] can hominy, rinsed and drained

1 cup [100 g] coarsely grated cheddar cheese

6 scallions, roots and dark green tops trimmed off, white and light green parts thinly sliced

1 egg

2 tsp Sriracha or your favorite hot sauce

Kosher salt

Neutral oil, such as canola, grapeseed, or safflower, for frying

A handful of roughly chopped fresh cilantro and some lime wedges for serving

In the bowl of a food processor, combine the hominy, cheddar, scallions, egg, Sriracha, and 2 tsp salt and pulse until the mixture is well mixed and pulling away from the sides and bottom of the bowl; it will be thick.

Line a plate with paper towels and set aside.

In a large heavy skillet, preferably well-seasoned cast-iron or heavy nonstick, over medium-high heat, add about 3 Tbsp oil (the exact amount depends on the size of your pan, but you're looking for enough oil just to coat the entire pan so that the fritters can brown evenly—you are essentially searing them, not deep-frying them). Once the oil is hot (a little bit of the hominy mixture will sizzle upon contact), drop tablespoonfuls of the batter into the skillet,

without crowding them, and use the back of the spoon to press down each mound into a flat round. Cover the pan with a splatter screen, if you have one, and be careful—this mixture contains a lot of moisture, so it tends to pop as it cooks. Cook the fritters until the undersides are browned, about 2 minutes, then carefully turn them and cook until the second sides are nicely browned, about 2 minutes longer. Transfer the fritters to the prepared plate and fry the remaining batter in batches, adding more oil to the pan as necessary.

Sprinkle the warm fritters with a little salt and the cilantro. Serve immediately, with the lime wedges for squeezing.

SPIN-OFFS

SUBSTITUTE BLACK BEANS for the hominy and keep the Southern/Southwestern vibes going.

FOR FALAFEL-LIKE FRITTERS, swap chickpeas for the hominy and feta for the cheddar. Skip the hot sauce and add a handful of finely chopped parsley and/or dill.

FOR HOPPIN' JOHN FRITTERS, soften a finely copped small yellow onion and a stalk of celery in a little oil and transfer to the food processor. Add a can of rinsed and drained black-eyed peas along with a handful of cooked rice and an egg and pulse to combine. Pan-fry as directed and serve sprinkled with thinly sliced scallions.

FOR WHITE BEAN AND PARMESAN FRITTERS, substitute white beans for the hominy, ½ cup [50 g] Parmesan for the cheddar, and parsley for the scallions. Omit the hot sauce. Serve with lemon wedges.

FOR KOREAN BINDATTEOK, soak 1 cup [180 g] dried mung beans and 2 Tbsp sweet rice in a bowl of cold water for a few hours, up to overnight. Drain and put them in a blender with ¼ cup [60 ml] fresh water, a generous pinch of salt, and a few dashes each fish sauce, toasted sesame oil, and soy sauce. Blend until smooth. Pan-fry small spoonfuls of the mixture in neutral oil, as directed in the main recipe. Make a dipping sauce of equal parts soy sauce and rice wine vinegar and add a handful of thinly sliced scallions. Serve the browned pancakes sprinkled with salt and the dipping sauce alongside.

Orecchiette with Spicy Sausage + Parmesan

SERVES 4 TO 6

I have a soft spot for old-school Italian American restaurants. I love how they all pretty much have the same menus and how each one promotes one or two signature pasta dishes that, according to my very unofficial research, always seem to have a bit of sausage meat and cream (like the legendary Rigatoni Pitti at Bar Pitti on Sixth Avenue in New York). This orecchiette—full of spicy Italian sausage and sweet onions, with a final warm bath of a little cream and plenty of Parmesan—is my rendition. It's also my favorite thing to eat on a cold night, preferably on the couch in front of a movie (though it does make for a great, simple dinner-party dish, and then all you need is a salad and something sweet for afterward). The **small victory** here is all about taking the pasta out of the boiling water before it is totally done and finishing it in the sauce. I like to think of dried pasta as a sponge that swells with whatever you're boiling it in when you cook it. Trading the last few minutes of cooking in water for something more flavorful gives you pasta with the most impact. Also, save some of the starchy pasta cooking water for finishing the dish. It lets you elongate the sauce and better coat the pasta without having to add more cream.

2 Tbsp extra-virgin olive oil, plus more as needed

8 oz [230 g] spicy Italian sausage, casings removed

2 large yellow onions, very thinly sliced

Kosher salt

1 lb [455 g] orecchiette or a short pasta such as penne or garganelli

8 oz [230 g] baby spinach

¼ cup [60 ml] heavy cream or ¼ cup [60 ml] milk plus 2 Tbsp half-and-half

Grated zest of 1 large lemon

1 cup [90 g] finely grated Parmesan cheese

In a large skillet over medium-high heat, warm the olive oil and crumble in the sausage. Cook, stirring now and then, until the sausage is really well browned, all of its fat is rendered, and little bits of meat are sticking to the bottom of the pan, about 10 minutes. Use a slotted spoon to transfer the sausage to a plate and set aside.

Add the onions to the pan, sprinkle with a large pinch of salt, and turn the heat to medium-low. Depending on how much fat the sausage released, your pan might be almost dry; if so, add 1 to 2 Tbsp olive oil. Cook the onions, stirring them every so often, until they've completely collapsed, are dark brown, and have picked up all the stuck bits of sausage, about 30 minutes. Transfer the onions to the plate with the sausage.

Meanwhile, bring a large pot of generously salted water to a boil. Add the orecchiette, bring the water back to a boil, and cook for 2 minutes less than the package tells you to (or until the orecchiette is cooked through but maintains a little bite). Use a mug to collect about 1 cup [240 ml] of the cooking water and set it aside.

Drain the orecchiette in a colander, give it a good shake, and then return it to the now-empty pot over low heat. Add the reserved sausage and onions and stir everything to combine. Add the spinach in handfuls, tossing to wilt each handful before you add the next. Then add the cream, lemon zest, and half of the Parmesan. If the orecchiette seems a bit dry, add some of the reserved cooking water (I will leave the amount to your discretion—it depends on how much water ended up in the pot when you transferred the orecchiette from the colander). Season to taste with salt.

Transfer the orecchiette to a serving bowl or to individual bowls and top with the rest of the Parmesan. Serve immediately.

SPIN-OFFS

FOR PENNE VODKA, heat a slick of olive oil with some minced garlic in a skillet and add a can of whole peeled tomatoes that you've crushed with your hands (the tomatoes, not the can). Add a splash of vodka and simmer for 20 minutes, then add a splash of cream. Finish cooking the penne in the sauce and serve with grated Parmesan.

FOR PENNE ARRABBIATA, do the garlic, oil, and tomato thing, but also add a generous pinch of red pepper flakes or a few crushed dried red chile peppers.

FOR SPAGHETTI PUTTANESCA, heat a slick of olive oil with some minced garlic and anchovies in a skillet and add a can of whole peeled tomatoes that you've crushed with your hands. After it all simmers for 20 minutes, stir in some capers and crushed olives and then finish cooking your spaghetti in the sauce. Serve topped with lots of chopped parsley.

FOR FETTUCCINE AMATRICI-ANA, sauté some diced guanciale or pancetta (or prosciutto or even bacon), sliced onions, and a pinch of red pepper flakes in a skillet until the pork is crisp and the onions are tender. Add a can of whole peeled tomatoes that you've crushed with your hands and simmer for 20 minutes. Finish cooking your fettuccine in the sauce. Serve topped with lots of grated Parmesan.

A Nice Lasagna

SERVES 6 TO 8

The definition of a make-ahead dish, this lasagna is my absolute favorite thing to serve to a big group of friends. It is also one of my best friend Ivan's favorite foods, and I like to gift it to him on his birthday (I assemble it in a disposable aluminum pan, wrap it up, and include instructions for baking it on the card). There are three **small victories** here. The **first** is using a food processor to make the pasta dough, which takes a lot of the fear out of homemade pasta (there's no precarious mound of flour to navigate or work surface to scrub). The **second** victory is skipping both the American tradition of using ricotta (which can get watery and even tough when baked) and the Italian tradition of adding béchamel (who wants to dirty another pot and worry about lumps?) and go straight for crème fraîche. It gives you the requisite creaminess that all great lasagnas need to have, but without any effort. I mix it right into the tomato sauce rather than layering it on separately, because the whole point is for them to combine anyway. The **third** small victory is a high sauce-to-pasta ratio, the ticket to baking lasagna without boiling the noodles first. This way, the pasta absorbs the sauce and gets full of flavor and you get to skip a whole lot of labor. You can skip making homemade pasta (but try it sometime—it's fun!) and use store-bought pasta sheets or a box of no-cook lasagna noodles.

SAUCE

Two 28-oz [794-g] cans whole peeled tomatoes

3 Tbsp extra-virgin olive oil

4 garlic cloves, thinly sliced

Kosher salt

1 cup [230 g] crème fraîche

PASTA DOUGH

2¼ cups [270 g] all-purpose flour, plus more as needed

3 eggs

1 tsp kosher salt

1 cup [100 g] finely grated Parmesan cheese

1 cup [100 g] coarsely grated whole-milk mozzarella cheese

2 large handfuls fresh basil leaves, torn into small pieces if large

TO MAKE THE SAUCE: In a large bowl, crush the tomatoes with your hands (this is a messy but fun job—it's a very good one for children) until they are in bite-size pieces.

In a large saucepan over medium-high heat, warm the olive oil, add the garlic, and cook, stirring, until it begins to sizzle, about 1 minute. Add the tomatoes and 1 tsp salt and bring to a boil. Lower the heat and let the sauce simmer, stirring every so often, until it is slightly reduced, about 30 minutes.

Whisk the crème fraîche into the sauce and season to taste with salt. Set the sauce aside to cool to room temperature while you conquer the pasta.

(Continued)

TO MAKE THE PASTA DOUGH: In the bowl of a food processor, combine the flour, eggs and salt and run the machine until a firm ball of dough forms around the blade, cleans the side of the processor bowl, and doesn't stick to your fingers when you touch it. If the dough is too dry, add a little water, 1 tsp at a time, until the dough comes together. If, on the other hand, it's sticky when you touch it, add a little flour, 1 tsp at a time, until the dough comes together. (The exact amount of moisture in the dough depends on how you measured your flour, how large your eggs are, even the humidity in the air.) Once your dough is good to go, dust it lightly with flour and wrap it tightly in plastic wrap. Let it rest at room temperature for 1 hour.

Line a baking sheet with parchment paper and have more parchment paper at hand.

Cut the rested dough into six pieces. Working with one piece at a time (keep the rest covered with plastic), lightly dust the dough with flour and press it down with the heel of your hand. Run the dough through your pasta machine, starting on the widest setting and working your way through the narrower settings, rolling it through each setting twice, until it is very thin but not too thin. I usually stop at 6, but your machine might be different from mine, so I'll just say that the final pasta should be the thickness of an envelope—which is to say thin, but not at all transparent. You don't want it to disappear into the finished lasagna. If the dough sticks during the rolling, simply dust it with a little flour. Lay the rolled-out pasta on the prepared baking sheet. Repeat the process with the rest of the dough, keeping the rolled pieces separated with parchment paper.

Preheat your oven to 400°F [200°C].

Ladle a thin layer of room-temperature sauce onto the bottom of a 9-by-13-in [23-by-33-cm] baking dish. Spread the sauce with a spoon to cover the surface of the dish. Add a layer of pasta (brush off any excess flour), cutting the pasta and arranging it as needed to form an even single layer. Spoon over just enough tomato sauce to cover the pasta and then scatter over some of the Parmesan, mozzarella, and basil. Repeat the layering process until you've used up all of your components, ending with sauce and cheese (not naked pasta or basil, both of which would burn if exposed).

Bake the lasagna, uncovered, until it's gorgeously browned and the edges are bubbling, 35 to 40 minutes. Let it rest at room temperature for 15 minutes, just like you would a steak, before slicing and serving. This lets the pasta fully absorb all of the bubbling sauce, so you don't end up with soupy slices.

SPIN-OFFS

FOR A MEAT LASAGNA, brown 8 oz [230 g] each ground beef and sweet Italian sausage meat in the oil with the garlic and then add the tomatoes. Continue as directed. This simple meat sauce is also great on its own on pasta, especially rigatoni. Serve dotted with ricotta and with plenty of grated Parmesan. Yum.

FOR A MORE SUBSTANTIAL VEGETARIAN LASAGNA, add cooked spinach, broccoli rabe, mushrooms, or cubes of butternut squash (or a combination of vegetables) to each layer.

CUT THE HOMEMADE PASTA INTO ROUGH SQUARES, boil it, and toss it with browned butter and minced sage. Serve with lots of grated Parmesan. Simple and good.

USE THE HOMEMADE PASTA FOR RAVIOLI by filling with a mixture of mashed peas and ricotta scented with minced fresh mint and black pepper. Serve with butter and cream and Parmesan (if you've gone to the trouble of making fresh pasta, it's not the time to be concerned about calories).

MEAT + POULTRY

Country Ham with Henley Mustard Sauce

SERVES 6 TO 8; MAKES 1½ CUPS [360 ML] SAUCE

This mustard sauce, ham's best friend, hails from my mother-in-law's family and is as essential to my wife's family's Christmas spread as matzo balls are to my family's Passover Seder. The sauce is a **small victory** not only for its familial significance but also because it demonstrates how to perfectly balance sweet with sour—the key to so many successful things in the kitchen (think great salad dressing or cocktails). I was introduced to the sauce alongside a pile of thinly sliced country ham and plenty of warm biscuits (store-bought are fine), which I love, but it also makes for a great glaze for grilled pork chops or chicken (check out the Spin-Offs for even more ideas). Store any leftover sauce (unlikely) in an airtight container in the refrigerator for up to a week (warm over low heat before serving).

1 cup [200 g] sugar

1 egg

1 Tbsp yellow mustard powder

¼ cup [60 ml] white wine vinegar

8 oz [230 g] country ham, thinly sliced

12 warm Everything Biscuits (page 53), made without the seeds

In a small saucepan over medium heat, combine the sugar, egg, mustard powder, and vinegar and whisk together. Bring to a boil, whisking constantly, and boil until thick and glossy, about 3 minutes. Transfer the sauce to a serving bowl and serve warm alongside the ham and biscuits.

NOTE: If you find yourself with a not-totally-smooth sauce (i.e., with bits of cooked egg), simply strain it through a fine-mesh sieve before serving.

SPIN-OFFS

SUBSTITUTE ENGLISH MUSTARD POWDER to make the sauce even sharper. Or add hot sauce and/or cayenne pepper to make it extra spicy.

DRIZZLE THE SAUCE ON BACON toward the very end of frying to glaze it. Alternatively, place strips of bacon on a rack set over a baking sheet, brush with the sauce, and bake at 400°F [200°C] until crisp.

TO TURN THE SAUCE INTO MUSTARD BBQ SAUCE (à la South Carolina), substitute light brown sugar for the regular sugar and add 1 Tbsp Worcestershire sauce to the mixture. Serve with pulled pork, on grilled pork tenderloin, or even on broiled salmon. Oh, and ribs! Put it on ribs!

Roast Pork Loin with Herbs + Cream Cheese

SERVES 8

There's something so pleasingly old-school about flattening something, stuffing it, rolling it, and tying it. While this might all seem intimidating, I'm a true believer that if you can tie your shoe, you can tie a roast. Try this for your next special-occasion dinner—say, when your in-laws come over or it's a good friend's birthday . . . or even, "Yay, it's Friday!" The **small victories** here—how to butterfly the pork loin (you can ask your butcher to do it, but it is easy to do yourself) and how to tie it up—are good tricks to have up your sleeve for any stuffed and tied dish you might want to try (chicken Cordon Bleu, anyone?). You could also make this with two butterflied pork tenderloins instead of a whole pork loin (be sure to cut the roasting time in half).

2 garlic cloves

1 cup [40 g] fresh Italian parsley leaves

¼ cup [10 g] fresh basil leaves

1 Tbsp fresh thyme leaves

3 oz [85 g] cream cheese, at room temperature

Kosher salt

Freshly ground black pepper

One 3-to 4-lb [1.4-to 1.8-kg] pork loin

2 Tbsp extra-virgin olive oil

¼ cup [60 ml] white wine, chicken stock, or water

Preheat your oven to 400°F [200°C].

With the food processor running, drop the garlic into the feed tube and process until finely chopped. Add the parsley, basil, and thyme and pulse until everything is finely chopped. Add the cream cheese, 1 tsp salt, and a few grinds of pepper and pulse until everything is well combined. Set the mixture aside.

Put the pork loin, fat-side down, on your work surface with one of the short ends pointing toward you. Using a sharp chef's knife, hold it parallel to the board and make a sharp incision along the length of the pork, cutting into the meat about ½ in [12 mm]. Continue to slice into the meat while lifting the top part with your other hand until the pork loin is opened out and totally flat and about 1 in [2.5 cm] thick.

Season the newly exposed side of the pork aggressively with salt. Spread the cream cheese mixture over the pork, using your hands or a rubber spatula. Starting from a short side, roll the pork up tightly so that it resembles its old self, this time with the herb mixture spiraled throughout it. Lay five 12-in [30.5-cm] pieces of kitchen string about 1 in [2.5 cm] apart on your work surface and carefully lift the pork and put it on top of the string, seam-side down. Tie the pieces of string tightly around the pork loin so that it is even and compact. Trim off the excess string.

Transfer the pork, fat-side up, to a large baking dish and drizzle the olive oil over it. Sprinkle the pork with a generous pinch of salt and a few grinds of pepper. Pour the wine around the pork.

(Continued)

Roast the pork until it is browned, is firm to the touch, and registers 145°F [63°C] when you test it in the thickest part with an instant-read thermometer, 1 to 1½ hours depending on the thickness of meat (start testing it at 1 hour). Transfer the pork to a cutting board and cover it loosely with aluminum foil.

Let the pork rest for 10 minutes, then cut off and discard the string. Slice the pork, arrange on a serving platter, and spoon over some of the pan juices. Serve immediately.

NOTE: If you're using a pork tenderloin instead of a whole pork loin, since it's smaller, you can flatten it more easily. Simply slice the pork lengthwise in half, without cutting through the entire loin, so that you can open it up like a book. Cover the pork with plastic wrap and use a meat mallet or a small heavy pot to pound the meat until it's an even 1 in [2.5 cm] thick. This is a good way of flattening other types of protein too, especially chicken breasts and beef tenderloins.

SPIN-OFFS

LEFTOVER PORK can be sliced and crisped in a hot skillet slicked with a little olive oil. This makes for an excellent and hearty breakfast alongside runny fried eggs (see page 31). The crisped pork also makes for a great filling for a sandwich on a soft roll piled with arugula that's been dressed with a lot of bright, fresh lemon juice.

FOR PORK THAT'S SALTIMBOCCA-ISH, season the flattened pork with salt and pepper and then lay over an even layer of sage leaves and thinly sliced prosciutto. Roll it up, lay some more sliced prosciutto on top, and then tie it and roast it.

Ribs with Gochujang, Fish Sauce + Honey

SERVES 4 HUNGRY ADULTS, 6 IF YOU'VE GOT A LOT OF SIDE DISHES

One **small victory** here is all about cooking ribs ahead of time by parking them in a low oven to get tender, and then finishing them on the grill or under the broiler with a sticky, super-flavorful glaze. Post-oven and pre-grill, the ribs can wait for you in the refrigerator for up to a week, which makes for make-ahead magic. Hello, dinner party! The sauce could easily be a bottle of barbecue sauce, but here I use a most addictive mixture of not-too-spicy Korean pepper paste (*gochujang*), salty soy sauce, punchy fish sauce, and sweet honey. This mixture, a **small victory** of its own, is great on all sorts of things, including roast chicken, grilled pork tenderloin, and broiled tofu (and maybe even a shoe).

3 lb [1.4 kg] pork
baby back ribs

Kosher salt

Freshly ground black pepper

One 12-oz [355-ml] bottle beer
(any type) or 1½ cups [360 ml]
chicken stock or water

2 garlic cloves, minced

¼ cup [60 ml] gochujang
(Korean red pepper paste)
or Sriracha

¼ cup [85 g] honey

2 Tbsp fish sauce

2 Tbsp soy sauce

Preheat your oven to 300°F [150°C].

Sprinkle the ribs all over with 2 tsp salt and ½ tsp pepper and place them in a large roasting pan or pot that holds them comfortably in a single layer. Pour the beer around the ribs and cover the whole thing with a lid or very tightly with aluminum foil.

Roast the ribs until they're incredibly tender (test with a paring knife), about 2 hours. (At this point, the ribs can be cooled to room temperature in their liquid, covered, and refrigerated for up to 1 week.)

Set your oven rack so that it's 6 in [15 cm] from the broiler and preheat your broiler to high. Or prepare a grill for high heat (or heat a large grill pan set over a couple of burners) and make sure your grates are super-clean.

Use tongs to transfer the ribs to a foil-lined baking sheet. If you cooked the ribs in a roasting pan, pour the cooking liquid into a saucepan and set it over high heat. If the liquid is already in a pot, just set it over high heat. Whisk the garlic, gochujang, honey, fish sauce, and soy sauce into the cooking liquid and bring to a boil. Let the mixture boil vigorously until it's slightly thickened and syrupy, about 5 minutes. Season to taste with salt and pepper.

Brush the racks of ribs on both sides with some of the gochujang mixture. Broil or grill the racks, turning once, until the glaze is caramelized on both sides, about 2 minutes per side. Repeat the process one more time so that the ribs get a double layer of glaze. Transfer the racks to a cutting board and cut them into individual ribs.

(Continued)

Transfer the ribs to a serving platter and drizzle with the remaining sauce. Serve immediately, with lots and lots of napkins.

SPIN-OFFS

OTHER GREAT SAUCES FOR THE RIBS include Henley Mustard Sauce (see page 151) or half mustard and half honey or maple syrup. Or try ketchup mixed with gochujang, Sriracha, or harissa. Or try hoisin sauce thinned with rice wine vinegar and soy sauce.

You can **BRAISE ALL SORTS OF RICH MEATS** before finishing them on the grill or under the broiler. This goes for short ribs, brisket, and pork belly, and even chicken thighs.

FOR DRY-RUBBED RIBS, rub the racks with a mixture of equal parts salt, ground black pepper, brown sugar, garlic powder, and paprika. Let rest, covered, in the refrigerator for 24 hours. Cook in a covered baking dish, with 1 cup [240 ml] water, for 2 hours, until tender. (Reserve the liquid for cooking beans.) Brush the ribs with barbecue sauce (see page 266 or store-bought) and broil or grill the ribs so the sauce forms a nice glaze.

All-Day Pork Shoulder with Apple Cider

SERVES 8 TO 10

I've always wanted a slow cooker, but we lack the counter space to justify purchasing one. Sometimes I just tuck a piece of meat inside a pot, park it in a low oven all day, and pretend I have one. Pork shoulder, with all of its glorious fat, works especially well; and if you put it in the oven late in the morning, you can pull it out right in time for dinner. I especially love this because it makes me feel like I'm accomplishing something all day long. The **small victory** here is letting time take care of a tough cut of meat and letting all its toughness slowly transform into succulence. Sometimes the best thing to do is set it and forget it. And then, of course, remember it.

2 tsp kosher salt

¼ cup [60 ml] maple syrup, dark brown sugar, or honey

¼ cup [60 ml] Dijon mustard

One 4½-lb [2-kg] boneless, skinless pork shoulder (or pork butt or Boston butt—they're all the same thing), at room temperature, patted dry with paper towels

2 cups [480 ml] apple cider

Preheat your oven to 475°F [240°C].

In a small bowl, whisk together the salt, maple syrup, and mustard. Rub the pork all over with the mixture and put it fat-side up in a large roasting dish or cast-iron skillet that holds it comfortably. Pour the apple cider around, not over, the pork.

Roast the pork for 15 minutes, just long enough to let the maple syrup start forming a crust on top, then turn the temperature to 250°F [120°C]. Let the pork roast, turning it once every 2 hours, until the exterior is beautifully browned and the meat is incredibly tender, 7 hours (6 hours are okay, as are 8, this isn't too exact).

Transfer the pork to a cutting board and use a knife and/or tongs to shred the meat. Return the meat to the roasting dish to really saturate the pork with all of its juice. Serve it warm. Or, if you're making the pork ahead of time, shred it and let it cool to room temperature in its cooking liquid, then cover and refrigerate for up to 1 week. Warm in a 300°F [150°C] oven or over low heat on the stove top.

SPIN-OFFS

FOR FILIPINO-STYLE PORK ADOBO, substitute ¼ cup [60 ml] each soy sauce and white vinegar for the maple syrup and mustard. Substitute 2 cups [480 ml] chicken stock or water for the apple cider along with four crushed garlic cloves and two bay leaves.

FOR MEXICAN-STYLE BRAISED PORK, leave out the maple syrup and mustard. Use one 12-oz [355-ml] bottle beer instead of the apple cider. Add 2 tsp dried oregano, two chipotle chiles packed in adobo (chop them up or just mash them with a fork), and the grated zest and juice of one orange.

Grilled Skirt Steak with Pickled Jalapeño Relish

SERVES 4

The **small victory** here applies to every single cut of steak or other meat you prepare: Figure out which way the grain runs before you cook it. It's much more obvious when the meat is raw. Identifying the grain will make it easy to slice across it when the steak is cooked, which is the quickest route to ensuring that your steak is tender, not chewy and stringy. Any steak can work in this recipe (use whatever you like to eat), but a quick note about the grain in skirt steak—it goes the short way across the meat, not the long way. I know it looks like you should just be able to cut the cooked steak into slices without thinking too much, but it really is best to cut it into sections and then slice across the grain of the sections. This jalapeño relish is a great condiment, equally good tucked inside quesadillas or spooned over tacos. Oh, it's also delicious on cheeseburgers and hot dogs! You can find jarred or canned pickled jalapeños in just about every grocery store, usually next to the boxes of "crispy taco shells" in the Mexican food aisle. Check out page 93 for more ideas on what to do with the leftover brine.

½ cup [80 g] drained pickled jalapeño chiles, finely chopped

½ cup [20 g] finely chopped fresh cilantro

Grated zest and juice of 2 limes

½ cup [120 ml] extra-virgin olive oil

Kosher salt

2 lb [910 g] skirt steak, membrane and/or silver skin trimmed, at room temperature, patted dry with paper towels

Freshly ground black pepper

In a small bowl, combine the jalapeños, cilantro, lime zest, lime juice, and ¼ cup plus 2 Tbsp [90 ml] of the olive oil and stir to mix. Season the relish to taste with salt and set aside.

Prepare a grill for high heat (or heat a large grill pan set over two burners). Make sure your grates are very clean.

Rub the skirt steak with the remaining 2 Tbsp olive oil and sprinkle both sides with a generous pinch of salt. Place the steak on the grill and cook until well browned on the first side, 3 to 4 minutes. Turn the steak and cook until browned on the second side and just firm to the touch, another 3 to 4 minutes. (The exact

(Continued)

cooking time may vary, depending on the thickness of the steak.) Transfer the steak to a cutting board and let it rest for about 10 minutes.

Slice the steak across the grain and transfer to a serving platter. Sprinkle the steak with a little salt and plenty of black pepper. Serve the relish on top of or alongside the meat.

SPIN-OFFS

TRY FLANK STEAK WITH TERI-YAKI SAUCE, a.k.a. what my family ate just about every weekend when I was growing up. We were partial to Soy Vay sauce (which I do still love), but to make your own very easy teriyaki sauce, just mix equal parts soy sauce and honey. That's it! I like to marinate the steak in some of the sauce and save some for spooning over after you grill and slice the meat. Serve sprinkled with toasted sesame seeds and thinly sliced scallions.

FOR CALIFORNIA-STYLE GRILLED TRI-TIP STEAK (a popular cut in that sunny state), rub the meat with a mixture of equal parts kosher salt, black pepper, brown sugar, and garlic powder with a pinch of cayenne. This mixture is good on just about any cut of steak or on chicken.

FOR VIETNAMESE-STYLE STEAK, marinate the steak in equal parts fish sauce, granulated sugar, and water. Pat dry before grilling. Serve thinly sliced with lime wedges, cilantro, and pickled daikon.

Brisket with Apricots + Prunes

SERVES 8

The **small victory** here is all about the dampened, scrunched parchment that covers the brisket during its long braise. The parchment acts like a protective blanket (in this case, a wet blanket is a good thing!) and keeps the meat from drying out. My friend Susie Theodorou, an amazing food stylist, taught me this trick. A food stylist's perspective is so interesting because it's all about what makes food *look* the best, not always what makes it taste the best. (Susie, for the record, is one of those exceptional types who always gets both right.) This brisket is my favorite thing to serve not only for Passover but also on any cold winter night—especially for a dinner party, since it feeds a crowd and is even better if you make it the day before. The simplest way to turn it into a complete meal would be to serve it with plenty of crusty bread or with egg noodles tossed with melted butter and chopped parsley, or mashed potatoes, or polenta (anything to help soak up the great sauce). I also like a bright salad served alongside to cut the richness—an arugula salad with olive oil and lemon and lots of thinly sliced celery for crunch is perfect. If your brisket is too large to fit comfortably in your cooking vessel, just cut the meat into two pieces.

One 3½- to 4½-lb [1.6- to 2-kg] brisket (see Note), at room temperature, patted dry with paper towels

Kosher salt

3 Tbsp extra-virgin olive oil

1 large yellow onion, thinly sliced

1 tsp hot pimentón (Spanish smoked paprika) or paprika

¼ tsp ground cinnamon

6 leafy fresh thyme sprigs

4 garlic cloves, crushed

2 Tbsp tomato paste

One 15-oz [425-g] can whole peeled tomatoes

1½ cups [360 ml] beef or chicken stock

12 pitted prunes

12 dried apricots

Preheat your oven to 300°F [150°C].

Season the brisket aggressively on both sides with salt.

In a large deep ovenproof Dutch oven over medium-high heat, warm the olive oil. Add the brisket and cook, turning once, until well browned on all sides, about 5 minutes per side. Transfer the brisket to a large plate and set aside.

Turn the heat to medium and add the onion to the pot and cook, stirring now and then and scraping up whatever browned bits are left in the pan, until softened, about 10 minutes.

Add the pimentón, cinnamon, thyme, garlic, tomato paste, and a big pinch of salt to the onion and cook, stirring, until the whole mixture is brick-red from the tomato paste, about 1 minute. Add the peeled tomatoes and their juice. Pour the beef stock into the tomato can (this way you get all the bits left inside the can), swish it around, and pour it into the pot. Turn the heat to high and bring the mixture to a boil. Turn off the heat, stir in the prunes and apricots, and nestle the brisket on top of the aromatic mixture; pour whatever juice has accumulated on the brisket plate on top.

Scrunch up a large piece of parchment paper with your hands and wet it under cold running water. Spread the wet parchment paper over the surface of the brisket and cover the pot tightly with a lid. Put the brisket in the oven until it's incredibly tender (uncover it and check with a paring knife or fork), about 4 hours.

If you're going to serve the brisket immediately, slice it across the grain and serve with all of its aromatic sauce. If you're making it ahead of time, allow the brisket to cool in the sauce, cover, and refrigerate for up to 1 week. Then slice the brisket across the grain and reheat it in the sauce either over low heat on the stove top or in a 300°F [150°C] oven until warm. You could slice it ahead of time, but I find it dries out more quickly. I don't remove the thyme stems before serving because (a) I often forget that they're there and (b) it's nice for things to be a little rustic, but feel free to find them and discard them.

NOTE: Brisket is often sold as "first cut," a leaner cut, and "second cut," which has more fat. First cut is often easier to find; I like the extra fat of the second cut. Both work—choose whichever you prefer.

SPIN-OFFS

FOR PORK SHOULDER RAGÙ, substitute boneless pork shoulder for the brisket, leave out the cinnamon and dried fruit, and use red wine instead of beef stock. Shred the cooked pork and serve it on a wide pasta like pappardelle or on creamy polenta. Either way, top with chopped parsley and plenty of grated pecorino or Parmesan.

FOR A COZY DINNER FOR A GROUP, substitute a dozen chicken thighs for the brisket. Leave out the tomatoes and substitute apple cider for the stock. Use dried cherries in place of both the prunes and apricots. Really delicious. Oh, and these will need only 1 hour in the oven.

FOR BRISKET TACOS—warm corn tortillas (see page 276) and pile with brisket and a crunchy slaw made of shredded cabbage, salt, lime juice, minced jalapeño, and chopped cilantro.

Homemade Merguez with Herby Yogurt

SERVES 4 TO 6

I like to make my own sausage so that I know exactly what's going into it. But I'm not about to deal with casings and all that. The realization that sausage is essentially highly seasoned ground meat formed into a patty is a **small victory** for any ambitious but not-too-ambitious DIYer. You'll see in the Spin-Offs that this recipe is really just a concept—there are infinite variations you can make with all different types of ground meat, spices, and even toppings. If you want to use all ground spices for this (i.e., if you have ground cumin in your cupboard and not cumin seeds and you're like, *Do I have to really buy a jar of cumin seeds for a measly 1 tsp???* the answer is NO!), just toast the ground spices in 1 Tbsp olive oil and then mix them into the lamb mixture; no grinding necessary.

½ cup [120 ml] plain yogurt

A small handful of finely chopped leafy fresh herbs, such as parsley, cilantro, mint, chives, basil, and/or dill (any single one is good, and a mix is even better), plus a few roughly chopped for serving

1 tsp red wine vinegar

Kosher salt

½ tsp cumin seeds

½ tsp coriander seeds

½ tsp fennel seeds

1 tsp sweet paprika

2 garlic cloves, minced

2 Tbsp harissa paste (or any hot sauce)

1 lb [455 g] ground lamb, at room temperature

3 Tbsp olive oil

A handful of shredded red cabbage and/or thinly sliced radishes and lemon wedges for serving

In a small bowl, combine the yogurt and finely chopped herbs and whisk in the vinegar. Season to taste with salt. Cover the sauce with plastic wrap and refrigerate while you prepare the merguez.

In a skillet over medium heat, combine the cumin seeds, coriander seeds, and fennel seeds and toast the seeds, swirling the skillet now and then to keep them from burning, until they're lightly browned and fragrant, about 3 minutes. Transfer the seeds to a coffee grinder and blitz them for a few seconds, until they're coarsely ground. (Alternatively, you can use a mortar and pestle. Or cool the spices, then transfer

them to a resealable plastic bag and crush them with a rolling pin or the bottom of a heavy saucepan.) Transfer the spices to a large bowl and stir them together with the paprika, garlic, harissa, and 1½ tsp salt.

Add the lamb to the bowl and use your hands to gently combine everything. Gently form the mixture into twelve evenly sized patties. (At this point, you can cover the merguez with plastic wrap and refrigerate for up to 3 days. Be sure to bring the patties to room temperature before proceeding.)

(Continued)

In a large skillet, preferably cast-iron, over medium-high heat, warm the olive oil. (Or, if you have a grill and it's a nice day, grill these!) Add the merguez patties, in batches as necessary to keep from crowding the skillet, and cook, without disturbing them, until the undersides are quite beautifully browned, 3 to 4 minutes. Carefully turn the patties and cook until the second sides are browned and the patties are firm to the touch, another 3 to 4 minutes. Transfer the merguez to a serving platter and cook the remaining patties.

Drizzle the merguez with the reserved yogurt mixture and scatter with the roughly chopped herbs and the cabbage. Serve immediately with lemon wedges for squeezing over.

SPIN-OFFS

To make the best **CHICKEN-APPLE-MAPLE BREAKFAST SAUSAGE PATTIES**, mix 1 lb [455 g] ground chicken (preferably dark meat) with a peeled and coarsely grated green apple, 2 Tbsp maple syrup, 2 Tbsp minced fresh sage, and lots of salt and pepper. Shape and pan-fry or grill. These are great alongside scrambled eggs.

To make **SPICY PORK SAUSAGE PATTIES**, combine 1 lb [455 g] ground pork with two minced garlic cloves, 2 Tbsp minced fresh parsley, 1 tsp red pepper flakes, 1 tsp fennel seeds, and 2 tsp kosher salt. Shape and pan-fry or grill. These are great on a breakfast sandwich with roasted red peppers (see page 61 or use store-bought), fried eggs, and mayonnaise.

I had the pleasure and privilege of enjoying hot dogs at the late, great Hot Doug's in Chicago before it closed. One of the hot dogs that particularly stands out in my memory is the **GREEN CURRY SAUSAGE**. To make similarly flavored sausage patties, combine 1 lb [455 g] ground pork with 3 Tbsp Thai green curry paste and 1 tsp kosher salt. Shape and pan-fry or grill. Serve drizzled with peanut butter that you've thinned with coconut milk until it's drizzle-able (season with salt and/or soy sauce) and scatter with toasted peanuts, toasted unsweetened coconut flakes, and plenty of chopped fresh cilantro. Very delicious and particularly great with a simple salad of thinly sliced cucumbers seasoned with salt and sugar and dressed with white wine vinegar.

To make **MERGUEZ BURGERS**, form the mixture into four patties instead of twelve. Serve in pita breads or on buns with the yogurt sauce, shredded cabbage, and additional herbs.

To make **INCREDIBLE ROAST CHICKEN**, use the spice, garlic, and harissa combination from the main recipe and rub it over the outside and under the skin of a chicken. Let the rubbed chicken sit at room temperature for 1 hour before roasting at 425°F [220°C] until it registers 170°F [70°C] on an instant-read thermometer, about 1 hour and 15 minutes (start checking it at 1 hour to be safe).

Turkey + Ricotta Meatballs

The first thing I ever cooked for my wife, Grace, were these meatballs. I made the mixture at my apartment, then packed it up with a box of pasta, ingredients for sauce, and a pot (she told me she had only a skillet) and took it all to her apartment . . . which soon became my apartment, too. A **small victory** here is not only about getting someone to marry you (!), but also about making meatballs that are incredibly light and tender by incorporating a generous amount of ricotta cheese in the mixture. In fact, I've found that by adding ricotta, you can skip the usual bread crumbs and eggs (which also makes this recipe gluten-free, if that's important to you)—I love any addition that allows you to let go of a few things. Another **small victory** is baking the meatballs instead of frying them. It's much less messy and so easy—win-win. Please note that while most of the recipes in this book serve four, I've made this one a bit larger because whenever I make meatballs, I like to make a ton so that I can freeze some. That way, I can have meatballs on the spur of the moment. I thought you might like that too, but feel free to cut the recipe in half if you prefer. Serve the meatballs with pasta, polenta, rice, garlic bread, or just on their own! Whichever way you choose, be sure to sprinkle them with plenty of grated Parmesan cheese.

Two 28-oz [794-g] cans whole peeled tomatoes

7 Tbsp extra-virgin olive oil

7 garlic cloves; 4 thinly sliced, 3 minced

Kosher salt

1 cup [40 g] fresh basil leaves, finely chopped

1 cup [40 g] fresh Italian parsley leaves, finely chopped

1½ cups [300 g] fresh whole-milk ricotta cheese

½ cup [50 g] finely grated Parmesan cheese

2 lb [900 g] ground turkey (preferably dark meat), at room temperature

Pour the contents of the tomato cans into a large bowl (set the cans aside) and crush the tomatoes with your hands (this is a messy but fun job, and a very good one for children). Rinse one of the cans with about ¼ cup [60 ml] water, pour it into the second can and swish it around to get all the excess tomato out of the cans, and then pour the water into the tomato bowl.

In a large saucepan or pot over medium-high heat, warm 3 Tbsp of the olive oil, add the sliced garlic, and cook, stirring, until it begins to sizzle, about 1 minute. Add the tomatoes and a very large pinch of salt and bring to a boil. Lower the heat and let the sauce simmer, stirring every so often, until it is slightly reduced and has lost any tin-can taste, about 30 minutes.

(Continued)

Meanwhile, preheat your oven to 425°F [220°C]. Line a baking sheet with aluminum foil. Drizzle 2 Tbsp olive oil on the baking sheet and use your hands to rub it over the entire surface of the sheet. Set aside.

In a large bowl, combine the minced garlic, basil, parsley, ricotta, Parmesan, turkey, and 1 Tbsp salt. Blend everything together gently but authoritatively with your hands (they're the best tool for the job) until well mixed. Then, use your hands to form the mixture into golf ball–sized meatballs; the mixture will be sticky, so wet your hands with a bit of water to help prevent the meat from sticking to them. Transfer the meatballs to the prepared baking sheet as you form them (it's okay if they are touching a little). Drizzle the meatballs with the remaining 2 Tbsp olive oil and roast until they're browned and firm to the touch, about 25 minutes.

Use tongs or a slotted spoon to transfer the meatballs to the simmering sauce (discard whatever juice and fat is left on the baking sheet). Cook the meatballs for 10 minutes in the sauce (they can be left in the gently simmering sauce for up to 1 hour) and serve.

SPIN-OFFS

FOR SAUSAGE AND RICOTTA MEATBALLS, instead of ground turkey, use 2 lb [910 g] of your favorite sausage meat. Just take it out of its casings and proceed as directed. I like using half sweet and half spicy Italian sausage.

FOR A SLIGHTLY MOROCCAN RIFF, use ground lamb instead of turkey and finely crumbled feta instead of Parmesan. Leave out the ricotta. Add a handful each of toasted pine nuts and raisins to the mixture, and use mint instead of basil. Add a cinnamon stick to the tomato sauce (remove it before serving the meatballs).

Dad's Chicken + Leeks

SERVES 4

This easy braised chicken, thick with sweet leeks in a fragrant broth, is my father's signature dish and I could not love it more. It's a perfect one-pot meal—you need nothing more than a good loaf of bread to sop up all of the broth from the pot. Sometimes my dad adds small creamer potatoes and roughly chopped carrots to really bulk it up, but I sort of love the minimalist simplicity of all leeks. Braising is the **small victory** here. Browning chicken (or any type of meat or poultry) and then simmering it gives you the best of both worlds—a browned crust full of flavor and tender meat, too. Braising works with all sorts of combinations of meat and vegetables. Chicken with mushrooms (finish with a bit of cream and mustard) is great, as are cubes of pork with red onions and red cabbage. Lamb with butternut squash. Big pieces of halibut with leeks and saffron. Anything! I've included a few great braised chicken dishes in the Spin-Offs, but the only real limit to braising is your imagination. I must also mention that a glug of heavy cream or crème fraîche stirred in at the end of this, or anything for that matter, would not be bad at all.

One 3½-lb [1.6-kg] chicken, cut into 10 pieces (2 wings, 2 legs, 2 thighs, and 2 breasts cut in half across the bone), backbone discarded (or saved for another use, like stock), at room temperature, patted dry with paper towels

Kosher salt

Freshly ground black pepper

3 Tbsp extra-virgin olive oil

4 large leeks, root ends and dark green tops trimmed off and discarded (or reserved for another use, like stock)

1½ cups [360 ml] chicken stock

A small handful of finely chopped fresh chives

Season the chicken pieces generously on both sides with salt and pepper. In a large heavy pot over medium-high heat, warm the olive oil. Add the chicken, skin-side down, in batches as necessary so that the pieces don't crowd the pot, and cook, without moving the chicken, until it is well browned on the bottom, about 8 minutes. Once the chicken is nicely browned and you are able to move it without any resistance (the gorgeous brown crust will release the chicken from the cooking surface), turn it over and cook until it's browned on the second side, another 8 minutes. Be patient, and don't push and poke the pieces too much (I find it's good to clean the leeks, make a phone call, or do

something similarly distracting while browning the chicken . . . my dad always plays Solitaire!). Transfer the chicken to a plate and set aside. Don't wash the pot.

Meanwhile, cut each leek in half lengthwise and then across into 1-in- [2.5-cm-] thick semicircles. Put the leeks into a large bowl full of cold water and swish them around so that any dirt that's clinging to them (as it tends to) sinks to the bottom. Gently scoop the leeks up and out of the water and let them drain in a colander. Do NOT just pour the leeks and their soaking water into the colander, or you will just end up pouring all the dirt back over them.

Put the leeks and chicken stock into the reserved pot and bring to a boil over high heat. While it's coming to a boil, scrape the bottom of the pot with a wooden spoon to loosen any browned bits from the surface; flavor! Once the stock has come to a boil, turn the heat to medium-low so that it rolls along at a gentle simmer. Return the chicken to the pot, along with any juice that has accumulated on the plate. Cover the pot with a lid that's ever so slightly ajar and cook, uncovering the pot once or twice to give the whole thing a stir, until the chicken is tender, about 30 minutes.

Season the broth to taste with salt and pepper and serve the chicken sprinkled with the chives. I like to serve this straight from the pot. This is also very good gently reheated the next day, and it freezes nicely.

SPIN-OFFS

FOR A SPANISH VARIATION, season the chicken not only with salt and pepper but also with a bit of hot pimentón (Spanish smoked paprika). Substitute a jar of rinsed and drained Piquillo peppers for the leeks and add a few minced garlic cloves and a handful of small Spanish olives (either pitted or give your friends a warning before eating).

FOR A HEARTY AND HEALTH-FUL ONE-POT MEAL, substitute a bunch of chopped dark leafy greens for the leeks and add two diced sweet potatoes or a peeled and diced butternut squash.

FOR SLIGHTLY VIETNAMESE BRAISED CHICKEN, leave out the leeks and add a packed ¼ cup [55 g] dark brown sugar, ¼ cup [60 ml] soy sauce, 1 Tbsp fish sauce, and two minced garlic cloves along with the chicken stock. Once the chicken is cooked through, stir in a head of chopped napa cabbage and let it wilt. Serve over rice.

Roast Chicken with Fennel, Rosemary + Lemon

SERVES 4

Including this recipe might make me a bit of a cookbook broken record, but roast chicken is truly the equivalent of a great song: It never gets old. This recipe is pretty simple, as roast chicken should be, and it includes two very helpful **small victories** that are useful not only for roast chicken but for all sorts of protein cooking. The **_first_** is, let your chicken (or other protein) come to room temperature before cooking so that it cooks evenly. **_Second_**, salt your chicken and let it air-dry at room temperature for 2 hours (or, better yet, uncovered in the fridge for up to 2 days) before cooking it. This lets the skin get nice and dry and also lets the salt really season the bird.

1 lemon	1 Tbsp minced fresh rosemary	One 3½-lb [1.6-kg] chicken, patted dry with paper towels
1 Tbsp fennel seeds	1 Tbsp kosher salt	

Remove the zest from the lemon with a fine grater (such as a Microplane) and place it in a mortar; set the lemon aside. Add the fennel seeds, rosemary, and salt and bash everything together with a pestle (or just stir everything in a bowl).

Rub the chicken with the salt mixture, inside and out, really massaging it into all of the crevices. Let the chicken sit uncovered for 2 hours at room temperature.

Preheat your oven to 425°F [220°C].

Place the chicken in a skillet or a baking dish (anything that holds it comfortably). Cut the zested lemon in half and put the halves into the cavity of the chicken.

Roast the chicken until the skin is browned and the leg feels nice and loose when you wiggle it and the thigh joints register 170°F [70°C] on an instant-read thermometer, about 1 hour and 15 minutes (start checking it at 1 hour to be safe). (Many cookbooks will tell you a lower temperature is okay, but then the chicken always seems to be undercooked, which, to me, is a bummer.)

Let the chicken rest for about 10 minutes before carving. Squeeze the juice from the lemon halves over the chicken when serving.

SPIN-OFFS

EXPERIMENT WITH SEASONINGS; try mixing the salt with cumin and coriander seeds. Or hot pimentón (Spanish smoked paprika) and minced garlic.

Or, if you can get your hands on some Ethiopian berbere spice, try that! Or use za'atar. You get the idea.

Use this same method (salting and seasoning ahead and bringing the bird to room temperature before roasting) for your **THANKSGIVING TURKEY**.

Jennie's Chicken Pelau

SERVES 4

My babysitter, Jennie, took great care of me and my brother for a decade, starting when I was three years old. Now, more than twenty-five years since we met, she and I maintain a close relationship. When I was a kid, the kitchen, unsurprisingly, was my favorite place to spend time with Jennie, especially when she cooked dishes native to St. Vincent, the small island in the Caribbean where she's from. Chicken pelau, a one-pot meal of chicken, rice, and vegetables (that stretches a little chicken into a lot of food), was something she made all the time. It's not unlike arroz con pollo or even paella. I thought that since I'd eaten pelau so many times, I could probably cook it on my own just by remembering the flavors. But every time I made it, something was missing. Recently I asked Jennie to show me how she makes it, and she started by burning sugar in oil until it was smoking. I couldn't believe this first step nor would I have ever figured it out on my own. **Small victory**: You really can learn something new every day. Another **small victory**: Have a few one-pot meals up your sleeve—they're perfect for when you want a home-cooked meal but don't feel very much like cooking (check out the Spin-Offs for a few more ideas). I've added coconut milk to this (something, just for the record, Jennie never used) because I love its sweet, rich undertone, but feel free to just use chicken stock or water in its place. Finally, the preparation belies the long ingredient list. This recipe is very easy to make and so very comforting, and burning the sugar lets you feel like you get to break the rules.

1 tsp garlic powder

1 tsp sweet paprika

Kosher salt

1 lb [455 g] boneless, skinless chicken breasts or thighs, cut into 1-in [2.5-cm] cubes, at room temperature

2 Tbsp vegetable oil

2 Tbsp sugar

1 small yellow onion, finely diced

2 carrots, diced

1 large or 2 small celery stalks, diced

1 small green bell pepper, cored, seeded, deribbed, and finely diced

3 garlic cloves, minced

½ jalapeño chile, halved, seeded, and minced

Leaves from 4 fresh thyme sprigs, minced

2 Tbsp ketchup or tomato paste

One 13½-oz [400-ml] can full-fat coconut milk, shaken

1 cup [240 ml] water

One 15-oz can [425-g] green pigeon peas or black-eyed peas, rinsed and drained

1 cup [200 g] long-grain white rice

In a large bowl, stir together the garlic powder, paprika, and 1 tsp salt. Add the chicken and toss to coat with the spice mixture, rubbing it in with your hands to make sure each piece is evenly coated. Set aside.

(Continued)

Turn on your exhaust fan if you have one and open your kitchen window. In a large heavy pot over medium-high heat, combine 1 Tbsp of the vegetable oil and all of the sugar and cook, stirring constantly, until the sugar is not only dissolved, but totally black and smoking and burned, about 4 minutes. Immediately add the chicken pieces in an even layer and cook, stirring now and then, until they are deeply browned all over, about 4 minutes (this happens faster than usual because you're browning the chicken in burnt caramel, which is already incredibly hot and very dark).

Turn the heat to medium-low and add the remaining 1 Tbsp vegetable oil, the onion, carrots, celery, bell pepper, garlic, jalapeño, thyme, and a big pinch of salt. Cook, stirring now and then, until the vegetables are slightly softened, about 10 minutes.

Stir the ketchup, coconut milk, and water into the pot. Turn the heat to high and bring the mixture to a boil, stirring everything with a wooden spoon to scrape the bottom of the pot to release any flavorful bits that might be stuck. Then, turn the heat to low and stir in the pigeon peas, rice, and a big pinch of salt. Give everything a good stir, cover the pot, and cook until the rice is tender, about 20 minutes. Turn off the heat and let the pelau rest, covered, for 10 minutes.

Season the pelau to taste with salt. Serve immediately.

SPIN-OFFS

FOR A MEXICAN ARROZ CON POLLO, heat a slick of olive oil in a large pot and brown cut-up chicken that has been seasoned with cumin, salt, and pepper. Remove it to a plate. Add a large chopped onion, a few minced garlic cloves, and a chopped red bell pepper to the pot and cook until soft. Add 1 cup [200 g] white rice and stir until the grains are opaque. Add 2 cups [480 ml] chicken stock, return the chicken to the pot, and bring to a boil, then lower the heat and simmer until the rice is tender and the chicken is cooked through, about 25 minutes. Add a handful of frozen peas, cover the pot, and let it sit for 10 minutes, so the residual heat cooks the peas. Serve sprinkled with chopped cilantro.

FOR ARROZ CON CHORIZO, brown a diced chorizo sausage in some oil in a medium pot. Add 1 cup [200 g] white rice and stir until the rice is toasty. Add 2 cups [480 ml] stock or water, along with a can of rinsed and drained black beans. Cover and cook over low heat until the rice is tender, about 20 minutes. Scatter a large handful of frozen peas over the top, put the lid back on, and let the whole thing sit off of the heat until the peas are cooked in the residual heat. Fluff with a fork and serve with chopped cilantro, salsa, diced avocado, and sour cream.

FOR A ONE-BAKING-SHEET DINNER, season diced potatoes with salt, pepper, minced garlic, and olive oil. Roast, turning everything once or twice, until they're nearly tender and a little bit brown, about 20 minutes. Add seasoned bone-in chicken breasts (salt, pepper, maybe a little paprika if you'd like) and continue to roast until the chicken is browned and cooked through and the potatoes are tender, another 20 to 25 minutes. Add a big bowl of spinach that you've coated with olive oil and seasoned with salt and roast just until the greens wilt, a final 5 minutes.

FOR AN EASY ONE-POT PORK MEAL, brown large-ish cubes of pork in olive oil in a deep pot. Add a few diced carrots, a couple of diced parsnips, and a diced apple. Add enough stock, apple cider, or water to come halfway up the sides of the pork and vegetables and scatter over a handful of dried cherries. Simmer until the pork and vegetables are tender, about 1½ hours. Sprinkle with chopped parsley before serving.

Buttermilk + Pimentón Fried Chicken

SERVES 4

I love fried chicken but have always avoided making it at home because I imagined vats and vats of oil (and what do you do with it afterward?) and batches and batches of chicken and all sorts of dredging mess and just general sweating while dealing with hot, dangerous fat. Yikes! But then I discovered a few **small victories** that changed it all. *First*, let the chicken sit overnight in seasoned buttermilk to ensure that it's flavorful all the way to the bone, not to mention extremely tender because of all the acidity in the buttermilk (try soaking a whole chicken in buttermilk before roasting it—it's awesome). *Second*, dredge the chicken in seasoned flour that's cut with a bit of cornstarch to make the batter extra crunchy. *Third*, shallow-fry the chicken in a deep, big pot so that you're protected from the oil and have room to maneuver (you don't need to deep-fry to make great fried chicken), and use a good old-fashioned splatter screen while frying (they work!). *Fourth*, let the leftover oil cool in the pot, pour it into an empty bottle, screw on the lid, and toss it—easy and safe disposal. The *last* is that fried chicken doesn't have to be a huge event for a big crowd. I like frying up a single chicken, cut into pieces. It's the perfect amount for four people (if it's just two of you, there will be enough to have some cold the next day . . . the best part of fried chicken).

¼ cup [85 g] honey

½ tsp cayenne pepper

4 tsp hot pimentón (Spanish smoked paprika)

Kosher salt

1 cup [240 ml] buttermilk or ¾ cup [180 ml] whole milk mixed with ¼ cup [60 ml] plain yogurt

2 garlic cloves, minced

One 3½-lb [1.6-kg] chicken, cut into 10 pieces (2 wings, 2 legs, 2 thighs, and 2 breasts cut in half across the bone; see Note), backbone discarded (or saved for another use, like stock)

1 cup [120 g] all-purpose flour

2 Tbsp cornstarch

Neutral oil, such as canola, grapeseed, or safflower, for frying

In a small bowl, whisk together the honey, cayenne, 1 tsp of the pimentón, and ½ tsp salt. Cover the bowl and set it aside at room temperature for up to 1 day. This will get drizzled on the fried chicken once it's done . . . hoorah!

In a small bowl, whisk together the buttermilk, garlic, remaining 3 tsp pimentón, and 2 Tbsp salt. Pour into a large resealable plastic bag and

add the chicken. Close the bag and turn to coat the chicken. Refrigerate the chicken for at least 4 hours, preferably overnight.

Take the chicken out of the refrigerator 1 to 2 hours before you're ready to cook it so that it can come to room temperature.

In a large baking dish, whisk together the flour, cornstarch, and 1 tsp salt.

Pour ½ in [12 mm] oil into a large heavy pot over medium heat and let the oil heat up.

Meanwhile, take the chicken out of the bag, working with one piece at a time, and allow the excess buttermilk to drip back into the bag. Place the chicken into the flour mixture. Dredge each piece lightly on all sides and transfer to a plate. Discard the excess buttermilk and flour mixtures.

When the oil is hot enough that it bubbles around the chicken when the edge of a piece is dipped into it, use tongs to gently and carefully place a few pieces in the oil—don't crowd them (the number of pieces will depend on the size of your pot).

Cook the chicken, turning the pieces every few minutes and adjusting the heat as needed, until the skin is dark golden brown and the chicken is firm to the touch. An instant-read thermometer inserted in the thickest part of the chicken should register 170°F [70°C]; this will take about 15 minutes for the wings and breast pieces and 18 to 20 minutes for the legs and thighs. Transfer the cooked chicken to a paper towel–lined serving platter and continue frying the rest, adding more oil to the pot if necessary.

Serve immediately with the reserved honey mixture for drizzling and dipping. It's also just as good at room temperature and even great cold.

NOTES: If you're working with a larger chicken, anything at or over 4 lb [1.8 kg], cut each breast into thirds across the bone instead of in half to ensure even cooking and lots of crispy, browned pieces.

If you're making a big batch of chicken, you can keep the first pieces warm and crisp by placing them on a cooling rack set on a baking sheet in a 250°F [120°C] oven.

SPIN-OFFS

Instead of pimentón, use lots of cracked black pepper in both the buttermilk and the seasoned flour. Dust the hot fried chicken with finely grated pecorino cheese. **CACIO E PEPE CHICKEN!** Or drizzle it with maple syrup— **BLACK PEPPER AND MAPLE SYRUP** are very good friends.

FOR A MEXICAN RIFF, instead of pimentón, use ground cumin and ground coriander. Drizzle the hot fried chicken with some of the juice from a jar of pickled jalapeños and scatter with chopped cilantro.

FOR A INDIAN RIFF, marinate the chicken in yogurt (thinned with a bit of milk or water) instead of buttermilk and use curry powder instead of pimentón. Serve the chicken with raita and mango chutney.

Indecision Grilled Chicken

SERVES 6

A couple of years ago, while making an impromptu birthday dinner for our friend Lacey, I scavenged in the fridge and couldn't decide between marinating chicken in herbs, or just with lemon, maybe with mustard, or maybe, better yet, honey mustard? I just decided to throw caution to the wind and go for all of the above. **Small victory**: Indecision is sometimes the best decision because this marinade was a total hit (which I was able to gauge by a full inbox the next morning with e-mails asking for the recipe). Another **small victory** is using boneless, skinless chicken thighs when grilling. Their extra fat means the chicken won't dry out as it tends to do when confronted with high heat. You can absolutely do half dark meat and half white meat if you prefer, or try the marinade on chicken legs or wings.

1 garlic clove, minced

2 Tbsp minced fresh Italian parsley

1 Tbsp minced fresh sage

Grated zest and juice of 1 lemon, plus lemon wedges for serving

1 Tbsp Dijon mustard

2 Tbsp seeded mustard

1 tsp honey

¼ cup [60 ml] extra-virgin olive oil

½ tsp kosher salt

¼ tsp freshly ground black pepper

1½ lb [680 g] boneless, skinless chicken thighs and/or breasts

In a large bowl, whisk together the garlic, parsley, sage, lemon zest, lemon juice, both mustards, the honey, olive oil, salt, and pepper. Add the chicken and use your hands to coat each piece with the mixture. Let the chicken marinate for 30 minutes to 1 hour at room temperature (or up to overnight, covered, in the refrigerator; bring to room temperature before proceeding).

Preheat the grill for high heat (or heat a large grill pan set over a couple of burners). Make sure your grates are super-clean.

Grill the chicken, turning the pieces occasionally, until it is nicely browned and is firm to the touch, about 5 minutes per side. Transfer the chicken to a platter and serve immediately or at room temperature with lemon wedges for squeezing over.

NOTE: Alternatively, you can roast the chicken in a 425°F [220°C] oven, turning the pieces halfway through cooking, for about 25 minutes total or broil them for about 5 minutes on each side.

SPIN-OFFS

MAKE PLAIN GRILLED CHICKEN (just coat it with olive oil and season with salt) and serve with Cilantro + Scallion Sauce (page 257); Arugula + Walnut Pesto (page 259); Chile, Lemon + Parsley Crème Fraîche (page 261); or Henley Mustard Sauce (see page 151).

TRY A DRY RUB INSTEAD OF A MARINADE—one of my favorites is a mixture of equal parts salt, brown sugar, and gochugaru (Korean red pepper flakes). This mixture also works really well on steaks and pork chops. Simply rub the chicken pieces with the rub and let them sit for about

1 hour at room temperature (or up to overnight in the refrigerator) before grilling. For great barbecued chicken, use this dry rub and then serve the chicken slathered with store-bought barbecue sauce or Molasses Barbecue Sauce (page 266).

Chicken + Pea Skillet Pie

SERVES 8

There are two major **small victories** here. The *first* is all about taking the fear out of pie crust. One bowl and your hands are all you need. Just keep your butter and your water cold and work with lightness in your fingertips (it's not a delicate process, but you just don't want to create too much heat, because cold butter = pockets of butter in your crust = pockets of steam = flaky dough). A little vinegar is a secret magical ingredient, since the acid basically curbs the gluten activity and keeps the dough flaky, instead of elastic (like you would want it for bread). Finally, roll out your piecrust on a piece of parchment paper. That way, your crust won't stick to your counter, it's easy to transfer, and cleanup is a real cinch. The *second* lies in the generous amount of crème fraîche in the filling, which takes the place of the traditional béchamel sauce often used in pot pie. It's easy, it doesn't get too heavy, and it lets the flavors of the roast chicken, sweet peas, and sharp shallots come through. This pie can be assembled up until the point of baking a day ahead of time (cover and refrigerate). Put in the oven when the doorbell rings. Best dinner party . . .

3½ lb [1.6 kg] skin-on, bone-in chicken breasts

2 Tbsp extra-virgin olive oil

Kosher salt

Freshly ground black pepper

¼ cup [60 ml] water

2 tsp apple cider vinegar

A handful of ice cubes

1¼ cups [150 g] all-purpose flour

8 Tbsp [110 g] very cold unsalted butter, diced

1 cup [230 g] crème fraîche

¼ cup [60 ml] Dijon mustard

One 10-oz [285-g] package frozen peas

A large handful of minced fresh Italian parsley

6 large shallots, thinly sliced

1 egg, beaten

Preheat your oven to 375°F [190°C].

Put the chicken breasts, skin-side up, in a 12-in [30.5-cm] skillet. Drizzle them with the olive oil, season aggressively with salt and pepper, and rub everything in with your hands. Roast the chicken until it's firm to the touch and nicely browned, about 40 minutes. Set the chicken aside until it's cool enough to handle. Leave the oven on.

Meanwhile, combine the water, vinegar, and ice cubes in a small pitcher and set it aside. In a large bowl, combine the flour, butter, and ½ tsp salt. Using your hands, work the butter into the flour mixture, rubbing it between your fingers until the mixture turns into coarse crumbs. Drizzle half of the ice water mixture (not including the ice cubes!) over the flour mixture and use a spoon or a rubber spatula to stir the ingredients together. Drizzle in more of the water, 1 Tbsp at a time, mixing until a dough forms and you haven't left any flour behind. (You might not need all of the water; the exact amount is hard to say because it depends on all sorts of variables, including how the flour was measured, how much humidity there is in the air—trust your instincts and pay attention to the way the dough feels; it should *just* come together). This could also all be done in a food processor if you'd like. Just pulse the flour, butter, and salt together and then, with the machine running, stream in the cold water and vinegar. Stop right when a dough starts to form.

Transfer the dough to a large, lightly floured piece of parchment paper and form it into a disk. Using a floured rolling pin, roll the dough into a circle that measures about 14 in [35 cm] across. Set the dough aside.

At this point, the chicken and the skillet should be cool enough to handle (if not, just wait a little longer). Remove the skin and separate the meat from the bones, discarding the skin and bones. Shred the meat directly into the skillet, capturing all of the juice. Add the crème fraîche, mustard, peas, parsley, shallots, 1 tsp salt, and ½ tsp pepper. Stir everything together (I think the best tool for this is your hands) until it's well mixed.

Pick up the dough round, using the parchment, and invert it on top of the filling. Peel off and discard the paper. (I don't mind if the dough looks a little uneven or haphazard, I like to let it just find its place naturally, but feel free to trim and crimp the edges if you'd like.) Brush the pastry with the beaten egg (I use my hands for this so I can be very gentle and achieve even coverage, and don't have to wash a brush afterward). Discard whatever egg mixture is left over (or save for another use such as a tiny omelet). Sprinkle the top of the pie with a generous pinch of salt. Use a paring knife to cut a few decorative slits in the top of the dough (these will also help steam escape).

Bake until the crust is dark golden brown and the filling visible through the steam vents is bubbling, 50 minutes to 1 hour.

Let the pie rest at room temperature for about 10 minutes before serving. I like to set the skillet right on the table (on a board or cloth) and just scoop up this rustic, homey dish with a large serving spoon.

SPIN-OFFS

FOR PIECRUST COOKIES (my favorite thing to make when I was a kid), cut the rolled-out dough into shapes or use your favorite cookie cutters. Transfer the cookies to parchment-lined baking sheets. Brush with melted butter, and sprinkle with a mixture of cinnamon and sugar. Bake in a 375°F [190°C] oven until golden brown, about 15 minutes. Transfer the cookies to a rack to cool (they will crisp as they cool).

TURN THE CRUST INTO A FRUIT PIE by doubling it and putting one rolled-out circle in the bottom of a pie dish and then filling with a generous 2 lb [910 g] fruit. Try peeled and sliced apples with cinnamon, or sliced ripe peaches mixed with blueberries. Or raspberries and sliced nectarines. Or fresh cranberries and sliced apples. You get the picture. Whatever fruit you choose, toss it with enough sugar to make it taste really more like itself (which is usually ¼ to ½ cup [50 to 100 g]), 3 Tbsp cornstarch, the juice of half a lemon, and a pinch of salt. Cover with the second rolled-out circle of pie crust. Crimp the edges, brush with egg, score the top, and bake at 375°F [190°C] until dark brown and the juices are bubbling, about 1 hour.

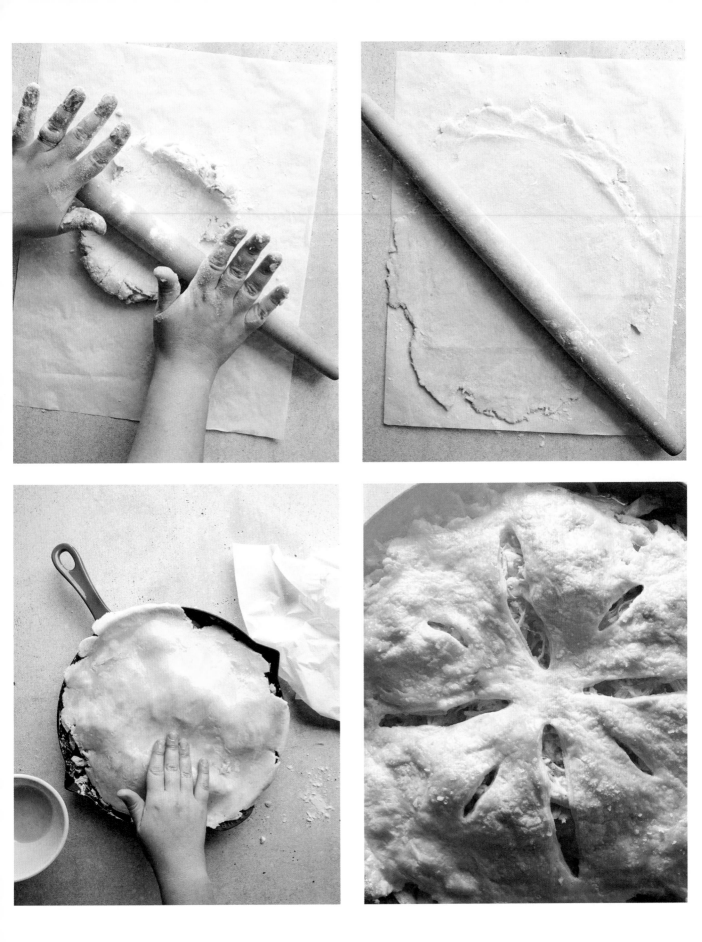

SHELLFISH + FISH

Greek-ish Grilled Shrimp

SERVES 4

Small victory: Use two skewers per shrimp kabob when grilling shrimp. This is a tiny bit more work on the front end, but the reward, a small (shrimp-size?) victory for sure, is that you create a stable raft of shrimp that can be cooked, flipped, and retrieved with confident ease. These can be cooked on a grill pan or under the intense heat of a broiler if you don't have an outdoor grill. Serve with a simple tomato salad dressed with torn herbs, olive oil, and lemon. You could grill some pita breads, too, or toss cooked orzo with butter and dill.

1½ lb [680 g] medium shrimp, peeled and deveined

6 Tbsp [90 ml] extra-virgin olive oil

½ tsp kosher salt

2 lemons, halved

¾ cup [90 g] crumbled feta cheese

1 tsp dried oregano

Soak twenty-four wooden skewers in warm water for about 1 hour (this keeps them from burning on the grill). Drain the skewers and set aside.

Prepare the grill for medium-high heat (or heat a large grill pan set over a couple of burners) and make sure your grates are super-clean.

Meanwhile, put the shrimp in a large bowl, drizzle with 3 Tbsp of the olive oil, and sprinkle with the salt. Use your hands to toss everything together so that each shrimp gets properly oiled and salted. Thread the shrimp onto the skewers, using two skewers per kabob, so that you end up with a dozen sturdy kabobs.

Transfer the shrimp kabobs and the lemon halves, cut-side down, to the grill. Let the shrimp cook until the undersides are ever so slightly charred,

about 2 minutes. Flip the kabobs and cook until the shrimp are slightly charred on the second side, opaque, and firm to the touch, just about 1 minute longer. At this point, the cut sides of the lemons should be nicely charred.

Transfer the shrimp and lemon halves to a serving platter and use tongs to help you remove the skewers (discard the skewers; they've done their job). Scatter the feta and oregano over the shrimp and drizzle with the remaining 3 Tbsp olive oil. Use your tongs to help you squeeze the smoky juice from the lemons over the shrimp. I like to leave the juiced halves on the platter along with the shrimp so you and your guests can get a little bit more juice out of them as you eat the shrimp, plus they're kinda beautiful, don't you think? Serve immediately.

SPIN-OFFS

TO MAKE GRILLED SHRIMP WITH BARBECUE SAUCE, oil and salt them as directed and thread them on double skewers. As they're grilling, brush them with your favorite barbecue sauce, or try the Molasses Barbecue Sauce (page 266), the gochujang mixture from the ribs on page 155, or Henley Mustard Sauce (see page 151). Be sure to serve with more sauce on the side.

The double-skewer method is also great for **CHICKEN YAKITORI**. Simply thread strips of chicken breasts onto skewers along with some large pieces of scallion. Brush with the soy sauce–maple syrup mixture from the salmon on page 205. Kids love these!

Old Bay Shrimp Cocktail

I'm a big fan of using every part of everything I buy, especially when it comes to expensive ingredients. In this shrimp cocktail (Old School!), I make a very quick stock out of the shrimp shells and use it to poach the shrimp, coaxing all of the potential flavor from the shellfish. The flavorful stock, a **small victory** in and of itself, not only boosts the flavor of the shrimp, but also becomes its own useful ingredient. You can save it (it freezes well) and use it to poach more shrimp the next time a shrimp cocktail–craving strikes, or use it as the base of a risotto, chowder, or gumbo (check out the Spin-Offs). I love getting two things out of one ingredient—a shrimp cocktail now and a whole bunch of possibilities later. I call for Old Bay seasoning everywhere in this recipe, because I *lovvvve* it, and some mayonnaise in the cocktail sauce—which might not be classic, but makes it almost like Russian dressing with a horseradish kick. This sauce would also be delicious with any type of fried seafood or even on roasted potatoes or chicken.

¼ cup [65 g] ketchup

¼ cup [60 g] mayonnaise

2 Tbsp prepared horseradish

1 Tbsp red wine vinegar

1 tsp Old Bay Seasoning, plus 1 Tbsp and more for dusting

1 lb [455 g] medium shrimp, unpeeled

2 garlic cloves

4 cups [960 ml] water

1 lemon, cut into wedges

In a small bowl, whisk together the ketchup, mayonnaise, horseradish, vinegar, and 1 tsp Old Bay. Cover the bowl with plastic wrap, pop it in the refrigerator, and proceed with the shrimp.

Peel and devein the shrimp, reserving the shells. Set the shrimp aside while you prepare the cooking liquid.

Put the shrimp shells into a medium saucepan and add the 1 Tbsp Old Bay, garlic, and water. Bring the mixture to a boil and cook until the liquid is extremely fragrant and a bit more concentrated than it was to begin with, about 10 minutes. Strain the stock through a fine-mesh sieve into a bowl. Rinse out the saucepan and return the stock to it. Discard the contents of the sieve.

Set up a bowl of ice water and put it near the stove. Bring the stock back to a boil, then lower the heat and add the shrimp. Simmer, stirring the shrimp once or twice, until they're bright pink and firm to the touch, about 2 minutes (shrimp cook quickly, so don't walk away or start doing anything else). Use a slotted spoon to transfer the shrimp to the ice water for just a minute to stop them from overcooking, then transfer them to some paper towels to drain and dry off. Put the broth in a heatproof airtight container, let cool to room temperature, and refrigerate for up to 3 days or freeze for up to 3 months.

(Continued)

Put the shrimp on a serving platter, along with the bowl of sauce for dipping and the lemon wedges for squeezing over. Dust the shrimp with a little shake of Old Bay. Serve immediately.

SPIN-OFFS *(NOTE THAT THE BROTH WILL BE PRETTY SALTY, SO BE SURE TO KEEP THAT IN MIND AND TASTE AS YOU GO WHEN YOU TURN IT INTO SOMETHING ELSE)*

FOR SHRIMP RISOTTO, warm the shrimp stock. In a separate pot, sauté a minced onion in olive oil and add 1 cup [200 g] Arborio rice and stir until it's opaque. Add a splash of white wine and cook until the wine evaporates. Add a ladleful of the shrimp stock and cook, stirring, until it has been absorbed. Continue adding the stock one ladleful at a time and stirring, adding more only once the previous addition has been absorbed, until the rice is cooked but still slightly al dente, about 20 minutes. If you run out of stock before the rice is cooked, just use simmering water. Stir in a good piece of butter. Serve topped with chopped chives. Add a few sautéed shrimp, if you like.

FOR SHRIMP CHOWDER, turn to page 73, but skip making the stock—you've already done that!

FOR A GREAT SHRIMP GUMBO, sauté a chopped onion, a chopped green bell pepper, a few chopped celery stalks, and a couple of minced garlic cloves in olive oil in a heavy pot. Once the vegetables are soft, add a few spoonfuls of flour and cook, stirring, until the flour is dark brown. Add a couple spoonfuls of tomato paste and a sprinkle of cayenne and cook until the tomato paste darkens a little, just a minute. Stir in the shrimp broth and let the whole mixture simmer until it's a bit thick, about 30 minutes. Stir in some peeled shrimp and as much crabmeat as you can afford and cook just until the shrimp are bright pink. Serve over rice and top with chopped parsley and/or thinly sliced scallions.

Korean Clambake

Ina Garten's first cookbook introduced me to the idea of an indoor clambake. A clambake in your kitchen? Sounds a little wild, but it's actually the easiest, most wonderful one-pot meal in the world. Talk about a **small victory**. You simply layer your ingredients in the order they'll cook in a large pot and let it hang out on the stove. That is that. Everything turns out perfectly, and then you pour it all out onto your table (I put large baking sheets on the table to catch all of the juice) and everyone rolls up their sleeves and digs in with their hands. It's fun! Following is my Korean version inspired by the wonderful and simple seafood stews I enjoyed in Korea when I worked on *The Kimchi Chronicles*, a PBS show. The kimchi-garlic butter is basically gold. Use it anywhere—drizzled over roast chicken, grilled clams, or even a bowl of rice with a fried egg on top.

8 Tbsp [110 g] unsalted butter, diced

1 Tbsp gochugaru (Korean red pepper flakes) or 1 tsp red pepper flakes

2 garlic cloves, minced

2 tsp kosher salt

One 16-oz [448-g] jar cabbage kimchi, including juice

1 lb [455 g] of the smallest potatoes you can find (creamers, fingerlings, or new potatoes are all great)

1 yellow onion, thinly sliced

4 ears corn, shucked and cut into 4 pieces each

1 lb [455 g] small clams, scrubbed

1 lb [455 g] shrimp in the shell

2 lb [910 g] mussels, scrubbed and debearded (i.e., using a paring knife, pull off the furry bit that is sometimes attached to the outside of the mussel)

1 cup [240 ml] light-colored beer or water

4 scallions, roots and dark green tops trimmed off, white and light green parts thinly sliced

In a small saucepan, combine the butter with the gochugaru, garlic, and salt. Set a sieve over the pan and pour in the contents of the kimchi jar so that all of the juice is added to the butter. Roughly chop the kimchi and set it aside. Put the saucepan over low heat and cook, stirring, until the butter melts. Let the butter mixture sit on the lowest heat to stay warm.

Put the potatoes in the largest pot you have. Scatter over the reserved chopped kimchi and the onion. Put the corn on top of the onions, followed by the clams, shrimp, and, last, the mussels. Pour the beer over the shellfish, set the pot, uncovered, over medium-high heat, and bring the mixture to a boil (there will be lots of steam). Cover the pot, turn the heat to medium-low, and cook for 20 minutes. At this point, transfer the shrimp (they should be pink and firm) and all of the clams and mussels that have opened to a sheet pan and cover with foil to keep them warm. Cover the pot again and continue cooking until the remaining clams and mussels open (there are always a few that take longer), 5 to 10 minutes. At this point, discard any that don't open (there are also inevitably always a few). Transfer the contents of the pot to the sheet pan with the shrimp. (Use a second pan if needed; large spoons are helpful in this messy but controlled endeavor.) Scatter the scallions on top and either drizzle everything with the warm butter mixture or serve the butter alongside for dipping, whatever you prefer (I like to pour it over everything). Put out lots of napkins and an extra bowl for shells, roll up your sleeves, and dig in.

(Continued)

SPIN-OFFS

FOR AN OLD-FASHIONED MAINE-STYLE CLAMBAKE, leave out the kimchi, substitute white wine or fish broth for the beer, and feel free to add steamers and/or lobsters to the mix. Instead of the kimchi butter, just serve with plain melted butter and be sure to have a bowl of lemon wedges for squeezing over everything.

FOR AN OLD BAY SHRIMP BOIL, use all shrimp instead of the mix of shellfish and leave out the kimchi. Add a halved lemon to the pot along with 1 Tbsp Old Bay Seasoning. Instead of the kimchi butter, just add some crushed garlic and a shake of Old Bay to melted butter.

FOR A CAJUN-STYLE CLAMBAKE, add 1 lb [455 g] sliced andouille sausage to the pot first and leave out the kimchi. If you can find crawfish, throw some in with the other shellfish. Instead of the kimchi butter, just add some cayenne pepper or Tabasco sauce and some minced garlic to melted butter.

Scallops with Chile-and-Parsley Bread Crumbs

SERVES 2; EASILY MULTIPLIED

This recipe is simple; and as with all simple dishes, each element has to be terrific and technique is paramount. The key is all in the sear. **Small victory**: Patience counts as an ingredient. Along with a hot, heavy pan, practicing restraint is rewarded with a deep, concentrated sear, the kind of browning that makes something like a sweet scallop taste like an exaggerated version of itself, bookended with crunch. Don't flip prematurely, as tempting as it is to get in there. To offset the richness of the scallops and counter their silky interiors, enter some very spicy, crunchy bread crumbs. These are also good friends with all sorts of seafood (use them as a topping for baked clams or scatter over a pot of cooked mussels), pasta (a bowl of spaghetti aglio e olio, see page 81, topped with these is heaven), or use as a topping for roasted vegetables or to add crunch to salads (especially Julia's Caesar, page 83). I made this recipe to serve just two, as scallops are pretty expensive and I like them for a "date night in," but feel free to multiply to serve more people (be sure to brown the scallops in batches as necessary).

4 Tbsp [60 ml] extra-virgin olive oil

1 small garlic clove, minced

½ tsp red pepper flakes

½ cup [150 g] coarse fresh bread crumbs (see headnote, page 118)

Kosher salt

1 Tbsp minced fresh Italian parsley

2 Tbsp unsalted butter

12 large sea scallops, tough connective muscle removed from each, patted dry with paper towels

Freshly ground black pepper

½ lemon

In a large, heavy nonstick or cast-iron skillet over medium-high heat, warm 2 Tbsp of the olive oil. Add the garlic and red pepper flakes and cook, stirring, until the aromatics just begin to sizzle, about 30 seconds. Add the bread crumbs and cook, stirring, until they're golden brown and crisp, about 5 minutes. Season the bread crumbs to taste with salt, stir in the parsley, and transfer to a small bowl. Set aside.

Wipe out the skillet with a paper towel, add the remaining 2 Tbsp olive oil along with the butter, and place it back over medium-high heat. Season the scallops generously on both sides with salt and pepper. Once the butter melts, add the scallops and cook, without disturbing them, until the undersides are really browned and gorgeous, about 2 minutes. Carefully turn the scallops and cook until the second sides are beautifully browned, 1 to 2 minutes.

Transfer the scallops to two plates or a serving dish and drizzle over the butter from the pan. Squeeze the lemon half over the scallops and scatter with the reserved bread crumbs. Serve immediately.

SPIN-OFF

Proper searing applies to all sorts of things, especially steaks and pork chops. To make a **PERFECT STEAK OR CHOP** at home, bring your protein to room temperature and then heat a little butter and a little oil in the heaviest pan you have; turn on your kitchen fan and open the window. Pat the steak or chops dry with paper towels and shower both sides with kosher salt and black pepper. Really aggressively season the meat—that's why steaks and chops taste so good at resaurants. Sear on both sides until a deep, dark crust forms. The meat will let you know when it's ready to turn—it should release easily from the pan. Tilt the pan and use a spoon to baste the meat with the butter mixture as it cooks on the second side. When it's nicely browned on the other side and is just firm to the touch, transfer to a cutting board and let it rest for about 10 minutes. Then, slice the meat, sprinkle with salt, and squeeze over a halved lemon, because rich meat and bright, acidic lemon are very good together. Some horseradish is nice, too.

Broiled Anything with Garlic + Parsley Butter

SERVES 4

I may have inherited my craving for unadorned broiled fish from my mother, who loves plain but elegant food. Whatever you broil, a good spread of garlic-and-parsley-flecked butter makes things a bit less austere and a lot more delicious. This compound butter is a **small victory** in and of itself because it transforms not just fish, but just about everything (try spreading it on toast or mixing it into scrambled eggs). The spin-offs are pretty much endless, and—bonus!— you can make a big batch and freeze it so that you can add it to anything at any time. It's money in the dinner bank.

4 Tbsp [55 g] unsalted butter, at room temperature

1 large garlic clove, minced

1 small shallot, minced

A small handful of fresh Italian parsley leaves, finely chopped

Kosher salt

1 lemon

1 Tbsp extra-virgin olive oil

1 lb [455 g] fish fillets, peeled shrimp, scallops, halved lobster tails . . . almost anything!

In a small bowl, combine the butter, garlic, shallot, parsley, and ½ tsp salt. Using a fine grater (like a Microplane), remove the zest from the lemon and add it to the bowl. Reserve the lemon. Mash the aromatics into the butter with a fork or potato masher and then use a wooden spoon to really beat the butter until it's nice and smooth and everything is evenly incorporated.

Set an oven rack so that it's 6 in [15 cm] from the broiler element and preheat your broiler to high. Line a baking sheet with foil and rub it with the olive oil.

Arrange the fish or shellfish evenly on the pre-pared baking sheet and sprinkle lightly with salt. Use two spoons (or just your hands!) to dot the butter mixture over the fish.

Broil until the fish flakes easily or the shellfish is firm to the touch. This will happen quickly, so don't step away or answer the phone or any-thing like that. The exact time will depend on what you're broiling and the strength of your broiler. For thin fillets such as sole or flounder or small shrimp, the time could be as short as 5 minutes. For thicker pieces of fish, like halibut, it could be more like 10 minutes.

Cut the zested lemon in half and squeeze the juice over the fish. Serve immediately.

(Continued)

SPIN-OFFS

GARLIC BREAD—spread the garlic butter on the cut sides of a halved baguette or a loaf of ciabatta. If you'd like, add a layer of grated Parmesan or pecorino cheese. Wrap the bread in aluminum foil and bake in a 375°F [190°C] oven until it's warm, 10 to 15 minutes. Cut and serve. Or grill slices of bread and spread with generous amounts of the garlic butter.

Use the garlic butter instead of the cream cheese mixture inside the **PORK LOIN** on page 152. Delicious!

STEAM A POT OF MUSSELS or clams and dollop with the garlic butter before serving.

USE THE BUTTER ON ANYTHING THAT JUST CAME OFF THE GRILL—fish, shellfish (halved lobsters are particularly impressive), chicken, pork, steak, or tofu. Or throw some clams and/or oysters on the grill, which will steam in their own juices and open up on their own, and top with the butter. Or hit grilled asparagus or zucchini with the butter while they're still warm.

MIX ANYTHING INTO SOFTENED BUTTER! Try grated orange zest, toasted cumin seeds, and a bit of harissa paste. Or miso paste and toasted sesame seeds. Or herbes de Provence. Or toasted fennel seeds, lemon zest, and minced garlic. Or gochugaru (Korean red pepper flakes), toasted sesame oil, and minced scallions. Or dill and paprika. Or Old Bay Seasoning. The list is only limited by your imagination. And remember, compound butters, wrapped tightly, freeze well.

Roasted Salmon with Maple + Soy

SERVES 4

The subtitle of this recipe could easily be "How to Get Your Kid to Love Fish." I like to think that my childhood was sponsored by Soy Vay, a bottled teriyaki sauce that my parents liked to marinate EVERYTHING in. Needless to say, I happily ate anything that was slicked with the stuff, so maybe there was something to it. The **small victory** here, an homage to my family's recycling bin filled with Soy Vay empties, is about combining something sweet with something salty to create a friendly introduction to new foods for kids. I have cooked for lots of kids who ordinarily hold their noses to fish, but when it's covered with this easy, sticky sauce, I can see their little minds change.

2 Tbsp maple syrup

2 Tbsp soy sauce

2 Tbsp extra-virgin olive oil

1 Tbsp minced fresh peeled ginger

One 1½-lb [680-g] salmon fillet, skin and any pin bones removed, cut into 1-in [2.5-cm] cubes

1 tsp black sesame seeds

Preheat your oven to 425°F [220°C]. Line a baking sheet or a large baking dish with parchment paper.

In a small bowl, whisk together the maple syrup, soy sauce, olive oil, and ginger.

Put the salmon pieces on the prepared baking sheet. Pour over the soy sauce mixture and use your hands to coat each piece of salmon on all sides. Arrange the pieces so that they have a little bit of space around them (as if you were baking cookies).

Roast the salmon until it's firm to the touch and beginning to flake when pierced with a paring knife, 10 to 15 minutes. Transfer the salmon to a serving platter and sprinkle with the sesame seeds. Serve immediately.

SPIN-OFFS

Use the sauce to coat **STIR-FRIED BEEF AND BROCCOLI** right at the end of stir-frying. Freeze the piece of beef for half an hour before slicing it—it will make cutting it thin very easy.

FOR ASIAN-STYLE LETTUCE WRAPS, use the sauce to glaze cooked ground turkey and then wrap it in pieces of lettuce. Serve with bowls of shredded carrots and thinly sliced cucumbers for topping. Kids love build-your-own kind of stuff, and this is also a great way to make vegetables a bit more exciting.

The other sweet condiment that kids love? **HONEY MUSTARD**. Try shaking some up with mustard and brown sugar or mustard and molasses. Coat chicken breasts or legs with the mixture and roast until the chicken is cooked through and the coating becomes a delicious glaze. You could also use Henley Mustard Sauce (see page 151) for the same effect.

Crispy Fish with Bacon + Chives

SERVES 4

Not only is cornstarch handy for thickening puddings and sauces, it's also the secret ingredient (**small victory!**) for the most shatter-inducing coating on all sorts of items, such as this pan-fried fish. If you eat fish but not pork, substitute 3 Tbsp olive oil for the bacon fat and add a shake of hot pimentón (Spanish smoked paprika) to the flour mixture for the requisite smokiness. The other important thing to note is that this is an occasion for your most slippery nonstick pan (meaning, that old pan that's all scuffed up won't do the trick). Any other type means that instead of looking beautiful on your plate, your dinner will be stuck to your pan.

3 Tbsp all-purpose flour

1 Tbsp cornstarch

Four 6-oz [170-g] white fish fillets, such as sole or flounder

Kosher salt

2 Tbsp neutral oil, such as canola, grapeseed, or safflower

4 oz [115 g] sliced bacon, roughly chopped

A small handful of finely chopped fresh chives

½ lemon

In a small bowl, stir together the flour and cornstarch. Season the fish fillets generously with salt on both sides and then dust them lightly all over with the flour mixture. You're looking for a really thin, even coating. Knock off any excess flour mixture. Set the fish aside.

In a large nonstick skillet over medium-high heat, warm the oil and add the bacon. Cook, stirring occasionally, until the bacon is crisp and the fat is rendered, about 5 minutes. Use a slotted spoon to transfer the bacon to a paper towel–lined plate, leaving the fat in the pan, and set aside.

Put the coated fish fillets into the bacon fat in a single layer and cook, regulating the heat so it doesn't get too hot, until the fillets are firm to the touch and crisp and golden brown all over, 2 to 3 minutes per side. The exact timing will depend on the thickness of the fish. To make sure it's cooked through all the way to the center, you can either break a fillet open with a fork to check or insert the blade of a paring knife into a piece (be sure not to poke through to the pan) and then touch the blade to see if it's nice and warm. Depending on the size of your fish and your pan, cook the fillets in two batches if necessary and keep the first batch warm on a baking sheet in a 275°F [135°C] oven.

Transfer the perfectly cooked, crispy fish to a serving platter. Sprinkle each fillet lightly with salt. Scatter the reserved bacon on top of the fish, along with the chives, and squeeze the lemon half over. Serve immediately.

SPIN-OFFS

FOR GREAT KOREAN-STYLE CHICKEN WINGS, season the flour-cornstarch mixture with a good amount of gochugaru (Korean red pepper flakes; or just use regular chili flakes), toss the wings in the flour mixture, and fry them (see page 180) until they're crispy. Toss with a mixture of one part fish sauce, one part honey, and one part soy sauce and sprinkle with more gochugaru to serve.

FOR PORK PICCATA, cut a pork tenderloin into ½-in [12-mm] slices and dust them with the flour-cornstarch mixture. Pan-fry in butter, then garnish with capers and chopped parsley and serve with lemon wedges.

FOR CHICKEN NUGGETS, simply toss cubes of chicken in the flour-cornstarch mixture, dip the coated cubes in egg, and dip them into the flour mixture again. Shallow-fry and serve with your favorite dipping sauce (spicy mayo for me!).

FOR CRISPY CALAMARI, thinly slice squid and toss it in the flour-cornstarch mixture. Deep-fry and serve with lemon and spicy marinara or tartar sauce.

Flounder with Roasted Tomatoes + Black Olives

SERVES 4

This is one of my go-to dishes when I have friends over for dinner. It's the easiest and tastiest way to make fish for a group. Even if you double the recipe, you can cook all the pieces at the same time; there's no splattering or mess whatsoever and there's no chance of the fish sticking to the pan. And you can serve straight from the sheet pan, because it looks gorgeous and has that "I just threw this together" vibe. If all of what I just said weren't **small victory** enough (yes, I just used "small victory" as an adjective), the roasted tomatoes themselves are a supreme **small victory**. The high heat blasts the juices out of the tomatoes, forming a quick, concentrated sauce that is not only great for roasting fish, it's also terrific tossed with pasta or as an accompaniment for scrambled eggs, roast chicken, grilled pork chops . . . the world is your tomato. To make this dish a complete meal, you need nothing more than arugula dressed with lemon and olive oil and a loaf of bread for sopping up the tomatoes.

1 shallot, thinly sliced

1 garlic clove, thinly sliced

2 pt [650 g] cherry tomatoes, left whole if small, halved if large

¼ cup [60 ml] extra-virgin olive oil, plus 2 Tbsp

Kosher salt

Four 6-oz [170-g] flounder or other flat fish fillets

½ cup [80 g] black olives (pitted if you'd like, okay if not)

A small handful of chopped fresh Italian parsley, chives, and/or basil

Preheat your oven to 400°F [200°C]. Line a rimmed baking sheet with parchment paper.

Put the shallot, garlic, and tomatoes on the prepared baking sheet. Drizzle with the ¼ cup [60 ml] olive oil and sprinkle with 1 tsp salt. Use your hands to mix everything together.

Roast the mixture until the tomatoes start to give off some of their juice and the juice is bubbling, about 20 minutes. If you are making this with not-great tomatoes (i.e., it's February in New England or something), feel free to roast the tomatoes for another 10 to 15 minutes to concentrate the flavors and compensate for the out-of-season produce.

Take the baking sheet out of the oven and give the tomato mixture a stir. Lay the flounder fillets on top of the mixture in a single layer (it's okay if they overlap a little bit). Drizzle the fish with the remaining 2 Tbsp olive oil and sprinkle evenly with 1 tsp salt. Scatter the olives on top of the fish and put the baking sheet back

(Continued)

in the oven. Roast until the fish is opaque and flakes easily when poked with a fork or a paring knife, 10 to 15 minutes longer.

Scatter the herbs on top of the fish. Serve immediately. It's okay if the fish falls apart when you serve it, that's part of its rustic beauty. If you're serving the olives unpitted, be sure to let your guests know.

SPIN-OFFS

RIFF ON YOUR PROTEIN: substitute just about any type of fish or shrimp for the flounder, or even cubes of boneless, skinless chicken breasts or thighs.

FOR A SLIGHTLY MOROCCAN VERSION, add a pinch of saffron threads, ½ tsp ground cumin, and a small handful of chopped dried apricots to the tomato mixture before roasting. Use Moroccan olives and sprinkle with mint and/or cilantro. Serve with couscous.

FOR A GREEK VERSION, add 1 tsp dried oregano to the tomato mixture before roasting, and be sure to use Greek olives. Sprinkle the fish with dill and/or parsley and squeeze over fresh lemon juice or drizzle with a little bit of red wine vinegar right before serving. Serve with orzo, toasted pita bread, rice, or roasted potatoes seasoned with dried oregano and fresh lemon.

FOR A SPANISH VERSION, add 1 tsp hot pimentón (Spanish smoked paprika) and a sliced jarred Piquillo pepper to the tomato mixture before roasting. Use Spanish olives; I particularly like the tiny ones called Arbequinas.

You can use drained **CANNED TOMATOES** here. In fact, roasted canned tomatoes are delicious. Try them on buttered rice. Yum!

Halibut with Chermoula in Parchment

SERVES 4

Living most of my life in New York City meant cooking in small kitchens with little, if any, proper ventilation. This was a situation I never fretted about, except when it came to cooking fish, especially in the series of studio apartments I called home for a long time when my kitchen was in my bedroom and vice versa. Parchment paper, one of my favorite tools in the kitchen, became my best friend. Wrapping fish in it, with something tasty like an herby chermoula (which is basically North African pesto), meant I could have gently cooked, odorless, splatterless fish with little effort and very little cleanup. Many **small victories** in one entrée, just my kind of thing. You could cut the fish into individual servings and cook them in separate packages (divide the chermoula accordingly), but I much prefer the ease of wrapping one package and the conviviality of serving family style. Your call.

1 garlic clove, minced

A small handful fresh Italian parsley leaves

A small handful fresh cilantro leaves

2 tsp sweet paprika

1 tsp ground cumin

½ preserved lemon, roughly chopped

¼ cup [60 ml] extra-virgin olive oil

½ tsp kosher salt

1½ lb [680 g] center-cut skinless halibut fillet, or another firm fish

Preheat your oven to 400°F [200°C]. Line a sheet pan with a 12-by-35-in [30.5-by-89-cm] piece of parchment paper.

In a blender or food processor, puree the garlic, parsley, cilantro, paprika, cumin, preserved lemon, olive oil, and salt together until the chermoula is smooth.

Put the halibut toward one side of the prepared pan and pour over the chermoula. Rub the chermoula all over the fish. Fold the empty half of the parchment over the fish so that it's completely enveloped in paper. Fold the edges of the paper together, making small overlapping folds as you go, so that the whole package is crimped. Once you get to the end, tuck the parchment fold underneath to keep it from opening.

Bake until the paper is dark brown and the fish is fragrant, 20 minutes. At this point, carefully (there will be hot steam!) cut a small slit in the top of the packet and test the fish with the blade of a paring knife; it should flake easily and be opaque throughout. If the fish is not cooked enough to your liking, just put it back in the oven for another 5 to 10 minutes. It's

(Continued)

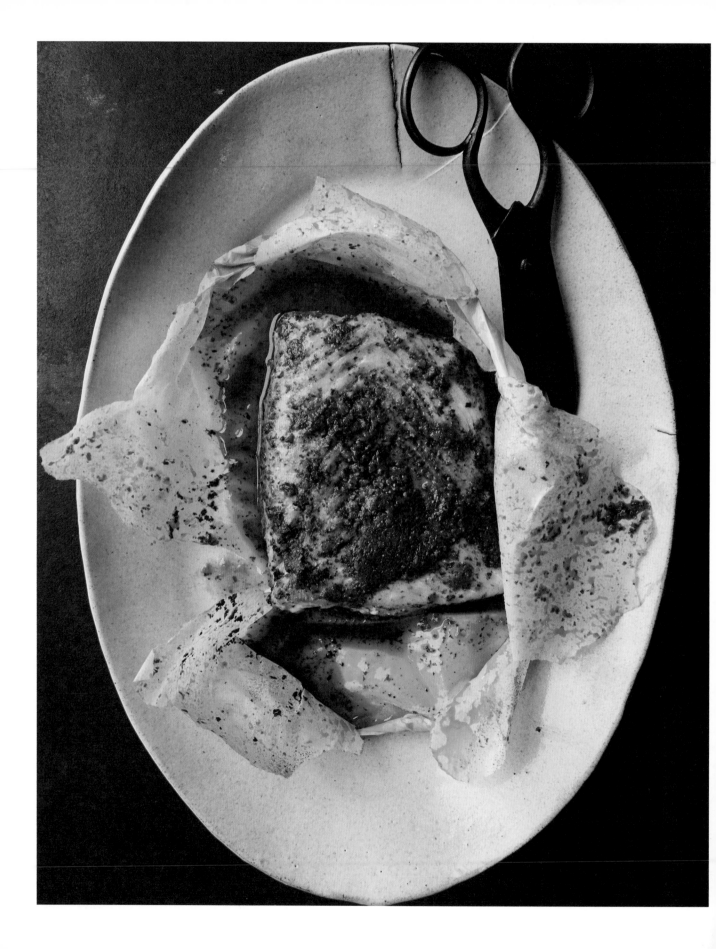

okay that the parchment is a little open, don't worry. Once the fish is cooked through, use two spatulas to transfer the parchment package to a serving platter and cut the package open with a paring knife or a pair of kitchen shears. Serve immediately.

SPIN-OFFS

FOR A ONE-PAN MEAL (an incredibly healthy one at that), add vegetables, such as cherry tomatoes, thinly sliced zucchini, shaved carrots, and/or string beans, to the package. Add a splash of water before crimping to create a little extra steam to help the vegetables cook through.

FOR A MORE ITALIAN VERSION, swap the chermoula for pesto.

INSTEAD OF HALIBUT, try any thick, firm fish that can stand up to the strong flavors of the chermoula (such as salmon or striped bass). Or try a more delicate fish with a less intense sauce, even just a simple pat of butter and a squeeze of lemon (and shorten the initial cooking time to 15 minutes).

GRILL THE PACKAGES instead of turning on the oven. Simply wrap the parchment packages in aluminum foil. And don't worry about having your fish stick to the grill!

DESSERTS

Sliced Citrus with Pomegranate + Pistachios

SERVES 4

This mix of gorgeous citrus fruits covered with jewel-like pomegranate seeds and crunchy pistachios is so satisfying but not at all heavy (and is a shout-out to my mom, who always orders the fruit plate, and to my dad, who has never met a pistachio he didn't like). The **small victory** here is all about how to get the seeds out of a pomegranate without splattering your kitchen (do the whole thing underwater).

3 lb [1.4 kg] assorted citrus fruits, including but not limited to oranges, grapefruits, clementines, and/or tangerines

2 Tbsp light brown sugar

1 pomegranate (choose a heavy one—that means it will be juicy!)

3 Tbsp toasted pistachios, roughly chopped

Working with one piece of citrus at a time, lop off the top and bottom of each fruit, cutting just deep enough to expose the fruit beneath the pith. Stand the fruit on your cutting board so that one of the cut ends is sitting on the board—it should be nice and steady. Cut the remaining peel and pith off the citrus in wide strips, working your way around the fruit, so that you end up with a completely peeled piece of fruit. Turn the fruit on its side and cut it into thin (but not too thin) rounds. Discard the peels or reserve them for another use (I like to simmer them with water and brown sugar, then strain the liquid and serve it over ice . . . a little gin mixed in doesn't hurt either).

Arrange the sliced citrus artfully, but not too preciously (this should look and feel casual), on a serving platter. Sprinkle the brown sugar on the slices as you go, being sure to get a little bit on each one. Let the fruit sit at room temperature for at least 10 minutes, or up to 2 hours.

Meanwhile, fill a large bowl with water. Cut the pomegranate into quarters (rinse the board off immediately afterward so that the juice doesn't stain it). Working with one section at a time, submerge the pomegranate in the bowl of water and dig the seeds out with your fingers. This keeps the bright red juice from spraying around your kitchen and also helps you separate the seeds from the white pithy membrane, as those bits will float and can easily be scooped off, while the seeds will sink. Once you've gotten all of the seeds loose, drain them and transfer them to a paper towel to dry a bit.

Scatter the seeds and pistachios over the sliced citrus. Serve immediately.

SPIN-OFFS

POMEGRANATE SEEDS ADD A POP OF TART, BRIGHT FLAVOR wherever they go. I especially love them in a colorful salsa made with chopped yellow cherry tomatoes mixed with lime juice, chopped cilantro, and very thinly sliced jalapeños. Great on grilled fish!

TRY FREEZING POMEGRANATE SEEDS and then dropping them into champagne glasses before pouring in any type of sparkling wine. Not only do they look pretty, but they also keep the wine nice and cold.

Blood Orange Granita with Mascarpone

SERVES 4

The first time I made this was for a dinner party I was hired to cook. I had never worked in my clients' kitchen before, so I made sure the menu didn't rely on equipment that might not be there or on any other hard-to-plan-for variables. To finish the meal, I settled on the simplest dessert I know—granita, a.k.a. frozen orange juice (**small victory** no. 1: Go for anything with a single ingredient and little effort). On that particular night, I figured I'd go a little "fancy" and use blood orange juice, which has a color nearly as striking as its deep flavor. I poured the juice into a large baking dish and stuck it in the freezer the minute I got into the kitchen (**small victory** no. 2: Make dessert ahead of the rest of the meal so you don't have to think about it). By the time the dinner guests were enjoying their spaghetti and meatballs, the mixture had frozen and I could scrape it with the tines of a fork, watching it turn into snow. To serve it, I alternated spoonfuls of the granita with mascarpone that had been thinned out with heavy cream (don't you just love the idea of thinning out one fat with another?). After the borderline-heavy meal, the dessert was a surprising and refreshing finish. Ina Garten, who had been one of the dinner guests, came into the kitchen and told me she loved it and that it reminded her of the Orange Julius drinks she used to enjoy when she was a teenager. Hearing that, I just about melted.

2 cups [480 ml] fresh blood orange juice or regular orange juice

½ cup [120 g] mascarpone

½ cup [120 ml] heavy cream

Pour the orange juice into a baking dish or another large container that fits comfortably in your freezer. Freeze until solid—at least 2 hours, or up to overnight (but not much longer, or else the flavor won't be as present).

Once the mixture is firm, scrape it with the tines of a fork so that it breaks into a zillion flakes. (You can do this up to a few hours in advance, and then just store it in the freezer.)

Just before serving, in a small bowl, stir together the mascarpone and heavy cream.

Alternate layers of the granita and the cream mixture in small glasses or side-by-side in small bowls, working quickly so that the granita doesn't melt too much. Serve immediately.

SPIN-OFFS

TRY ANY FRUIT JUICE in place of the blood orange juice. Grapefruit is particularly refreshing.

MAKE A TOMATO JUICE GRANITA, serve it with grated horseradish and a little vodka, and call it a Cold-Blooded Mary.

MAKE AN ARNOLD PALMER GRANITA—freeze equal parts lemonade and iced tea, and serve with a few dashes of bitters.

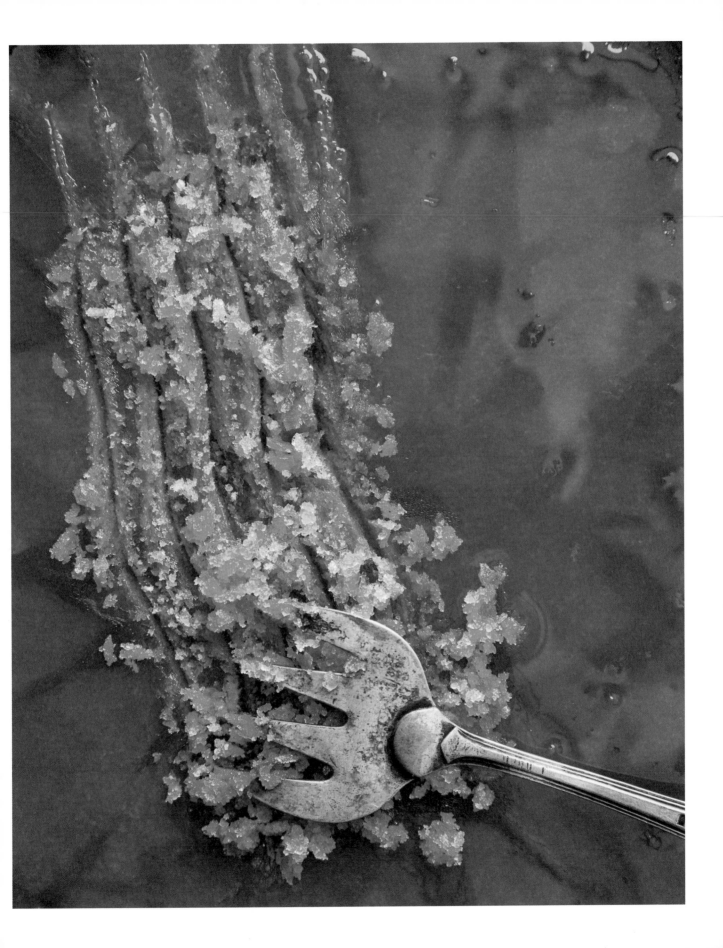

Coconut "Ice Cream" with Lime + Mango

SERVES 4, MAKES 1 PT [480 ML]

I like to make sure that everyone sitting at my table can enjoy whatever I am making. When you usually find yourself the exception (*I'm gluten-free! Vegan! No sugar!*), it's nice to have the same thing on your plate (or in your bowl) as everyone else. That's why this ice cream is so perfect—it's great for those who are gluten-free, sugar-free, and completely vegan and you don't even need to mention any of that. You can just call it *good*. Democracy is one **small victory** for sure, but so is the method: Freezing coconut milk (sweetened with maple syrup and flavored with lime) in ice-cube trays and then popping the cubes into a food processor means you can have a creamy dessert that's the texture of soft serve without making custard or owning (or taking out) a clunky ice-cream machine.

One 13½-oz [400-ml] can full-fat coconut milk, shaken

¼ cup [60 ml] maple syrup

Grated zest and juice of 1 lime

Pinch of kosher salt

1 ripe, juicy mango, peeled, pitted, and diced

In a small bowl, whisk together the coconut milk, maple syrup, lime zest, lime juice, and salt. Transfer the mixture into a pitcher or measuring cup with a spout, and divide it evenly among all of the wells of two standard ice-cube trays. It's okay if the wells aren't full—actually, it's better, as the ice cream will be easier to process if the cubes are smaller.

Freeze the mixture until solid, 4 hours. (You can make the cubes up to 1 week in advance. Once they are frozen, simply pop them into an airtight bag and store them in the freezer—leaving them exposed in the trays will compromise the flavor.)

Put the frozen cubes in the bowl of a food processor and pulse until roughly chopped, then let the machine run until the mixture is smooth and the texture of soft serve. Stop to scrape the sides of the bowl a few times during processing. If the mixture isn't getting smooth within 1 to 2 minutes, let it sit for a few minutes so that the coconut mixture defrosts slightly and then process again. (At this point, you can pack the ice cream into an airtight container and freeze for up to 1 week. Let sit at room temperature for about 10 minutes before serving.)

Scoop the ice cream into serving bowls and top with the mango. Serve immediately.

SPIN-OFFS

THROW SOME FROZEN FRUIT (raspberries, pineapple, mango, and cherries all work really well) into the food processor along with the coconut milk mixture.

TRY ALMOND MILK instead of coconut milk (leave out the lime and add a pinch of ground cinnamon).

For a nut-free version, use **RICE MILK** instead of coconut milk.

Peach + Bourbon Milkshakes

SERVES 4

I was once tasked with cooking an important dinner and the pressure in the kitchen was palpable. In an attempt to cross something off my list, I had decided to make dessert ahead of time and thought homemade peach ice cream, spiked with a bit of bourbon, would be a major hit—familiar but with a little edge, my favorite kind of thing to make and eat. Except later, when I took the lid off the container and dug my trusty scoop into the ice cream, the scoop immediately sank to the bottom. I, myself, just about froze. In retrospect, I realize I had added a bit too much bourbon (is there really such a thing?), so the ice cream could never freeze solid. As it luckily goes sometimes when the stress barometer is high and options are few and far between, a little lightbulb went off in my head. No one knew I had planned to serve ice cream, so I just switched the bowls for glasses, got some straws, and served great milkshakes. **Small victory**: Failure is sometimes just an invitation for a new name.

---

5 ripe peaches, peeled (see Note), pitted, and sliced, or one and a half 10-oz [284-g] bags frozen peaches, still frozen for an extra thick shake, defrosted for a smoother shake

1 Tbsp fresh lemon juice

1 tsp vanilla extract

¼ cup [60 ml] whole milk

½ cup [120 ml] bourbon

3 Tbsp honey

Pinch of kosher salt

1 pt [480 ml] vanilla ice cream, slightly softened

Put four tall glasses in the freezer to chill.

In a blender, combine the peaches, lemon juice, vanilla, milk, bourbon, honey, and salt and puree until smooth. Add the ice cream and blend until smooth.

Divide the milkshake among the chilled glasses. Serve immediately, with both straws and long spoons.

NOTE: To peel the peaches, first score them on the bottom with a paring knife (make a little X) and then drop them into boiling water until the skin starts to break, about 1 minute. Immediateley plunge them into ice water to stop them from cooking and to make them easy to handle. Drain them and peel with a paring knife.

SPIN-OFFS

Blend frozen strawberries and/or raspberries with some honey and rosé wine. Serve in chilled glasses for the most **ELEGANT SLUSHIE** around.

FOR A BOOZY LEMON FIZZ, serve scoops of lemon sorbet in juice glasses and top off with Prosecco. Serve with straws and spoons.

FOR AN UPDATED RUM RAISIN-ISH MILKSHAKE, blend vanilla ice cream with pitted dates, grated orange zest, and rum.

Happy Wife, Happy Life Chocolate Cake

MAKES ONE TWO-LAYER 8-IN [20-CM] CAKE

This is Grace's favorite cake and I bake it often for that reason. A mash-up of recipes inspired by my favorite food blogs, it's incredibly easy to make and is decadent without being too heavy or too sweet. The frosting, a total **small victory** because of its simplicity and ingenuity, was inspired by a post that I bookmarked years ago from Deb Perelman's Smitten Kitchen. To make it, you simply whisk together room temperature sour cream with melted chocolate and a little maple syrup. How smart is that? The cake itself, a riff on one from Jenny Rosenstrach's Dinner: A Love Story, is a classic "dump cake," (the worst name ever, I know), which means you put everything in one bowl and stir it together. **Small victory**: No huge mess, no creaming butter and sugar, no fuss whatsoever. I use raspberry jam in between the layers, but you could swap it for any flavor jam you like (or make an extra batch of frosting and use that). A great sum of simple parts, this is my kind of baking. This cake is great right away after you assemble it, but is truly at its best served cold out of the refrigerator.

CAKE

1¼ cups [150 g] all-purpose flour

1 cup [200 g] sugar

¾ cup [75 g] Dutch-processed cocoa powder (such as Guittard or Dröste), sifted if lumpy

1 tsp baking soda

1 tsp baking powder

½ tsp kosher salt

8 Tbsp [110 g] unsalted butter, melted and cooled

2 eggs, lightly beaten

1 cup [240 ml] strong black coffee, at room temperature

1 cup [240 ml] buttermilk or plain yogurt

1 tsp vanilla extract

FROSTING

¾ cup [130 g] semisweet chocolate chips or roughly chopped semisweet chocolate

¾ cup [180 ml] sour cream, at room temperature

1 Tbsp maple syrup

½ cup [160 g] raspberry jam (seeded or seedless, whatever your preference)

Raspberries for serving (optional)

TO MAKE THE CAKE: Preheat your oven to 350°F [180°C]. Use your hands to butter the bottom and sides of two 8-in [20-cm] cake pans, then line the bottom of each with a circle of parchment paper (see headnote, page 229). For good measure, butter the parchment paper. Set the pans aside.

In a large bowl, whisk together the flour, sugar, cocoa powder, baking soda, baking powder, and salt. Add the melted butter, eggs, coffee, buttermilk, and vanilla and whisk until the batter is smooth. Divide the batter evenly among the prepared cake pans (my friend Larry suggests using a cup measure to be accurate).

Bake until the cakes are firm to the touch and a toothpick inserted in the centers comes out clean, about 30 minutes. Transfer the cakes, still in their pans, to a wire rack and let them cool completely. Once cool, use a dinner knife to loosen the edges of the cakes from the pans and invert them onto your work surface (you might need to give the pan a little whack). Peel off and discard the parchment.

TO MAKE THE FROSTING: Meanwhile, bring a small pot of water to a boil and then lower the heat to a simmer. Put the chocolate chips in a large stainless-steel or heatproof glass bowl and set it over the pot (the water should not touch the bowl—if it does, simply pour some out). Stir until the chocolate is melted. (Alternatively, you can melt the chocolate in a microwave in 15-second increments, stirring between increments.) Remove from the heat and whisk in the sour cream and maple syrup. The frosting should be smooth and quite silky. Refrigerate the frosting until the cakes have cooled. It will thicken as it cools (a good thing).

Once the cakes are cool, put one on a serving platter upside-down so that the flat side is facing up. Spread the jam over the top. Put the second cake on top of the jam-slathered cake, again flat-side up—this way you get a nice flat top. (If the jam makes the layers slip and slide a bit, use a couple of skewers to hold the layers together while you frost the sides and then remove the skewers to frost the top). Using a small offset spatula or a dinner knife, spread the frosting all over the sides and top of the cake. There's no need to be perfect with this; I like it kind of rustic looking. But if you're more of a type-A person, go ahead and smooth the top and sides (and you could even stick strips of parchment paper under the bottom of the cake before frosting it to keep your serving platter clean). Whatever makes you happy.

Let the cake sit for about 1 hour before serving. There's something about letting each element get to know the others that serves this cake very well. In fact, I prefer to make it the day before and refrigerate it overnight, and serve it cold. Either way, slice and serve with some fresh raspberries alongside if you'd like.

NOTE: If you only own a single cake pan, fear not! Simply pour the batter into the pan and bake it until a toothpick tests clean (it will take 10 to 15 minutes longer in the oven than the two separate layers). Once the cake cools completely, use a serrated knife to cut it into two layers. Voilà.

SPIN-OFFS

FOR CUPCAKES, distribute the cake batter in a standard 12-well muffin tin lined with paper liners and bake until firm to the touch, about 20 minutes. Top with raspberry jam and/or the frosting.

FOR VANILLA CAKE, leave out the cocoa powder and coffee.

FOR THE QUICKEST VANILLA FROSTING, whip ½ cup [120 ml] heavy cream until stiff peaks form and fold in ½ cup [120 ml] room-temperature sour cream. Sweeten with powdered sugar and add a splash of vanilla extract.

Afternoon Cake

MAKES ONE 8-IN [20-CM] CAKE

This not-too-sweet, very simple cake is perfect for that "it's four o'clock and I need a little something with a cup of coffee" moment. Fragrant with orange, rich with ground nuts, and not at all dry since there's plenty of olive oil, the cake needs nothing, though a spoonful of crème fraîche on top of a slice certainly wouldn't be unwelcome. The only thing more satisfying than eating this cake is making it—it is seriously easy and therefore hard for even a complete baking novice to screw up. It's also one of those baked goods that just gets better if it sits for a few hours, even a day or two. The **small victory** is not just having a straightforward cake up your sleeve but also embracing parchment paper, one of my favorite kitchen tools.

To cut a piece of parchment paper into a perfect circle to fit your cake pan (which is like an insurance policy that your cake won't stick), rip off a piece of parchment that's a bit bigger than your pan. Fold it into a square, then fold it in half to make a triangle and fold it in half again to make an even more narrow triangle. Place the tip of the triangle in the center of the pan. Use scissors to cut off the excess parchment that extends beyond the sides of the pan. Unfold the parchment and, voilà, you have a perfect circle that fits into your pan. Another **small victory** for parchment? Put a piece on your work surface and use it almost like a place-mat when you are measuring a dry ingredient like flour. Then you can pick up the edges of the paper when you're done and scoot the excess flour back into its container.

1 cup [120 g] all-purpose flour	2 eggs	Grated zest of 1 orange, plus ¼ cup [60 ml] fresh orange juice
½ cup [50 g] finely ground nuts (see Note)	½ cup [120 ml] extra-virgin olive oil	Powdered sugar for dusting
1½ tsp baking powder	½ cup [100 g] granulated sugar	
½ tsp kosher salt	½ tsp vanilla extract	

Preheat your oven to 350°F [180°C]. Use your hands to butter the bottom and sides of an 8-in [20-cm] cake pan, then line the bottom with a circle of parchment paper. For good measure, butter the parchment paper. Set the pan aside.

In a medium bowl, whisk together the flour, ground nuts, baking powder, and salt.

In a large bowl, whisk the eggs until the whites and yolks are fully combined. Add the olive oil and granulated sugar and whisk until the sugar is dissolved (test by rubbing some of the mixture between two fingers). Whisk in the vanilla, orange zest, and orange juice. Whisk in the flour mixture.

(Continued)

Pour the batter into the prepared pan, being sure to use a rubber spatula to get it all out of the bowl. Hold the pan just a little bit above the counter and then drop it on the counter to eliminate any air bubbles.

Bake until the cake is beautifully golden brown and a toothpick inserted in the center comes out clean, 25 to 30 minutes. Transfer the cake, still in its pan, to a wire rack and let it cool completely. Once cool, use a dinner knife to loosen the edges of the cake from the pan and invert it onto your work surface (you might need to give the pan a little whack). Peel off and discard the parchment. Invert the cake one more time onto a serving platter so the flat side is down and the domed side is up.

Just before serving, dust the cake with powdered sugar.

NOTE: Any nut works well in this cake. To make ground nuts, just put whichever type of nut you'd like (I've made this cake successfully with walnuts, almonds, hazelnuts, and pistachios, and am sure pecans and pine nuts would also be great) in the food processor and blitz until they're as fine as cornmeal. Or use a mortar and pestle. Or purchase ground nuts, which often go by the name "meal" or "flour" as in "almond meal" or "almond flour." For a nut-free cake, simply omit the ground nuts and add an additional ½ cup [60 g] flour.

SPIN-OFFS

Feel free to **SUBSTITUTE ANY CITRUS** in place of the orange. Clementine, tangerine, blood orange, and grapefruit zest all work very well.

FOR A LEMON–POPPY SEED CAKE, use lemon zest and juice instead of orange and add 1 Tbsp poppy seeds to the batter.

If you're using ground almonds, add ½ tsp **ALMOND EXTRACT** to the batter for a more intense almond flavor.

Just before you put the cake in the oven, dot the top with ¼ cup [80 g] **RASPBERRY JAM** and use a fork or the tip of a paring knife to swirl in the jam.

Apricot Upside-Down Skillet Cake

SERVES 8

This recipe is for my dad who asked me to include something that he could flip over—how could I resist a request like that? I came up with this upside-down cake for him, as he is a great cook but an uneasy baker who owns neither a mixer nor a cake pan. This requires a single bowl and a well-seasoned cast-iron skillet (which, incidentally, could be swapped for a buttered cake pan lined with parchment paper). A caramelized, fruit-heavy cake that looks impressive, this is about as easy to prepare as a boxed mix and doesn't involve any difficult techniques like creaming butter, folding ingredients, whipping egg whites, or making caramel. For all of the beginner bakers out there, here is a **small victory**, turned upside-down. If your apricots (which could easily be substituted with any stone fruit) are a little underripe, that's okay. The fruit will get rich and concentrated as it bakes.

11 Tbsp [150 g] butter, at room temperature

Packed 3 Tbsp [35 g] dark brown sugar

Kosher salt

1 lb [455 g] fresh apricots, pitted and cut into thick wedges

¾ cup [150 g] granulated sugar

2 eggs

½ cup [120 ml] whole milk

1 tsp vanilla extract

2 tsp baking powder

2 cups [240 g] all-purpose flour

Vanilla ice cream, whipped cream, or crème fraîche for serving (optional)

Put a large piece of aluminum foil, to catch any drips, on the oven rack below the one you're going to bake the cake on. Preheat your oven to 350°F [180°C]. Lightly butter the sides of an 8-in [20-cm] cast-iron skillet with the butter wrapper (don't worry about the bottom, it will get plenty of butter in a moment).

In a large bowl, use your hands to work 3 Tbsp of the butter together with the brown sugar and ½ tsp salt. Spread the mixture on the bottom of the skillet. Set the bowl aside.

Arrange the apricot wedges in a single layer on top of the butter mixture. You could do this in concentric circles if you'd like, but I like it slightly more human and haphazard. You might feel like you have too many apricots, but keep in mind that they will release water as they cook and shrink, so squeeze all the slices in there.

In the same bowl, using a whisk, combine the remaining 8 Tbsp [110 g] butter with the granulated sugar until smooth. Whisk in the eggs until smooth. Whisk in the milk and vanilla. At this point, the mixture might look a little curdled (especially if your milk is cold, which will harden the butter). No worries! I just wanted to mention so you didn't think you did anything wrong because you absolutely did not. Whisk in ½ tsp salt and the baking powder. Whisk in the flour until just combined. Use a rubber spatula to gently scrape the batter over the apricots, being cautious not to disrupt the apricots too much (you want them to stay on the bottom of the pan and not get mixed into the batter).

(Continued)

Bake until the cake is golden brown and a toothpick inserted in the center (just through the cake, not all the way down to the apricots) comes out clean, about 45 minutes. Let the cake cool in the skillet for 30 minutes (I like to set it on the stove top so that air can circulate, or you can use a cooling rack if you have one). Use a dinner knife to loosen the cake from the skillet. Put a serving dish on top of the pan and put one hand on top of the dish and hold the handle of the skillet with your other hand (it should be cool enough to grab now, but if not use a towel). Carefully but assertively turn the whole thing over to invert the cake onto the serving dish. If any of the brown sugar mixture and/or apricots stick to the pan, simply use a knife or a spoon to dislodge it/them and put them back on top of the cake.

Serve warm or at room temperature with vanilla ice cream on each serving, if you'd like.

SPIN-OFFS

INSTEAD OF APRICOTS, use 1 lb [455 g] pitted and sliced plums, nectarines, or peaches. Or try pitted and halved cherries or an equal amount of blueberries, raspberries, and/or blackberries. Or sliced and cored pears. Or a mix of fruit. You get the idea.

MIX UP THE CAKE—feel free to swap up to ¾ cup [90 g] of the flour for whole-wheat flour, almond or walnut meal (or any nut flour), or coconut flour. You could also use nut milk, rice milk, or coconut milk in place of the whole milk.

IF YOU LOVE ALMOND-FLAVORED CAKE, use ½ tsp almond extract in place of the vanilla extract (it's stronger than vanilla so you only need half the amount). This is especially good with cherries or pears on the bottom (or is it the top???).

Berry + Buttermilk Cobbler

SERVES 8

The main **small victory** here is having a really delicious, incredibly easy dessert up your sleeve. Plus, all you need is one baking dish and one bowl (and a couple of measuring devices). To save on cleanup, I melt the butter right in my measuring glass in the microwave and then just add the buttermilk to it (a very **small victory**, but a victory nonetheless). The cobbler topping could be used on top of any fruit mixture, and the topping itself can be varied—check out the Spin-Offs for more ideas. One final bit of advice: Don't use a smaller baking dish (such as a pie plate) because the filling-topping ratio will be way off. If you don't have a 9-by-13-in [23-by-33-cm] baking dish, use the largest skillet you have, preferably one that's 12 in [30.5 cm] in diameter.

2 lb [910 g] mixed berries, rinsed (strawberries are not ideal because they contain so much water)

2 Tbsp fresh lemon juice

½ cup [100 g] sugar

Kosher salt

2 Tbsp cornstarch

1 cup [120 g] all-purpose flour

1 tsp baking powder

4 Tbsp [55 g] unsalted butter, melted

½ cup [120 ml] buttermilk

Vanilla ice cream for serving

Preheat your oven to 375°F [190°C]. Lightly butter the bottom of a 9-by-13-in [23-by-33-cm] baking dish with the butter wrapper.

Put the berries in the prepared dish and drizzle with the lemon juice. Add ¼ cup [50 g] of the sugar and a generous pinch of salt. Use your hands to combine all of the ingredients. (Taste the berries to check the sugar and lemon levels. If you're at the height of berry season, they should taste perfect—sweet enough for dessert, but cut with enough lemon so not too sweet.

If you're making this with not-amazing berries, fear not . . . just add a little more sugar to taste.) Mix in the cornstarch and set aside.

In a large bowl, combine the remaining ¼ cup [50 g] sugar, the flour, baking powder, and ½ tsp salt. Whisk everything together. Drizzle the butter and buttermilk over the dry ingredients and stir with a wooden spoon until a shaggy dough forms.

(Continued)

Use two teaspoons to dollop the dough evenly over the berries. Put the baking dish on a parchment-lined baking sheet to catch any drips and make clean-up a breeze.

Bake the cobbler until the topping is dark golden brown and the berries are bubbling, about 1 hour. Let stand at room temperature for about 15 minutes before serving so that the juices collect themselves and don't run everywhere.

Serve the cobbler warm with vanilla ice cream.

SPIN-OFFS

Substitute 2 lb [910 g] of just about **ANY TYPE OF FRUIT** for the berries, or use other fruit in combination with the berries. I like a mixture of sliced nectarines (I don't bother peeling them) with blueberries. Or try all fresh cherries (pitted) when they're in season (a mix of sweet and sour cherries is terrific). A plum and blackberry cobbler is lovely, as is a fresh apricot and raspberry one. Whatever you choose, keep the lemon juice, sugar, cornstarch, and pinch of salt.

The **COBBLER TOPPING** can be made with all-purpose gluten-free flour. Or use ½ cup [60 g] whole-wheat flour in place of half of the all-purpose flour. Or try substituting ¼ cup [30 g] of the flour with cornmeal or almond meal. Almond meal goes really nicely with cherries—and you can even add a couple drops of almond extract to the topping, along with a handful of sliced or chopped almonds, if you go down that nutty road.

Feel-Better-Soon Cookies

MAKES ABOUT 36 COOKIES

Fact: There's comfort in cookies. Once, when a friend had gone through something really tough and it was one of those times where there's not much you can do except be there, I decided to make some cookies for my visit. I wasn't sure if she'd want something with chocolate, or something on the oaty spectrum, or maybe dried fruit? That indecision became a more-is-more moment, and I just threw it all into the bowl. I now love these little-bit-of-everything cookies; they hit all the right spots. There are two **small victories** here. *First*, if you make cookies a lot, get yourself a mini ice-cream scoop so that you can easily and efficiently scoop cookies that are all the same size (I'm not usually one for gadgets, but this is worthwhile, and please get one with a little lever so that the dough pops out easily). *Second*, whenever you go to the trouble of making cookie dough, double the batch and freeze half of the portioned cookie dough on a baking sheet until the dough is firm, then stow the unbaked cookies in an airtight container or bag in the freezer so that you can bake a few at a moment's notice for fresh, warm cookies anytime. Or you can just eat the frozen cookie dough (a totally acceptable choice).

16 Tbsp [220 g] unsalted butter, at room temperature

Packed 1 cup [200 g] dark brown sugar

1 tsp vanilla extract

2 eggs, beaten

1 tsp baking soda

½ tsp kosher salt

1½ cups [180 g] all-purpose flour

1 cup [100 g] rolled oats

½ cup [90 g] semisweet chocolate chips or chopped-up dark chocolate bar

½ cup [80 g] dried fruit, chopped if large (apricots, cherries, and/or raisins are all great)

Position racks in the upper and lower thirds of the oven and preheat your oven to 350°F [180°C]. Line two baking sheets with parchment paper and set aside.

In a large bowl and using a wooden spoon, beat together the butter and brown sugar, really whipping them so that the mixture becomes light and creamy. If it's hard to get the butter going at first, get in there with your hands and squish it until it softens (it's messy but kinda fun). Add the vanilla, eggs, baking soda, and salt and stir everything until the mixture is uniform. Stir in the flour until just combined, then gently stir in the oats, chocolate chips, and dried fruit.

Using a small ice-cream soup, drop mounds of the dough onto the prepared baking sheets, spacing them about 2 in [5 cm] apart.

Bake the cookies until they're lightly browned, about 10 minutes if you like them quite soft or up to 15 minutes if you prefer them a bit darker and crisper. (My friend Julie says 8 minutes is great if you like them underdone.) However long you bake them, halfway through baking, switch the bottom baking sheet to the top rack and vice versa, so that the cookies bake evenly.

Transfer the cookies to a wire rack to cool completely before eating—if you have that kind of patience. Store in an airtight container at room temperature for up to 3 days.

(Continued)

SPIN-OFFS

FOR A SORTA NUTELLA-EQSUE EFFECT, substitute chopped toasted hazelnuts for the cherries and apricots.

TRY PISTACHIOS instead of chocolate chips, and all dried cherries in the fruit department.

SUBSTITUTE GROUND NUTS FOR THE OATS. Walnuts work especially well, and you can just grind them in your food processor—or put them in a plastic bag and bash them with a rolling pin or a heavy pot.

FOR CHOCOLATE-PEANUT COOKIES, use ½ cup [100 g] chopped, salted peanuts instead of dried fruit and add 3 Tbsp creamy peanut butter to the batter.

FOR GORP COOKIES, use ½ cup [100 g] salted peanuts instead of the chocolate chips and use all raisins in the dried fruit category.

FOR BREAKFAST COOKIES, use granola instead of rolled oats. Keep or skip the chocolate depending on what type of morning person you are.

Hope + Winky's Cookies

MAKES 15 COOKIES

My dogs, Hope and Winky, like many dogs, are nuts for peanut butter, and every now and then, when I'm feeling especially domestic and maternal in a canine sort of way, I'll make them these treats. Every ingredient included is beneficial. The peanut butter is packed with protein, the olive oil gives dogs' coats a good shine, and the oats and cornmeal are full of fiber. I'm not going to lie—I've tried these and they're actually pretty good! If you don't have your own furry friend, you can take a doggy bag (couldn't resist) of these to your nearest and dearest pup. The **small victory** here is sharing the love with *every* member of the family!

½ cup [130 g] smooth peanut butter

¼ cup [60 ml] olive oil

½ cup [120 ml] chicken or beef stock or water

½ cup [50 g] rolled oats

1 cup [140 g] cornmeal

Pinch of kosher salt

Preheat your oven to 350°F [180°C]. Line a baking sheet with parchment paper and set aside.

In a large bowl, combine the peanut butter, olive oil, chicken stock, oats, cornmeal, and salt. Stir together—vigorously!—with a wooden spoon until a stiff dough forms. Using your hands, roll the dough into golf ball–size balls and transfer to the prepared baking sheet, leaving 2 in [5 cm] between each treat. Press each one gently to flatten it into a circle.

Bake the treats until they smell nutty, look very dry, and are lightly browned, about 20 minutes. Cool completely on the pan (otherwise, they will crumble into a zillion pieces).

Store in an airtight container at room temperature for up to 2 weeks. Sit and stay before eating!

SPIN-OFF

IN THE SUMMER, try mixing one part plain yogurt with one part water and freeze the mixture in ice-cube trays for high-calcium treats that will help cool off your dog.

A FEW DRINKS +
SOME THINGS
TO KEEP ON HAND

Ginger + Honey Arnold Palmers

SERVES 4

My go-to drink all summer long is an Arnold Palmer, and I especially love it with a hit of spicy fresh ginger. A **small victory** here is all about peeling the ginger. Instead of a vegetable peeler or a paring knife (which both usually end up taking off a lot of the ginger itself), use a spoon to scrape the piece of ginger. The spoon will take off the brown skin and nothing else. Another **small victory**, how to make iced tea quickly when you don't already have it brewed, is rooted in impatience: Brew an extra-strong cup of tea and dilute it with ice.

1 cup [240 ml] boiling water

1 Tbsp minced peeled fresh ginger

¼ cup [85 g] honey

3 English Breakfast or other black tea tea bags

¼ cup [60 ml] fresh lemon juice

4 cups [720 g] ice cubes, plus more for serving

In a large bowl, whisk together the boiling water, ginger, and honey. Add the tea bags and let sit until the tea has infused the mixture, 3 to 5 minutes. Remove and discard the tea bags. Stir in the lemon juice and ice cubes.

Much of the ice will melt, which is intentional since it will perfectly dilute the strong tea.

Fill four tall glasses with more ice and fill with tea. Serve immediately.

SPIN-OFFS

Instead of black tea with lemon, try **RED ZINGER OR HIBISCUS TEA** with fresh lime or grapefruit juice. So refreshing!

Swap the black tea for **CHAI TEA** and use milk instead of lemon juice.

Trade black tea for **EARL GREY** and use fresh orange juice instead of the lemon juice.

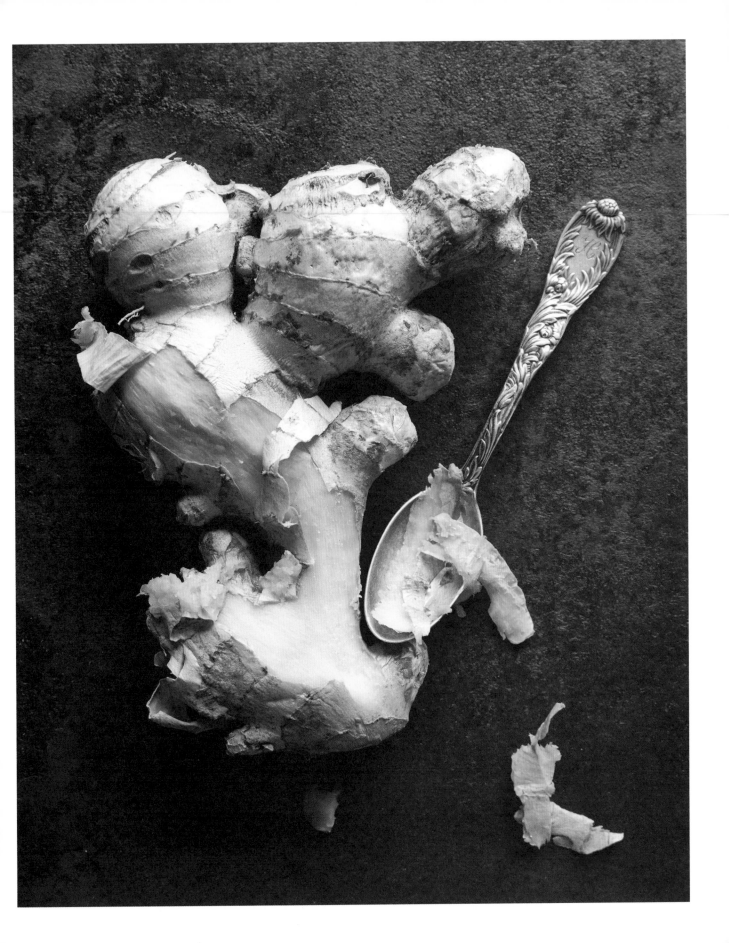

Whiskey + Maple Syrup Sour

Confession: I hate cocktail shakers. In my experience, they either leak when you shake them or the two parts seem to glue themselves together. In fact, I once splurged on a shaker with my initials engraved on it and it very soon ended up in a recycling plant somewhere because after trying every trick in the book, it was still stuck. For life. Nowadays I just whisk the ingredients together in a bowl and pour the mixture over ice. **Small victory**: Trade your fussy shaker for a whisk and never let a cocktail stress you out again.

1 Tbsp maple syrup

2 Tbsp fresh lemon juice

3 Tbsp whiskey

A few dashes of Angostura bitters

Ice cubes for serving

¼ cup [60 ml] seltzer water

In a medium bowl, whisk together the maple syrup, lemon juice, whiskey, and bitters.

Fill a highball glass to the top with ice and pour the whiskey mixture into it. Top with the seltzer and give it a stir. Serve immediately.

SPIN-OFFS

FOR THE BEST, SIMPLEST MARGARITA, whisk together the juice of one lime with 1 Tbsp agave nectar and 3 Tbsp good-quality tequila. Serve over plenty of ice.

FOR AN EXCELLENT COSMO-POLITAN (which my dad was drinking before *Sex and the City*, a fact I love), whisk together 3 Tbsp vodka, 2 tsp Cointreau, 1 Tbsp cranberry juice, and 2 tsp fresh lime juice. Add a handful of ice cubes and stir until the drink is nice and cold, then strain it into a chilled glass.

FOR A TOM COLLINS–ISH DRINK, whisk together 3 Tbsp gin, 1 Tbsp lime juice, and 1 Tbsp sugar or honey until the latter dissolves. Pour into a tall glass filled with ice. Top off with seltzer, stir, and serve.

Paloma Slushies

I love a classic margarita (see Spin-Offs, page 247), but I hate making more than one or two at a time. For a group of friends, enter the paloma: A mix of fresh lime and grapefruit juices and tequila, it's the perfect drink for a crowd, especially because you can easily make big batches without squeezing a gazillion limes and there's no need to mix individual drinks. The **small victory** here, beyond embracing pitcher drinks for a crowd, is peeling the limes and then putting them in the blender whole instead of juicing them. This way you get more bang for your buck per lime—plus, it's an excuse to make the drink into slushies. I like to add a bit of salt to the actual drink rather than salt the rims of the glasses, mostly because it's a lot less work! It also helps the lime and grapefruit taste a bit more pronounced (I like to think of salt here like an exclamation point).

4 limes	1 cup [240 ml] grapefruit juice	½ tsp kosher salt
¼ cup [85 g] honey	1 cup [240 ml] silver tequila	4 cups [720 g] ice cubes

Peel three of the limes by lopping off the tops and the bottoms of each one, cutting just deep enough to expose the fruit beneath the pith. Stand each lime on your cutting board so that one of the cut sides is sitting on the board—it should be nice and steady. Cut the remaining peel and pith off the limes in wide strips, working your way around the fruit, so that you end up with a complete, peeled piece of fruit. Discard the peels or reserve them for another use (I like to simmer them with water and brown sugar, then strain the liquid and serve it over ice . . . a little tequila mixed in wouldn't hurt one bit.) Cut the remaining lime into thin slices.

Put the peeled limes in a blender; add the honey, grapefruit juice, tequila, and salt; and blend until combined. Add the ice and let the machine run until the ice is totally blitzed and the mixture is very smooth.

Pour into four glasses and garnish with the lime slices. Serve immediately.

SPIN-OFFS

SUBSTITUTE POMEGRANATE JUICE for the grapefruit juice. Not only is the resulting drink a stunning color, it's wonderfully tart.

FOR HIBISCUS PALOMAS, put three hibiscus tea bags into 1 cup [240 ml] boiling water, along with 2 Tbsp agave nectar, and let cool to room temperature. Discard the tea bags. Substitute the strong tea for the grapefruit juice. Gorgeous!

FOR AN ALT-CITRUS PALOMA, substitute 1 cup [240 ml] fresh tangerine, blood orange, or clementine juice for the grapefruit juice.

Black Pepper Bloody Marys

SERVES 4

A couple of years ago, thanks to my friend Carla, I discovered the Unicorn mill (which really does live up to its name). I swear by it. One **small victory** here is not only landing on a not terribly expensive yet highly functioning pepper mill that will last a lifetime but also discovering how to fill it with peppercorns without having them go all over your counter. Simply pour a small handful of peppercorns onto a piece of paper and pick up the edges of the paper so that you essentially make a chute, allowing the peppercorns to easily enter the opening in the mill. Another **small victory** is to take a few minutes sometime to measure how many turns of your mill makes 1 tsp. Then write that on the mill itself so that you can always measure pepper easily (for the life of me I have no idea how to balance a measuring spoon and a pepper mill at the same time). All of this pepper talk brings me to these Bloody Marys that are heavy on the pepper, just the way I like them. Feel free to serve the vodka on the side, though, for friends who might not want any (and for friends who might want a lot).

4 cups [960 ml] tomato juice

2 Tbsp prepared horseradish

1 Tbsp Worcestershire sauce

¼ cup [60 ml] fresh lemon juice, plus 4 lemon wedges

1 cup [240 ml] vodka

1 tsp kosher salt

Coarsely ground black pepper

Ice cubes for serving

8 celery stalks

In a large pitcher, stir together the tomato juice, horseradish, Worcestershire, lemon juice, vodka, salt, and 2 tsp pepper.

Fill four tall glasses generously with ice and divide the tomato mixture among the glasses. Squeeze a lemon wedge into each drink and then drop the wedge into the glass. Garnish each drink with two celery stalks (this way, your drink counts as a health food!) and an extra grind of black pepper. Serve immediately.

SPIN-OFF

Try topping a **GIN AND TONIC** with a grind of black pepper. There's something special about juniper and black pepper together. In addition to the customary squeeze of lime, add a slice of cucumber or a long, slender cucumber spear to use as a swizzle stick.

Apple Cider + Ginger Beer Punch

SERVES 10

I like having friends over for drinks, but I hate making individual drinks for everyone. Punch to the rescue! The **small victory** here is all about the ice cubes. Freezing apple cider in ice-cube trays will keep a big batch of punch cold without diluting it. Note that the bourbon could easily be swapped for rum.

5 cups [1.2 L] apple cider

Three 12-oz [355-ml] bottles spicy ginger beer

2 cups [480 ml] bourbon

½ cup [120 ml] fresh lemon juice

Pour 2 cups [480 ml] of the apple cider into all of the wells of two standard ice-cube trays. Freeze until the cubes are solid, about 3 hours.

Meanwhile, in a large punch bowl or pitcher, stir together the remaining 3 cups [720 ml] apple cider with the ginger beer, bourbon, and lemon juice. Refrigerate until well chilled, about 2 hours.

To serve, pop the cider cubes out of the trays and add them to the punch to keep the punch nice and cold. Or put the ice cubes in glasses and pour the punch over.

SPIN-OFFS

Make a **SEA BREEZE PUNCH** (so old school, but very delicious) with 2 cups [480 ml] each orange juice, cranberry juice, and vodka and a 750-ml bottle of sparkling white wine. Chill it down with ice cubes you've made with orange juice (feel free to drop a few cranberries into the ice cubes for added pizzazz).

Make a large batch of **PIMM'S CUP**, and instead of fresh fruit and ice cubes use frozen fruit.

Make a large pitcher of **DARK-AND-STORMY COCKTAILS** and chill with ice cubes made with spicy ginger beer.

Make **RUM PUNCH** with ½ cup [120 ml] fresh lime juice, 1 cup [240 ml] pineapple juice, 1½ cups [360 ml] rum, and 2 cups [480 ml] sparkling white wine or spicy ginger beer. Make the ice cubes with pineapple juice, or just chill it down with chunks of frozen pineapple.

Roasted Hazelnut Milk with Cinnamon

MAKES 3½ CUPS [840 ML]

This drink came from a moment of desperation. My wife, Grace, loves a warm, milky coffee, and especially loves when there's a hint of hazelnut involved, but was told by her doctor that the acid in coffee was doing her no favors in the health department. I started making homemade nut milks for her so she could still have a mug of something comforting in the morning. Here, the **small victory** isn't just finding a substitution for coffee but also about roasting the hazelnuts before turning them into a creamy nut milk. The roasting amplifies their flavor and is a small step with a big impact—my favorite kind of small victory.

1 cup [140 g] raw whole hazelnuts

1 tsp ground cinnamon

¼ tsp ground nutmeg

½ tsp kosher salt

2 Tbsp honey

Preheat your oven to 400°F [200°C].

Put the hazelnuts on a baking sheet and roast, stirring them a couple of times, until they're dark brown and very fragrant, about 15 minutes.

Transfer the hot hazelnuts to a large bowl and add enough cold water to cover them. Cover the bowl tightly with plastic wrap and refrigerate for at least 2 hours, up to overnight.

Drain the hazelnuts and discard the soaking liquid. Put the hazelnuts into a blender, along with 4 cups [960 ml] fresh cold water, and blend until completely smooth. Pass the mixture through a nut milk bag or a fine-mesh sieve into a bowl (discard the contents of the bag/sieve, or try using it to exfoliate—seriously!). Whisk the cinnamon, nutmeg, salt, and honey into the milk. (Taste to make sure it's to your liking; feel free to add more spice or honey if you'd like.)

Store in an airtight container in the refrigerator for up to 4 days. Shake the container before enjoying the milk cold in tall glasses over ice or heating in a small pot over low heat and pouring into mugs. Either way, stir before serving.

SPIN-OFFS

FOR A DELICIOUS CHAI, iced or hot, combine three chai tea bags with 1 cup [240 ml] boiling water and let sit until it reaches room temperature. Discard the tea bags and mix the strong tea with a batch of the hazelnut milk. Serve cold over ice or warmed and in mugs.

FOR AN EASY SHAKE, combine 1 cup [240 ml] of the hazelnut milk with a diced banana and a handful of ice cubes in a blender and blend until smooth.

FOR GREAT VEGAN HOT CHOCOLATE, add 3 Tbsp cocoa powder to the hazelnut mixture. Warm the mixture in a pot and serve in mugs.

Cold Elixir

SERVES 4

Whenever I get a cold, I make endless batches of this mixture. While it might just be something to do while I'm sniffling and shuffling around in thick socks, I feel like ever since I've started drinking it, my colds don't last as long. **Small victory**: A natural remedy that works. I like to make this in a big batch and store it in the refrigerator (for up to 2 days) and heat it up as I need it. This is also good cold and served over ice (which can help soothe a sore throat).

3 cups [720 ml] boiling water

One 3-in [7.5-cm] piece fresh peeled ginger, crushed

¼ cup [60 ml] apple cider vinegar

¼ cup [85 g] honey (preferably raw)

Two 3-in [7.5-cm] cinnamon sticks, each broken in half

½ tsp cayenne pepper

Pinch of kosher salt

In a large bowl or jar, combine the water, ginger, vinegar, honey, cinnamon sticks, cayenne, and salt and stir until the honey dissolves. Strain and drink immediately.

SPIN-OFFS

FOR A FRESH GINGER STOMACHACHE SOOTHER, double the ginger and leave out the vinegar and cayenne.

I once read that **ROSEMARY CAN HELP WITH HEADACHES**. If you find yourself with a bad headache, try steeping a roughly chopped branch of rosemary in boiling water. Stir in a bit of honey, too.

FOR EXTRA VITAMIN C, add the grated zest and juice of a lemon and/or an orange to the elixir.

TO HELP YOU SLEEP, add a chamomile tea bag or a little dried lavender to the elixir. Leave out the cayenne.

Fromage Fort

MAKES 1 CUP [250 G]

Fromage fort translates literally to "strong cheese," and I could not be a bigger fan. It's an old-fashioned recipe that's all about using up the little leftover ends and bits of cheese kicking around in your refrigerator. By combining these scraps with garlic and a splash of white wine, you get a spreadable mixture that takes toast to another level and is probably the best thing that's ever happened to the inside of a baked potato. I remember seeing Jacques Pépin make this with Julia Child on television when I was a kid and thinking, *well, there's a brilliant man.* **Small victory**: The ends of a bunch of things can be the beginning of a great thing.

1 small garlic clove

8 oz [230 g] assorted pieces of cheese (cut soft cheeses into small pieces and coarsely grate hard cheeses)

1 Tbsp butter, at room temperature

3 Tbsp white wine

Kosher salt

Freshly ground black pepper

Toast or crackers for serving

With the food processor running, drop the garlic into the feed tube and process until finely chopped. Add the cheese, butter, and white wine and process until smooth. Season to taste with salt and pepper (the amounts will depend on the types of cheese you use).

Serve right away on toast or crackers, or store in an airtight container in the refrigerator for up to 1 week (it will harden a bit in the fridge, so bring it to room temperature before serving).

SPIN-OFFS

FOR PIMENTO FROMAGE FORT, use mostly cheddar cheese and add some diced jarred pimento peppers. Use a spoonful of cream cheese instead of the butter (or, who am I kidding, use both).

FOR BLUE CHEESE FROMAGE FORT, use all of your leftover blue cheeses and serve on toast. Top with a shaved celery salad that you've dressed with olive oil and lemon juice and then douse with hot sauce. Fancy Buffalo wing-style toast! Or serve the toasts alongside a Cobb or iceberg wedge salad.

FOR A SPECIAL SANDWICH, spread fromage fort on two slices of bread and sandwich with a layer of thinly sliced apples. Pan-fry as you would a grilled cheese sandwich. So strong and so good! Cut into small squares and enjoy with cocktails.

FOR A SOUP TOPPER, top slices of toasted baguette with fromage fort and run them under the broiler to get a little bit melty. Enjoy on top of bowls of onion soup or alongside tomato soup.

Cilantro + Scallion Sauce

MAKES ABOUT 1 CUP [240 ML]

I love a green, herby sauce. It can be as simple as chopped parsley mixed with olive oil and seasoned with salt or as complex as a basil pesto studded with ground nuts and cheese. This cilantro-scallion version is very much an ode to the scallion sauce from Great NY Noodle Town, a wonderful restaurant in New York City's Chinatown, where the door doesn't close until late at night (actually, early in the morning) and the duck is always crispy. The sauce, celebrated and copied by many chefs in New York and beyond, is a simple mix of thinly sliced scallions and minced ginger made spoonable with oil, soy sauce, and vinegar. I added cilantro because I love it, and the **small victory** here is all about cilantro stems—they have flavor, too! Don't discard them, just finely chop them (this goes for any recipes using soft, leafy herbs with tender stems like cilantro). The sauce is great on grilled or roast chicken, stirred into cooked rice or scrambled eggs, swirled into a bowl of noodle soup, or spooned over baked or stir-fried tofu and/or vegetables.

6 scallions, roots and dark green tops trimmed off, white and light green parts thinly sliced

½ cup [20 g] finely chopped fresh cilantro (including tender stems)

2 tsp minced peeled fresh ginger

¼ cup [60 ml] canola oil

1 Tbsp soy sauce

1 Tbsp rice wine vinegar or sherry vinegar

Kosher salt

In a bowl, combine the scallions, cilantro, ginger, canola oil, soy sauce, and vinegar and stir to mix. Season to taste with salt.

Serve immediately, or store in an airtight container in the refrigerator for up to 2 days. Bring to room temperature before serving.

SPIN-OFFS

FOR A MEDITERRANEAN HERB SAUCE, mix a large pile of finely chopped parsley with a tiny bit of minced garlic and some chopped capers. Add enough olive oil to make it spoonable and season with something acidic (a little fresh lemon juice or a few drops of vinegar will do) and salt. A few finely chopped olives would be nice in here, too.

FOR A KOREAN RENDITION, mix a large pile of finely chopped cilantro with a large pile of finely chopped cabbage kimchi and stir in some of the liquid from the kimchi jar. Season with toasted sesame oil and salt and throw in a few toasted sesame seeds, too.

FOR A WASTE-NOT, WANT-NOT VERSION, mix a large pile of finely chopped carrot tops and/or fennel fronds with some chopped parsley and a tiny bit of minced garlic. Add enough olive oil to make it spoonable and season with red wine vinegar and salt.

Arugula + Walnut Pesto

MAKES 1⅓ CUPS [300 G]

This recipe comes from my love of making pesto in big batches and freezing it in small portions so I don't have to defrost a big container just to use a little bit (plus, it's not great to keep refreezing things because they start to taste like . . . the freezer). The **small victory** here is using an ice-cube tray to facilitate the process. A cube of flavor at a moment's notice, how great is that? This arugula and walnut pesto, as delicious as tradtional pesto, not only takes well to freezing but it's also incredibly versatile. Toss it with a bowl of spaghetti or with roasted vegetables. In the summer, drizzle it over a platter of sliced tomatoes, or thin it with lemon juice for a salad dressing. Or mix it with an equal measure of crème fraîche, yogurt, or mayonnaise to make a dip for raw vegetables (which is a wonderful way to get kids to eat vegetables).

2 small garlic cloves

½ cup [60 g] raw walnuts

Packed 4 cups [80 g] baby arugula

½ cup plus 2 Tbsp [150 ml] extra-virgin olive oil

¼ cup [8 g] finely grated Parmesan cheese

Kosher salt

With the food processor running, drop the garlic into the feed tube and process until finely chopped. Add the walnuts and pulse until finely chopped. Add the arugula and, you guessed it, pulse until finely chopped. Add the olive oil and Parmesan and process, stopping to scrape the sides of the bowl as necessary, until everything is well combined. Season to taste with salt.

Use immediately, or divide evenly among the wells of a standard ice-cube tray. Freeze until the cubes are solid, about 2 hours. Then, pop the cubes into an airtight bag and store them in the freezer for up to 2 months.

SPIN-OFFS

FOR VEGAN PESTO, leave out the Parmesan and call it a day. Or, for a similar edge, add the grated zest of a lemon and/or some minced sun-dried tomatoes.

FOR A NUT-FREE PESTO, just leave out the walnuts.

FOR CLASSIC BASIL PESTO, swap fresh basil leaves for the arugula and pine nuts for the walnuts.

Chile, Lemon + Parsley Crème Fraîche

MAKES 1 CUP [240 ML]

I have always been obsessed with cookbooks. Even as a teenager, I couldn't go to bed without taking in a chapter or two. Imagining my grown-up life when I could prepare dinner parties of my own lulled me to sleep on a nightly basis. My favorite books, hands down and still to this day, were and are Lee Bailey's. He was a master at evoking a particular atmosphere in his writing. One of the things he wrote about, the rule of four, is an idea I have subscribed to big-time. Usually we think that a protein, a vegetable, and some sort of grain or carbohydrate makes a complete meal, but Lee insisted on adding a fourth thing to the mix to make every meal special. This could be a skillet of homemade cornbread or a jar of interesting pickles; but for me, whisking something assertive (e.g., horseradish, lemon zest, or garlic) into a creamy base (e.g., mayonnaise or yogurt) is the instant condiment I make most regularly and that, **small victory**, takes any meal from totally fine to a little bit more remarkable. Here's my favorite version, especially when roast chicken is on the docket (which is often in my house). It's also great on fried eggs, grilled zucchini, roasted potatoes, or even as a dip for potato chips. Honestly, it is perfect on everything.

¾ cup [170 g] crème fraîche

Grated zest and juice of 1 lemon

3 Tbsp minced fresh Italian parsley

1 garlic clove, minced

1 small red chile, halved, seeded, and minced, or 1 Tbsp chile paste or hot sauce

1 tsp kosher salt

In a small bowl, combine the crème fraîche, lemon zest, lemon juice, parsley, garlic, chile, and salt and stir until everything is well mixed.

Serve immediately, or store in an airtight container in the refrigerator for up to 1 day (stir and taste for seasoning before serving as the cold temperature and time both tend to mute the flavors, so feel free to perk up the sauce with extra salt and lemon).

SPIN-OFFS

FOR HORSERADISH SAUCE, substitute horseradish for the lemon zest and juice and swap the parsley for chives. Add 1 tsp sherry vinegar and leave out the chile. This is excellent on all sorts of potatoes, especially ones served alongside meat or roast chicken.

FOR GARLIC + HERB SAUCE, put a clove of garlic and two large handfuls of fresh basil leaves in a food processor or a large mortar and pestle and crush them together. Or just finely chop them. Mix with ¾ cup [170 g] crème fraîche and season with salt. This is really excellent on a tomato salad.

No-Sweat Vinaigrette

MAKES ABOUT ¾ CUP [180 ML]

Vinaigrette seems to inspire fear in many home cooks, with the whole slowly-whisking-in-oil-drop-by-drop thing. I say throw caution to the wind and, **small victory**, just throw everything into a clean jar and shake with abandon. Then you can leave the vinaigrette in the jar and pull it out anytime you need to dress a little green salad or a platter of roasted vegetables or pep up a roasted chicken . . . the list of uses for vinaigrette is endless. Even better than a clean jar, and major **small victory**, is a jar of mustard that you've scraped just about clean but there's still some clinging to the sides that your sandwich knife just can't seem to reach. Make the dressing in *that* jar, and win-win: Salad dressing, plus you kept something useful from ending up in the recycling bin.

1 just-about-empty jar of Dijon mustard or 2 tsp Dijon mustard

3 Tbsp sherry vinegar

½ cup [120 ml] extra-virgin olive oil

1 tsp honey

1 garlic clove, minced

Kosher salt

Freshly ground black pepper

Open the lid to the mustard jar (or use a clean jar and add the 2 tsp mustard to it) and add the vinegar, olive oil, honey, garlic, ½ tsp salt, and a few grinds of pepper. Screw on the top and shake vigorously to combine. Season to taste with salt.

Use immediately, or store in the refrigerator for up to 1 week (bring to room temperature before using, as oil tends to solidify when refrigerated).

SPIN-OFFS

FOR A SLIGHTLY GREEK DRESSING, substitute red wine vinegar for the sherry vinegar and add 1 tsp dried oregano.

FOR A MORE FRENCH DRESSING, substitute white wine vinegar for the sherry vinegar and add a minced shallot and a tiny bit of dried herbes de Provence or minced fresh thyme and/or tarragon.

FOR SEEDED MUSTARD DRESSING, simply add a spoonful of seeded mustard along with the Dijon.

FOR A REALLY '80S DRESSING, substitute balsamic vinegar for the sherry vinegar.

Spicy Honey

Grace and I used to live in Greenpoint, Brooklyn, near a lot of great restaurants, including Paulie Gee's, one of the most fun pizza places in New York. My favorite pie there is called the Hellboy, and it is basically a great margherita topped with thin slices of spicy soppressata and drizzled with Mike's Hot Honey, a terrific product that bills itself as "The World's Most Versatile Condiment." Honey with chiles and vinegar, it's one of my favorite things, and this is my rendition. I have a bunch of suggestions for how and what to use it on in the Spin-Offs, but all you really need to know is that it's good on everything. The **small victory**? Before you measure honey, coat your measuring cup with cooking spray. The honey will slide out easily, so not only will the cup be easy to clean but you also won't waste a drop of precious honey. Keep this in mind each time you have to measure something sticky.

¾ cup [255 g] honey

¼ cup [60 ml] red wine vinegar

2 tsp kosher salt

2 tsp red pepper flakes

In a small heavy saucepan over high heat, stir together the honey, vinegar, salt, and red pepper flakes. Bring to a boil, then turn off the heat and let the honey mixture come to room temperature.

Use immediately, or store in an airtight container at room temperature for up to 1 week.

SPIN-OFFS

DRIZZLE THE HONEY ON A PEPPERONI PIZZA for your own Hellboy!

DRIZZLE THE HONEY ON YOUR DINNER—it's especially good on fried chicken (see page 180), slow-cooked pork shoulder (see page 158), or ribs (see page 155).

TOP ROASTED CARROTS AND/ OR SWEET POTATOES with butter and a generous drizzle of the honey.

Spread **RICOTTA ON TOAST** and drizzle with the honey.

DRIZZLE THE HONEY ON COOKED BACON, either right before you take it out of the pan or the oven to really glaze it, or just before serving.

Thin the honey with extra vinegar and whisk it all together with some oil for an **QUICK SALAD DRESSING**.

Serve the honey with **HOT BIS-CUITS AND PLENTY OF BUTTER**. And give me a call so I can swing by because how good does that sound?

Molasses Barbecue Sauce

MAKES 1 CUP [240 ML]

I find that molasses tends to be an ingredient you use once or twice for a random recipe (e.g., gingersnaps) and then it lingers in the back of your cupboard forever, neglelected and taking up space. I devised this rich, intensely flavorful barbecue sauce as a way to use up the inevitable extra molasses we all have. Employing everything lurking in my cupboard is a **small victory** that I believe in very much (check out the Spin-Offs for more molasses ideas). This barbecue sauce is great on ribs (try it on the ones on page 155) or brushed on grilled chicken or pork toward the end of cooking. It also gives a tremendous depth of flavor to baked tofu and makes it taste almost meaty.

¼ cup [80 ml] molasses

2 large garlic cloves, minced

2 Tbsp Dijon mustard

2 Tbsp apple cider vinegar

½ cup [130 g] ketchup

1½ tsp hot pimentón (Spanish smoked paprika)

1 tsp kosher salt

In a small bowl, whisk together the molasses, garlic, mustard, vinegar, ketchup, pimentón, and salt. End of story.

Store for up to 1 week in a covered container in the refrigerator.

SPIN-OFFS

A very random but very delicious combination I picked up during a work trip to Spain is cubes of **RIPE PINEAPPLE DRIZZLED WITH MOLASSES AND DUSTED WITH GRATED LIME ZEST**. Sounds out there, but is very good and quite refreshing for a snack or a light dessert.

MAKE A DRINK by whisking equal parts molasses and fresh lemon juice or apple cider vinegar together. Dilute to taste with seltzer and serve over ice.

Try using molasses **IN PLACE OF HONEY OR MAPLE SYRUP** anywhere those ingredients are called for—such as in your favorite granola recipe.

FOR AN EASY GLAZE, whisk together equal parts molasses and soy sauce and brush on barbecued chicken, ribs, or steak, or glaze a ham.

Pickled Red Onions

MAKES ABOUT 1 PINT JAR [400 G]

I love a refrigerator pickle. As opposed to a canned pickle, you don't have to worry about sterilizing or boiling jars, or controlling bacteria, or anything like that. You just mix up some pickles, stick them in the fridge, and eat them either right away or within a couple of weeks. These pickled onions, perfect for topping tacos, chilaquiles (see page 36), brisket (see page 162), salads, or avocado toast (see page 26), could not be easier to make (**small victory**). Just put everything in a jar, give it a good shake, and park it in the fridge.

1 red onion, cut lengthwise in half and then into thin half-moons

1 garlic clove, thinly sliced

2 tsp sugar

1½ tsp kosher salt

½ cup [120 ml] white vinegar

½ cup [120 ml] water

In a pint jar, combine the onion, garlic, sugar, salt, vinegar, and water; screw on the lid tightly; and shake until the salt and sugar dissolve. Let sit for about 20 minutes at room temperature.

Eat straight away, or store in the refrigerator for up to 2 weeks.

SPIN-OFFS

SUBSTITUTE SHAVED CARROTS or thinly sliced radishes for the onions.

USE SLICED TURNIPS instead of the onions and add a coarsely grated small beet to turn them a stunning color.

TRY ADDING SPICES to your pickles, like mustard, cumin, and/or coriander seeds.

FOR KIMCHI-LIKE PICKLED ONIONS (or any vegetable, especially daikon), add 1 Tbsp gochugaru (Korean red pepper flakes) to the mix, along with two additional sliced garlic cloves and a splash of fish sauce.

A Jar of Raspberry + Blackberry Jam

MAKES 1¼ CUPS [375 G]

In the summer, my eyes tend to be bigger than my stomach and I often buy more fruit than I can eat. When my berries start to turn from pristine into a bit bruised and very "yesterday" looking, instead of wasting the last bits I mix them all together and turn them into a jar of jam. Just like Pickled Red Onions (page 267), making a single jar of jam means you don't have to worry about sanitizing jars or anything like that. It simply means, **small victory**, that your summer fruit will last a little while longer (and, another plus, you control how much sugar is in your jam, which is often way more than you would think in store-bought jars). This also makes a wonderful ice-cream topper and a filling for shortcakes—and a great gift.

3 cups [360 g] mixed raspberries and blackberries (just past their peak is okay)

1 Tbsp fresh lemon juice

½ cup [100 g] sugar

Pinch of kosher salt

In a large saucepan, combine the berries, lemon juice, sugar, and salt and crush everything together with your hands or a potato masher. Set the saucepan over medium-high heat and bring the mixture to a boil, then turn the heat to medium-low so that the mixture is simmering rapidly but isn't quite at a full boil.

Cook, stirring now and then, until the jam is thickened and a bit reduced, about 20 minutes. Use a spoon to remove any foam that rises to the top during cooking.

Transfer the jam to a clean jar and let it cool to room temperature (this will take 1 to 2 hours), then seal tightly with the lid. Store in the refrigerator for up to 2 weeks.

(Continued)

SPIN-OFFS

TRY JUST RASPBERRIES OR JUST BLACKBERRIES, or just blueberries or strawberries. Or a combination of any of these or other berries you can get your hands on.

FOR PEACH OR NECTARINE JAM—peel and pit the fruit (score the fruits with a paring knife, drop them into boiling water until the skin starts to break, and then plunge them into ice water to cool; drain and peel) and proceed as directed.

TRY SCENTING ANY SUMMER FRUIT JAM WITH SPICES (simply add whole or ground spice to the mix) or use a different acid instead of lemon juice. For example, peaches go beautifully with spicy red pepper flakes or aromatic coriander seeds, and strawberries go well with balsamic vinegar.

USE LIGHT OR DARK BROWN SUGAR instead of granulated sugar to give the jam a slight caramel undertone.

FOR RHUBARB JAM, up the sugar to 1 cup [200 g] and add a peeled and grated apple (which has enough natural pectin, which rhubarb lacks, to thicken the jam).

FOR CHERRY TOMATO JAM, substitute cherry tomatoes for the berries. This is so unexpectedly good. Try it on toast that's been spread with goat cheese.

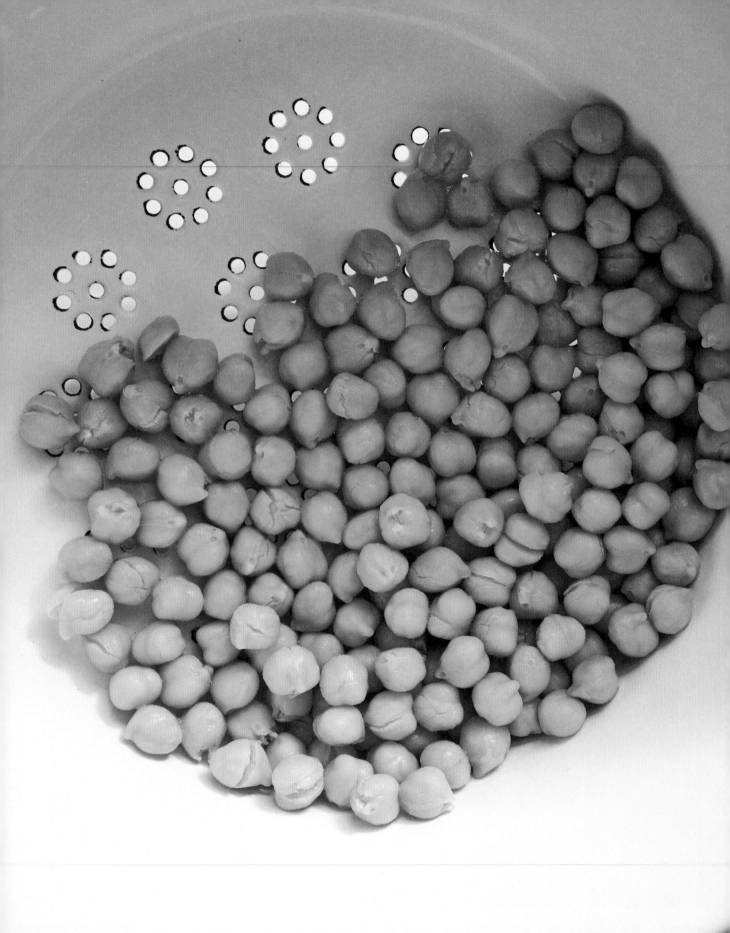

SEVEN LISTS

Seven Easy-but-Memorable Bites to Have with Drinks

ELIZA HONEY'S SPECIAL: Alternate slices of cucumber and white cheese (such as Montery Jack or a young Manchego or even sliced feta) on a platter and sprinkle with kosher salt and paprika.

AFFORDABLE CAVIAR: Top good potato chips with small spoonfuls of crème fraîche and salmon roe and sprinkle with chopped chives. Be sure to make these just as you eat them and not ahead of time (or else the chips will get soggy). You can also put out bowls of crème fraîche and salmon roe next to a bag of chips and let your friends assemble their own.

BITE-SIZE WEDGE SALADS: Cut large iceberg lettuce leaves into bite-size pieces. Top with chopped tomatoes and drizzle with blue cheese dressing (easily made by combining equal parts crumbled blue cheese and sour cream and thinning the mixture with red wine vinegar).

FANCY GRILLED CHEESE: Make grilled cheese sandwiches, cut them into quarters, and serve on your nicest platter.

CACIO E PEPE POPCORN: Sprinkle hot buttered popcorn with very finely grated pecorino cheese and tons of freshly ground black pepper.

BACON AND EGGS: Top Deviled-ish Eggs (see Spin-Offs, page 35) with crumbled cooked bacon and thinly sliced scallions.

MY FAVORITE HORS D'OEUVRE EVER: Put sliced chorizo in a cast-iron pan, set it under the broiler until the slices are hot and slightly crisp, and then drizzle with Spicy Honey (page 264). Serve with toothpicks.

Seven Things to Do with a Can of Chickpeas*

CRISPY CHICKPEAS: Toss the chickpeas with olive oil and salt, spread out on a baking sheet, and roast in a 425°F [220°C] oven, stirring now and then, until crispy, about 30 minutes. Add 1 tsp hot pimentón (Spanish smoked paprika) or red pepper flakes along with the salt if you like heat! Serve with cocktails, use as a garnish for a salad, or mix with roasted vegetables and serve as a side dish.

EASIEST, HEALTHIEST SOUP: Warm the chickpeas in 4 cups [960 ml] chicken or vegetable stock, then add a chopped bunch of kale and cook just until the greens are wilted. Serve in bowls with pesto alongside for swirling in.

THE MOST SAVORY BREAKFAST: Sauté a sliced onion with 4 oz [115 g] diced chorizo or bacon until the onion is softened and the meat is crisp and browned, about 10 minutes. Stir in the chickpeas and cook until they're a little browned, 5 minutes. You could wilt a bit of spinach in the mixture if you'd like. Serve with fried or poached eggs on top.

HUMMUS WITH YOGURT: Puree the chickpeas in a food processor with a minced garlic clove, the juice of a lemon, a heaping 1 Tbsp tahini, and 2 to 3 Tbsp each olive oil and plain yogurt. Season with plenty of salt.

HUMMUS-ISH SALAD: Mix the chickpeas with chopped cucumbers, tomatoes, sliced radishes, and torn herbs (parsley, chives, dill, and/or cilantro). Whisk together 2 Tbsp each tahini, lemon juice, olive oil, and warm water and season with salt. Drizzle the mixture over the salad.

CHICKPEA CURRY: Sauté a sliced yellow onion in olive oil with a heaping 1 tsp curry powder and lots of salt and black pepper until it's soft. Add 2 cups [480 ml] liquid (water, chicken or vegetable stock, whole milk, coconut milk, coconut water, or yogurt thinned with water) and bring to a simmer. Add the chickpeas, along with some chopped cauliflower and/or baby spinach, and cook until the vegetables are tender. Season with salt and serve on rice with lots of chopped cilantro on top.

CRISPY CHICKPEA CAKES: Use a food processor to crush the chickpeas and then mix in a handful each of chopped parsley and cilantro, the grated zest of a lemon, plenty of salt and pepper, and some ground cumin. Form into patties and pan-fry in olive oil until crispy.

*(drain and rinse the chickpeas before using)

Seven Things to Do
with Leftover Roast Chicken

TACOS: Heat corn tortillas one at a time over a gas flame until their edges are slightly charred. Stack them on a damp paper towel as you go and then wrap the stack in foil. Let them stand for a few minutes—this way they get some char but are also softened with a bit of steam. Top with warm shredded chicken, sliced avocado, and shredded red cabbage that you've tossed with lime juice and salt. Serve with hot sauce!

CHICKEN SALAD FRENCH-STYLE: Mix shredded chicken with creamy mustard dressing (see Spin-Offs, page 83) and serve on lightly dressed Bibb lettuce with plenty of blanched green beans and boiled potatoes alongside.

CHICKEN SALAD À LA MY FATHER: Mix shredded chicken with mayonnaise, salt, pepper, a chopped hard-boiled egg, and lots of finely chopped celery and onion. Great on toast.

CHICKEN AND BISCUITS: Check out the Spin-Off on page 54.

CHICKEN PHO: Make the broth from Snow-Day Udon Soup (page 70), with the addition of charred onions (stick a roughly chopped onion under the broiler!), a cinnamon stick, two star anise, and a handful of cilantro stems. Simmer for 30 minutes, then strain and serve in large bowls with shredded chicken and cooked rice noodles. Top with chopped fresh cilantro, basil, and mint. Serve with Sriracha and lots of lime wedges.

QUICK CHICKEN CHILI VERDE: Sauté a diced onion with a couple minced garlic cloves and a diced green bell pepper in olive oil. Add 1 tsp each ground cumin and chili powder. Add 1 lb [455 g] chopped tomatillos and 1 cup [240 ml] chicken stock. Bring the mixture to a boil, lower the heat, and let it all simmer for about 15 minutes and then add shredded chicken and a can of rinsed and drained white beans. Simmer for a final 15 minutes or so. Serve with sour cream, grated cheese, and thinly sliced scallions.

WHICH-CAME-FIRST SOUP (I.E., CHICKEN AND EGG DROP SOUP): First, make an easy chicken broth from the roast chicken carcass. In a pot, cover the carcass with 8 cups [2 L] water. Add a sliced onion and a chopped carrot and simmer for 1 hour. Strain the broth into another pot, add the shredded meat from the chicken to the broth, and season with salt and pepper. Bring it to a simmer. Whisk 3 eggs together and, while stirring constantly, slowly pour them into the simmering soup. The egg will feather itself into small pieces. Serve with plenty of grated Parmesan. If you'd like, whisk in the juice of a lemon.

Seven Things to Do with Ground Meat

PATTY MELTS: Season ground beef and form the mixture into super-thin burgers. Brown the burgers on both sides in a buttered pan. Place each burger between two slices of cheddar cheese and then between two slices of rye bread. Cook the sandwiches in the pan with plenty of butter until the bread is browned and the cheese is melted.

VIETNAMESE-ISH LETTUCE WRAPS: Thinly slice 4 shallots and sauté in 2 Tbsp canola oil until dark brown. Transfer to a plate and add 1 lb [455 g] ground pork, chicken, or turkey to the pan. Cook the meat until gorgeously browned, return the shallots to the pan, and hit the mixture with some brown sugar, fish sauce, and soy sauce (about 1 Tbsp of each). Serve with lettuce leaves and thinly sliced cucumbers, carrots, and jalapeños. Add some lime wedges and a pile of fresh herbs (cilantro, basil, and/or mint) to your platter. Go to town making bundles with any and all of the fillings.

MIDDLE EASTERN MEATBALLS: Sauté a finely diced onion, a few minced garlic cloves, and some minced ginger in olive oil and add 1 Tbsp curry powder and 2 tsp kosher salt. Let the mixture cool to room temperature and then mix it thoroughly into 1 lb [455 g] ground lamb, beef, turkey, or chicken. Form the mixture into small meatballs. Simmer them in a wide pan of tomato sauce (to which you've added a cinnamon stick) until firm to the touch.

KINDA SORTA KIBBEH: Season 1 lb [455 g] ground lamb with ground cumin, ground coriander, salt, and pepper (about 1 tsp of each). Add a large handful of finely chopped leafy herbs (think cilantro, parsley, and/or dill). Form into small patties and pan-fry, grill, or broil until browned on both sides and firm to the touch. Serve with garlicky yogurt.

STUNNING MEAT LOAF: Season 2 lb [910 g] ground meat with salt, pepper, and minced garlic. Put half of it on a sheet pan and pat it down so it looks like a thin meat loaf. Cover with a layer of roasted, peeled peppers, followed by a row of peeled hard-boiled eggs. Cover with the rest of the ground meat so the peppers and eggs are completely hidden. Bake at 400°F [200°C] until browned and firm to the touch, about 1 hour. Let the meat loaf rest for about 15 minutes before slicing.

EASY, DELICIOUS TACOS: In a pan, brown 1 lb [455 g] ground meat (any type except for lamb would work well here) in a bit of oil in a pan and then add a jar of your favorite salsa. Simmer until almost all of the liquid is evaporated. Serve in tortillas topped with sour cream, sliced radishes, and fresh cilantro.

LIGHTER MERGUEZ: Substitute ground turkey or chicken for lamb (see page 164).

Seven Ways with Mussels

SUPER-FRENCH MUSSELS: Sauté chopped shallots in butter, add mussels and a splash of white wine and a bit of Pernod, if you'd like. Cover and steam until the mussels open. Serve sprinkled with lots of chopped parsley and chives. You could also add a splash of cream or crème fraîche to the cooking liquid.

SLIGHTLY MEXICAN MUSSELS: Sauté a diced white onion in a little bit of olive oil with lots of chopped chorizo. Add the mussels and a bottle of Mexican beer (or any light, crisp beer). Cover and steam until the mussels open. Serve sprinkled with lots of chopped cilantro and finely diced white onion.

THAI-STYLE MUSSELS: Sauté some chopped peeled ginger, garlic, and lemongrass in neutral oil, then add the mussels, a can of coconut milk, and a splash of fish sauce. Cover and steam until the mussels open. Serve sprinkled with chopped cilantro and lime wedges for squeezing over.

KOREAN-STYLE MUSSELS: Sauté chopped cabbage kimchi and diced onions in neutral oil (add some chopped bacon too, if you'd like), then add a spoonful of gochujang (Korean red pepper paste) and cook until the whole mixture is brick-red. Add a Korean beer (like Hite or OB or any light, crisp beer) and bring to a boil, then add the mussels. Cover and steam until they open. Serve drizzled with melted butter to which you've added a minced garlic clove and a spoonful of gochujang.

INDIAN MUSSELS: Sauté some chopped peeled ginger and garlic with curry powder in neutral oil. Add a diced tomato, the mussels, and a can of coconut milk. Cover and steam until the mussels open. Serve sprinkled with chopped cilantro.

OLD BAY MUSSELS: Pour a bottle of beer into a pot and add a few generous shakes of Old Bay Seasoning. Bring to a boil, then add the mussels. Cover and steam until the mussels open. Serve with lemon wedges for squeezing over.

JAPANESE MUSSELS: In a pot, whisk a bit of miso paste into 1 cup [240 ml] boiling water, then add the mussels. Cover and steam until the mussels open. Serve sprinkled with toasted sesame seeds and thinly sliced scallions.

Seven Things to Do with Pizza Dough

FOCACCIA: Press the dough into a generously oiled sheet pan and drizzle with even more olive oil. A generous pour of olive oil is the key to great focaccia. Season with kosher salt and a sprinkle of fresh rosemary leaves. Bake at 450°F [230°C] until browned, about 20 minutes. Serve as is or use it to make sandwiches.

GRILLED PIZZAS: Form the dough into thin rounds and grill over a hot fire or in a grill pan over high heat until marked and lightly browned on both sides, just a minute or two on either side. Transfer the grilled dough to a baking sheet, top as you wish, and stick the pizza under the broiler so that your cheese gets not only melted but also beautifully browned, just a couple of minutes.

SQUARE PIZZA (A.K.A. A "GRANDMA PIE"): Press the dough into a generously oiled sheet pan and spoon over a thin layer of tomato sauce. Top with grated mozzarella and a bit of grated Parmesan cheese. If you'd like, add some sliced pepperoni or cooked and crumbled sausage. Bake at 450°F [230°C] until browned, about 20 minutes. Tear over some fresh basil and cut into squares.

GARLIC KNOTS: Roll the dough into small balls and then roll the balls into ropes. Tie the ropes into knots and put them on a parchment-lined baking sheet. Mix melted butter with minced garlic, brush the knots generously with the mixture, and sprinkle with salt. Bake at 450°F [230°C] until browned, 15 to 20 minutes.

CALZONES: Form the dough into thin rounds and transfer to parchment-lined baking sheets. For each calzone, spread a thin layer of tomato sauce over half of the round. Top the tomato sauce with ricotta (and whatever other fillings you'd like) and fold the undressed half of the dough over the cheese to form a half-moon shape. Pinch the edges together and brush with beaten egg. Bake at 450°F [230°C] until browned, about 20 minutes.

SWEET FOCACCIA: Press the dough into a generously buttered sheet pan and drizzle with even more melted butter. Dollop with ricotta cheese and sliced peaches (or plums or pitted cherries) and sprinkle with granulated sugar. Bake at 400°F [200°C] until the exposed dough and fruit are browned and the juices are bubbling, about 25 minutes.

FRIED DOUGH: Just break the dough into small pieces, deep-fry in neutral oil, and toss with powdered sugar.

Seven Easy-but-Memorable Desserts

DATES WITH MASCARPONE: Buy really good, juicy dates, halve and pit them, and spread the cut sides with mascarpone. These are seriously delicious and truly the easiest thing ever.

GRILLED CHOCOLATE SANDWICHES: Put a layer of roughly chopped dark chocolate between two slices of brioche and cook in butter, as you would a grilled cheese sandwich, sprinkling the sandwich with sugar as it cooks so that it gets crunchy and caramelized.

PINEAPPLE WITH PASSION FRUIT: Cut a ripe pineapple into cubes and put them on a serving platter. Scoop the pulp out of two or three ripe passion fruits onto the pineapple and serve. (Keep in mind a ripe passion fruit should look dry and crinkly and not at all attractive—that's how you know it's good!)

ICE CREAM WITH OLIVE OIL AND SALT: Top scoops of vanilla ice cream or gelato with a generous pour of grassy olive oil and a pinch of flaky salt. Seriously good!

VANILLA ICE CREAM WITH JAM: Serve scoops of vanilla ice cream with spoonfuls of jam. Mix the two together as you eat. Amazingly easy and good. My favorite is rhubarb jam for this—the combination tastes like pie à la mode.

ANY FLAVOR SEMIFREDDO: Let a 1-pt [473-ml] container of whatever flavor ice cream you love soften at room temperature until it's almost but not quite melted. Meanwhile, whip 1½ cups [360 ml] heavy cream until it forms stiff peaks. Fold the two together and transfer to a plastic wrap–lined loaf pan. Cover and freeze for at least 4 hours, or up to 24 hours. Invert the semifreddo onto a cutting board, remove the plastic, and slice (a knife dipped in hot water makes easy work of this). Let the slices soften a bit before serving.

PEACHES IN COLD WHITE WINE: Slice ripe peaches into halves or wedges (you can peel them first if you like) and put them in individual glass dishes. Cover with cold white wine and refrigerate for about 1 hour before serving.

Menu Suggestions

A LOW-KEY BREAKFAST FOR A GROUP ON SUNDAY: A few pitchers of Black Pepper Bloody Marys (page 251), Gravlax with Caper Cream Cheese (page 28), Green Eggs With (or Without) Ham (page 33), and a batch of Apple + Toasted Oat Muffins (page 46).

HANGOVER BREAKFAST: Coconut water on ice with lime and Chilaquiles with Roasted Tomato Salsa (page 36).

BREAKFAST IN BED FOR YOUR PERSON: Hot coffee, orange juice, and Sour Cream Pancakes with Roasted Blueberries (page 43).

WHEN YOUR PARENTS COME FOR LUNCH: Chilled white wine; Bibb Lettuce with Garlic Dressing (page 80); and Roast Chicken with Fennel, Rosemary + Lemon (page 174), cut into pieces and served at room temperature; Apricot Upside-Down Skillet Cake (page 231) served with crème fraîche for dessert.

DINNER IF YOU'RE A NEW COOK: Flounder with Roasted Tomatoes + Black Olives (page 209), a loaf of bread, salad greens with No-Sweat Vinaigrette (page 262), Berry + Buttermilk Cobbler (page 234).

THE MOST FUN DINNER (WHICH IS ALSO THE EASIEST DINNER): Korean Clambake (page 195) with plenty of rosé and beer.

DINNER WITH FRIENDS AND THEIR KIDS: String Beans with Pork, Ginger + Red Chile (page 103; made without the red chile), white or brown rice, and Roasted Salmon with Maple + Soy (page 205) with Cilantro + Scallion Sauce (page 257) served on the side for adults; Coconut "Ice Cream" with Lime + Mango (page 221) for dessert.

A BIG GROUP OF FRIENDS FOR SATURDAY DINNER: Lots of Italian red wine, Gus's House Salad (page 87), Cauliflower with Anchovy Bread Crumbs (page 118), and Orecchiette with Spicy Sausage + Parmesan (page 142). Buy ice cream and cookies for dessert.

YOUR BEST FRIEND'S BIRTHDAY: Zucchini + Nigella Fritters (page 107) and Smoky Eggplant Dip with Yogurt + Za'atar (page 122) with warm pita bread to start, then big platters of Chopped Chickpea Salad (page 139), Halibut with Chermoula in Parchment (page 211), and Best Rice Pilaf with Roasted Red Cabbage (page 129). End the meal with a platter of Sliced Citrus with Pomegranate + Pistachios (page 217), and assign the birthday cake to someone else!

DINNER FOR YOUR HEALTH-CONSCIOUS FRIENDS: Potluck Quinoa (page 132), Indecision Grilled Chicken (page 182), and sliced tomatoes showered with salt, lemon juice, and torn basil leaves.

A HOLIDAY COCKTAIL PARTY: Apple Cider + Ginger Beer Punch (page 252), Deviled-ish Eggs (see Spin-Offs, page 35), Old Bay Shrimp Cocktail (page 192), Fromage Fort (page 256) on toast, and Roasted Scallion + Chive Dip (page 119) with plenty of potato chips.

WHEN IT'S TOO HOT TO COOK DINNER INSIDE: Grilled Skirt Steak with Pickled Jalapeño Relish (page 159) with Tin-Foil Kale + Cherry Tomatoes (page 98) and grilled corn on the cob.

NEW YEAR'S EVE DINNER: A large batch of Whiskey Maple Syrup Sours (page 247) and Country Ham with Henley Mustard Sauce (page 151) to start, then Buttermilk + Pimentón Fried Chicken (page 180) with black-eyed pea salad (see Spin-Offs, page 139).

MOVIE NIGHT ON THE COUCH: Cacio e Pepe Popcorn (see page 274), Square Pizza (see page 281), Julia's Caesar (page 83), and Peach + Bourbon Milkshakes (page 222).

A JEWISH HOLIDAY: Aunt Renee's Chicken Soup (page 74), Kasha + Mushrooms with Crispy Salami (page 134), Brisket with Apricots + Prunes (page 162), Beet + Just-Barely-Pickled Cucumber Salad (page 88), and Afternoon Cake (page 229) for dessert.

DATE NIGHT AT HOME: Spring Pea, Leek + Herb Soup (page 67), Scallops with Chile-and-Parsley Bread Crumbs (page 200), and Grilled Chocolate Sandwiches (see page 282).

WHEN YOU CLOSE YOUR EYES AND PRETEND YOU LIVE IN ITALY: Parmesan Soup with Tiny Pasta + Peas (page 64), spaghetti topped with Arugula + Walnut Pesto (page 259), and Peaches in Cold White Wine (see page 282).

WINTER LUNCH: Snow-Day Udon Soup (page 70), Any Flavor Semifreddo (see page 282; made with green tea ice cream).

A MEAL TO BRING TO A FRIEND IN NEED: Corn + Potato Chowder (page 78), a container of Julia's Caesar dressing (see page 83) with a bag of washed and dried lettuce wrapped in a paper towel, and a batch of Feel-Better-Soon Cookies (page 237).

A MEAL TO GET SOMEONE TO MARRY YOU: Flutes of Prosecco with a splash of Aperol, Julia's Caesar (page 83), spaghetti with Turkey + Ricotta Meatballs (page 168), and ice cream.

Give Back

This cookbook, like most cookbooks, assumes that whoever is reading it has access to food and not only the desire, but also the time, energy, and means to cook. How great would it be if that were the case for everyone? I firmly believe that if you have the privilege of eating however much you want whenever you want, you should spend some time ensuring that others have the same opportunity. Here are a few organizations that are helping make that happen and are worth contacting if you have time to help, money to donate, and/or the ability to spread the word. Each meal is a small victory.

National Organizations

NO KID HUNGRY/SHARE OUR STRENGTH:
nokidhungry.org

FOOD RESEARCH AND ACTION CENTER:
frac.org

CHILDREN'S HEALTHWATCH:
childrenshealthwatch.org

ALLIANCE TO END HUNGER:
alliancetoendhunger.org

THE EDIBLE SCHOOLYARD PROJECT:
edibleschoolyard.org

International Organizations

HEALTH RIGHT INTERNATIONAL:
healthright.org

FEED PROJECTS: feedprojects.com

BREAD FOR THE WORLD: bread.org

New York City Organizations

EDIBLE SCHOOLYARD NYC: esynyc.org

GOD'S LOVE WE DELIVER: glwd.org

FOOD BANK FOR NEW YORK CITY: foodbanknyc.org

CITY HARVEST: cityharvest.org

GROWNYC: grownyc.org

NEW YORK CITY COALITION AGAINST HUNGER: nyccah.org

Local Organizations

Contact your local food pantry or soup kitchen to see if they could use volunteers or donations. These are often found in churches (though many are nondenominational). Also check out organizations that help with school lunches and after-school meal programs, such as the Patachou Foundation in Indianapolis (thepatachoufoundation.org) and support programs that employ and empower through food, such as D.C. Central Kitchen (dccentralkitchen.org), Hot Bread Kitchen (hotbreadkitchen.org), and Drive Change (drivechangenyc.org).

Also

If you have a little time to spare, watch *A Place at the Table*, an excellent documentary about hunger in America.

Acknowledgments

CHRONICLE BOOKS, thank you for believing so strongly in this book and being its shepherd. **SARAH BILLINGSLEY**, you are such a kind editor and I so value your input and support. Additional and tremendous thanks to **VANESSA DINA, DOUG OGAN, TERA KILLIP, STEVE KIM, AMY CLEARY, CHRISTINE CARSWELL**, and the rest of the Chronicle team.

KARI STUART (who is so good at her job), I am so happy to call you not only my agent but also my dear friend. And thank you to **PATRICK MORLEY**!

INA GARTEN, thank you for setting the bar so high. Your work and friendship inspire me on a daily basis. Thank you so much for your support.

A million thank-yous to **MARIO BATALI, APRIL BLOOMFIELD, SOFIA COPPOLA, DANA COWIN, SALLY FIELD, RUTH REICHL, MIMI SHERATON**, and **GAIL SIMMONS** for your kind words. Your support means the world to me.

JUDITH SUTTON, you are without a doubt the best copy editor in the world and I would not have felt right putting this book into the world without your eyes looking at it first. Thank you.

ANDREA GENTL and **MARTIN HYERS**, you made my dream come true when you said you would make the photos. Creating these images with you guys, **MEREDITH MUNN, MOE BARON**, and **LARRY RUHL**, were some of my happiest days. Your collective talent is inspiring and your collective kindness makes my heart feel warm. Let's do it again!

Speaking of **LARRY RUHL**, you have been the most incredible support in and out of the kitchen. This book got much better when I met you. Thank you.

ROB MAGNOTTA and his team at Edge, thank you for making my dream photo shoot possible.

A tremendous thank-you to my supportive and enthusiastic "Kitchen Cabinet," my friends and family who tried recipes and gave me incredibly helpful and productive feedback: **ROCHELLE AND DOUG TURSHEN, ELAINE BONNEY, KAIT TURSHEN, CLEO BROCK-ABRAHAM, AMELIA LANG, TIM MAZUREK, KARI STUART, ELIZA HONEY, JULIE KOHN, KATY WRIGHT, SAMIN NOSRAT, PHOEBE LAPINE**, and **SARAH BROWN**.

Thank you to **THE NEW YORK PUBLIC LIBRARY** for giving me a key to the Allen Room and, with it, a place to take myself seriously as a writer. I feel like I know what it's like to have a key to the city!

Thank you to **ALL OF MY FAMILY AND FRIENDS**, the people I most love to feed. Thank you in particular to those of you who patiently consumed the most eclectic meals while I worked on these recipes.

MOM AND DAD, I am eternally grateful for your bottomless cup of support. Thank you for helping me articulate what I wanted this book to look like and being so incredibly good at what you do. I love you so much.

GRACE, HOPE, WINKY, and **TURK**, my heart belongs to all of you. Thank you for taking such good care of it. Grace, my love, home is wherever you are.❤

Index